Creating Compassion

Creating Compassion

ACTIVITIES FOR UNDERSTANDING HIV/AIDS

Phyllis Vos Wezeman

THE PILGRIM PRESS • *Cleveland, Ohio*

United Church Press, Cleveland, Ohio 44115

© 1994 by Phyllis Vos Wezeman and Jude Fournier

This book contains the most current information to date on the HIV virus. It is advisable that you consult your local health department, the AIDS Network, or a physician for further advice.

Biblical quotations are from the New Revised Standard Version of the Bible, © 1989 by the Division of Christian Education of the National Council of the Churches of Christ in the U.S.A., and are used by permission.

Design and composition by John Reinhardt

Printed in the United States of America on acid-free paper

99 98 97 96 95 94   5 4 3 2 1

Library of Congress Cataloging-in-Publication Data
Wezeman, Phyllis Vos.
    Creating compassion: activities for understanding HIV/AIDS / Phyllis Vos Wezeman
        p. cm.
    Includes bibliographical references.
    ISBN 0–8298–0996–1 (alk. paper)
    1. AIDS (Disease)—Religious aspects—Christianity.   2. Activity programs in Christian
education.   I. Title
RC607.A26W484
362.'1969792'0071—dc20   94–27133
                                                                              CIP

To Robert G. and Linda S. Davidson
with appreciation for your dedication to developing and distributing
creative resources that strengthen and support numerous ministries.

Contents

ACKNOWLEDGMENTS

Thanks to: AIDS Ministries/AIDS Assist; American Red Cross; Michael Beatty; Patricia Cebelak; Tim Chartier; Judith Harris Chase; John A. Dalles; Wava Furlong; Tanya Harmon; Joanne Hill; Christine Hoover; Paul Kawata; Val Keller; Rita Kemble; Sr. Ethne Kennedy; Bob Kloos; Ann and Ron Liechty; Jim Morgan; Parish Resource Center of Michiana, Inc., and its board, staff, and volunteers; Morris Pike; Jaime Rickert; Marilyn and Gerald Sapak; Elizabeth Segal; Sr. Connie Shaw; Mary Anna Spellers; H. Ruth and Art Thiessen; Colleen Aalsburg Wiessner; Edna Wynn; and numerous others who have contributed to this project.

Additional thanks to Educational Ministries, Inc., for permission to adapt material from *Peacemaking Creatively Through the Arts*, by Phyllis Vos Wezeman (Prescott, Ariz.: Educational Ministries, Inc., 1990).

Special thanks to: Jude Dennis Fournier and Ken, Stephanie, David, and Paul Wezeman for suggestions and support.

CHAPTER 1
Introduction

The Problem

AIDS affects everyone. Countries throughout the world are engaged in efforts to stop the spread of the Human Immunodeficiency Virus (HIV) that causes Acquired Immune Deficiency Syndrome (AIDS). In the United States, huge sums of money are being spent by public and private organizations to find a vaccine to fight the infection that destroys the immune system. On a state-wide level, programs abound to educate citizens about HIV/AIDS issues. Community service agencies provide varied and valuable assistance to persons infected and affected by the virus. Neighborhoods focus on HIV/AIDS-related issues such as housing, employment, and medical care. Schools teach prevention methods. Congregations design ministries of compassion and care. Families face issues of acceptance and action. Individuals cope with choices and change. AIDS affects every person, both directly and indirectly.

The virus that causes AIDS is found in blood, semen, and vaginal fluids and is transmitted in many ways. HIV is passed from one person to another chiefly during unprotected sex or through the sharing of intravenous drug needles and syringes. Blood used for transfusions and for the treatment of the blood-clotting disorder hemophilia are tested for the virus in most countries; however, before 1985, untested blood products sometimes contained the virus that causes the infection. A woman infected with HIV may spread the disease to her child during pregnancy, during birth, shortly after birth, or through breast milk. Additional methods of transmission include sharing instruments for ear piercing or tattooing, organ donation, and medical equipment malfunction and accident.

HIV attacks the infected person's immune system, making it incapable of fighting diseases and infections. Without a functioning immune system to ward off other infections, the individual becomes vulnerable to bacteria, protozoa, fungi, and other disease-causing organisms, which may cause life-threatening illness, such as pneumonia, meningitis, and cancer.

As of June 30, 1994, the World Health Organization estimates that 17 million people—16 million adults and 1 million children—are infected with the HIV virus. Approximately 1 million of those infected live in the United States. Since all these individuals are assumed to be capable of spreading the virus sexually or by sharing implements for intravenous drug use, scientists predict that 30 to 40 million people will be HIV-infected by the year 2000. Currently there are 985,119 reported cases of AIDS worldwide, with 411,907 of them occurring in the United States. As a result of underdiagnosis, incomplete reporting, and reporting delay, it is estimated that there are actually closer to 4 million cases of AIDS in the world. At present there is no cure; therefore it is expected that those infected will eventually die from the disease.

At this time, there is no cure for or vaccine to prevent AIDS. For now, prevention education and universal precautions are the most effective tools against the spread of HIV. Everyone needs to know how HIV is transmitted and how it is prevented.

The Potential

Education of those who risk infecting themselves or infecting others is the only way we now have to stop the spread of AIDS. People must be responsible for their own behavior. If the AIDS epidemic is to be stopped, people must understand the disease—its causes, nature, and prevention.

Young people need to explore and experience a variety of HIV/AIDS themes and concepts in a positive and creative manner. Joanna Rogers Macy writes,

> It is, therefore, not sufficient to discuss the present crisis on the informational level alone, or seek to arouse the public to action by delivering ever more terrifying facts and figures. Information by itself can increase resistance, deepening the sense of apathy and powerlessness. We need to help each other process this information on an affective level, if we are to digest it on the cognitive level.[1]

The arts are a useful means of achieving this goal. Artistic media can help children to imagine a world without HIV/AIDS. The arts can help children go beyond imagining as well. As Duane Sweeney writes, "[S]tudents [are] stimulated to begin acquiring the knowledge and skills they will need to play a part in shaping the future they envision. . . . They [are] encouraged to create fresh solutions and express their own ideas."[2] Thus, by unleashing the creative imagination, young people can find hope for the future. Through artistic expression children can also participate in finding solutions to the difficult problems they face as they deal with HIV/AIDS issues in all aspects of life.

The Possibilities

This resource is a handbook of creative activities and learning experiences to enable youth, as well as people of all ages, to explore HIV/AIDS as it relates to nine themes:

- World
- Nation
- State
- Community
- Neighborhood
- School
- Congregation
- Family
- Self

Each section contains activities using each of the following art forms:

- Architecture
- Art
- Banners/Textiles
- Cartoons
- Creative Writing
- Culinary Arts
- Dance
- Drama/Clown/Mime
- Games
- Music
- Photography
- Puppetry
- Storytelling

An overview of each art form and its application to HIV/AIDS education is provided in this chapter. A glossary is included at the end of this book.

The Purpose

A purpose, or goal statement, is included at the beginning of each of the projects discussed in this book. Although these statements are specific to each particular exercise, the purpose of all of the activities may be summarized as follows:

- To heighten positive self-esteem in young people.
- To teach the importance of learning about HIV/AIDS in all spheres of life.
- To stress prevention through education.
- To portray HIV/AIDS themes in active rather than passive ways.
- To inspire and excite children about involvement in HIV/AIDS causes.
- To enhance young people's ability to think creatively about HIV/AIDS.
- To identify processes and skills necessary for addressing HIV/AIDS.
- To use the Bible's teachings and Jesus' example as guides for life.

The Participants

Although the activities are intended for use with young people, they may be easily adapted for use with any age group. The learning experiences also provide opportunities for working with multiple age groups.

Although the activities are particularly geared for use by religious educators, teachers in public, private, and parochial settings will find them an excellent means to educate youth about HIV/AIDS in positive, creative ways. The numerous projects may also be used in families as well as congregational and community youth clubs.

Procedure

The activities are designed to involve students as active participants in learning rather than as passive recipients of information. The more the student is engaged in the process, the more powerful will be the effect upon his or her life.

The exercises should be adapted to meet the learning abilities of the students. They have been designed as guides rather than lesson plans so that they can be used in many contexts.

The materials used are readily obtainable. The amount of time necessary for completion of each procedure has not been indicated as it will depend how the activity is used. Some require advance preparation. This is clearly indicated in the directions.

Themes may be explored in sequence as an HIV/AIDS curriculum or the activities for a particular art form, such as music, may be utilized to enhance existing lesson plans. Alternatively, exercises may be selected to supplement other learning materials.

Overview of the Arts

ARCHITECTURE Architecture is an important, but often overlooked, medium to use in introducing people to and involving them in HIV/AIDS activities. Topics to consider range from barriers to bridges, from health-care facilities, housing, and home environments to the structures in which HIV/AIDS-related policies are administered. Explore architecture to build new awareness of both short- and long-term HIV/AIDS projects. A suggested design for an activity using this art form is provided for each theme.

ART One art activity is included for each theme. The specific methods suggested emphasize craft, drawing, painting, and paper techniques. Additional experiences including art are spread liberally throughout the book. For example, one creative writing exercise suggests having children draw or paint their feelings; a banner and textile section contains complete instructions for incorporating batik into a project; and several of the storytelling activities offer art-related suggestions to reinforce comprehension or to provide closure.

The activities and exercises offered under the theme "Art" are only starting points. Any art technique, such as pottery or print-making, papier-mache, or plaster molding, can have an HIV/AIDS application added to it.

Art projects offer an excellent way to help children develop HIV/AIDS awareness; but, more important, they provide an opportunity for young people to explore and express their feelings. Art does more than educate people about HIV/AIDS. It releases the creative potential that is needed to address the issue.

BANNER/TEXTILES

Banner and textile projects, with or without the use of words, can proclaim messages pertaining to themes ranging from AIDS and self through AIDS and the world. Banners may be constructed from almost any fabric, even paper. The type of material is often determined by whether the piece will be used inside or outside. Color, a critical factor in the impact a banner makes, should be considered when selecting the material. The design may be sewn on or glued in place. The space in which a banner will hang determines its size. In a small space, use a banner that will not look crowded. In a large space, make sure it is big enough to be seen.

The banner and textile suggestions include both individual and group projects and present many techniques, such as patchwork and weaving. Fabric-based activities illustrate several topics such as the NAMES Project AIDS Memorial Quilt and ABC Quilts.

CARTOONS

Funnies. Comics. Cartoons. Regardless of what they are called, these illustrations and symbols provide an opportunity to help young people consider issues or communicate ideas. The activities included involve exploring existing cartoons or designing new ones. Use these entertaining, yet educational, messages in ways that will contribute to comic relief while inspiring careful reflection.

CLOWN/MIME

Clowning and mime are wonderful media to use to communicate HIV/AIDS concerns. Through involvement with these fresh, fun approaches, people can begin to comprehend and respond to serious, complicated issues.

CREATIVE WRITING

Writing activities and projects can be used to help students discover and develop creative, yet concrete, ways to address themes of HIV/AIDS. The techniques and topics to consider are unlimited. The expression of ideas and emotions should be emphasized rather than mastery of mechanics. The concentration should be on content instead of form. Assistance may be offered in spelling, punctuation, and grammar if a participant requests it or if a final editing is necessary.

Creative writing activities may be adapted to the ages and abilities of the students. Include younger children in projects by having them dictate their ideas to an older learner or an adult or by providing tape recorders into which they may speak their sentences and stories.

Positive, creative, experiential activities are suggested. The ideas may be combined to develop one lesson or used individually in a variety of ways.

CULINARY

Focusing on food is an experiential and educational way to help young people to explore concepts involving the world, nation, state, community, neighborhood, school, congregation, family, and self, and to address ways in which HIV/AIDS plays a part in each of these themes. Issues such as cooperation and prejudice and information about the immune system and World AIDS Day can be addressed in taste-pleasing and thought-provoking ways.

The activities suggested are intended to help young people become more aware of attitudes and actions that can be explored and experienced through the use of the culinary arts.

DANCE

"Dance has the power to renew—to enliven—to draw a people together. Dancing people are people who can shake off the failures and disappointments of life, feel the Spirit quicken within them, and face the future with hope."[3] Dance, therefore, is a powerful medium to use in HIV/AIDS education. Symbolic expression of the human body sometimes reaches the hearts and souls of people more effectively than spoken or sung messages.

A traditional form of worship in the early Christian Church, dance can be used in conjunction with readings, songs, and prayers to raise the level of spiritual awareness about HIV/AIDS issues.

Dance is available to everyone. Inexperienced and trained dancers can share equally in creating movements and pieces that range from simple to elaborate, from concrete to abstract. A learning activity using dance is provided for each theme.

DRAMA
Drama is a powerful method to use to educate about HIV/AIDS. For the nine themes, ideas for short plays and skits and suggestions for preparing and presenting short scenes and situations are offered. Plays addressing HIV/AIDS issues are also listed.

GAMES
People of all ages and abilities can enjoy and learn from games. They are a good way to mix people and, in the process, to strengthen friendships and relationships. The emphasis in games is on cooperation rather than competition. When people work together, the elements of advantage and the fear of failure are removed. Each player can feel good about himself or herself and these feelings are shared with others. The games suggested can be led by people with no prior experience or particular expertise. They do not require expensive equipment or time-consuming preparation.

MUSIC
Music is used extensively in the worship, education, and outreach ministries of a congregation. It is an art form and teaching tool familiar to both educator and pupil. Since it is a participatory learning activity, it is a good way to help a student discover his or her unique role in addressing HIV/AIDS.

For each of the nine themes, ideas for using music are provided. They involve activities incorporating music or offer ways to use songs, such as adapting a familiar tune to an HIV/AIDS theme by writing new words.

PHOTOGRAPHY
Taking pictures, showing films, making videos, viewing filmstrips, clipping newspaper or magazine photos—all are methods involving photography that are intended to educate, entertain, enlighten, and enrich. These methods enable learners to explore and experience a variety of HIV/AIDS-related activities and approaches.

Nine suggestions for learning about HIV/AIDS through photography are included. These are only a start. Develop others to meet specific curriculum needs and classroom circumstances.

PUPPETRY
Puppetry is the art of bringing an inanimate object to "life" and communicating a message. This ancient medium has been used around the world to entertain, to educate, and to enlighten. In Southeast Asia, shadow puppets dramatize religious epics. In Europe, priests introduced the marionette to help people visualize Bible stories. In Africa, carved figures are devices to transmit oral history.

The ideas for the nine themes focus on puppets that can be quickly and easily constructed from inexpensive or free, readily available items. The six basic types of puppets—hand, rod, marionette, shadow, finger, and body—are represented in the examples.

STORYTELLING
The art of storytelling has been used throughout the world for centuries. By means of this inviting, involving method, values and traditions have been passed from generation to generation. Jesus himself taught in parables as a way to help people understand complex and controversial issues.

Several storytelling methods are suggested in this book. These include helping students look at their perceptions through the use of folktales, locate and share statistical information by making shape books, and learn about transmission and prevention methods.

1. Joanna Rogers Macy, *Despair and Personal Power in the Nuclear Age* (Baltimore: New Society Publishers, 1983), p. xiii.
2. Duane Sweeney, "Peace Child: A Play for Children," *The Peace Catalog* (Seattle: Press for Peace, 1984), p. 133.
3. Adelaide Ortegal, *A Dancing People* (West Lafayette, Ind.: Center for Contemporary Celebration, 1976), p. 1.

CHAPTER 2
World

Activities in this chapter are designed to help young people explore many of the facts and issues connected with the worldwide AIDS epidemic. The learning activities are also intended to encourage participants to develop a caring and compassionate attitude toward people with HIV/AIDS.

Architecture

PURPOSE   To explore types of architecture throughout the world and to emphasize that no home is immune from AIDS.

PREPARATION   *Materials*

- Resource materials on styles of homes throughout the world
- Scissors
- Glue
- Tape
- Cardboard
- Wood
- Rope
- Fabric
- Miscellaneous materials for constructing models of homes
- *People* by Peter Spier (Garden City, N.Y.: Doubleday, 1980)

Advance Preparation

- Obtain pictures of dwellings in various countries

PROCEDURE   Home. It may be a cottage, chalet, cliff dwelling, cave, or camper. Regardless of what it's called, home is the place where people live. A home provides protection for the people who live in it. The types of homes in which people live are as varied as the inhabitants; however, all houses have something in common. They provide shelter and security for people. Whether it is a houseboat or hacienda, igloo or Native American long house, tepee or tent, homes have something else in common: No home is immune from AIDS. People in all parts of the world, regardless of the type of dwelling in which they reside, are infected and affected by HIV/AIDS.

Show the participants photographs, illustrations, slides, videos, or models of homes in various parts of the world. Pictures are available in reference and resource books as well as magazines such as *National Geographic*. An excellent book to use for this activity is *People*. In this spectacularly illustrated picture book, Peter Spier reminds the reader that even with the billions of people in the world, each person is unique, different from everyone else, and deserving of the respect and tolerance of others. Two of the large pages in *People* contain drawings of twenty-five types of homes found throughout the world.

Invite each person to choose one country and to make a model of one type of home found in that particular place. Provide the supplies necessary for the project, including materials such as glue, scissors, tape, cardboard, wood, rope, and paper. Allow time for the builders to construct representations of dwellings typical of various parts of the world. To remind the group that AIDS does not discriminate on the basis of age, race, religion, sex, or the type of home in which a person lives, challenge the participants to locate statistics and stories about AIDS transmission and prevention in various parts of the world. For example, it is estimated that in Australia, North America, and Western Europe, heterosexual transmission is increasing among urban populations. In Latin America and the Caribbean, there has been a substantial increase in reported AIDS cases among women, which leads to a large number of babies born HIV infected. Perinatal transmission is extremely common in Africa. Injecting drug users are the predominant transmitters of HIV in Southeast Asia. In East Asia and the Pacific a large number of those affected are hemophiliacs, who contracted HIV infection from contaminated blood products. Unsterile equipment accounts for many HIV/AIDS cases in Eastern Europe. Statistics are available from the sources listed in the resource section of this book. Emphasize that AIDS strikes people no matter where they live in the world.

For a cooperative project, challenge the participants to work together to create the model homes. Divide the group into two or more teams and assign a country and type of home to each team. For example, one team might be told to make a reed house from Bolivia; a second team, a jhuggi from India; and the third team, a Italian villa. Explain that each team will be involved in a relay race and that their task is to build a model home from the materials provided. Indicate the areas in which the teams will work and ensure that each group has basic supplies, such as scissors, glue, tape, and string. Place additional materials, such as cardboard, rope, wood, paper, and fabric, on a table at one end of the room; have the teams stand at the opposite end of the room. When the leader says "Go," the first person on each team runs to the other side of the room, takes an item from the table, and returns to the group's construction site. Each player is to select one item that he or she thinks will help make a good model. That item is then added to the home the team is building. Continue until each player has had a turn. If necessary, the relay may take place a second time until enough materials are gathered for the models. When time is up, have each team display its newly created home. Gather the models to form a large collage that can be displayed in a prominent place in the congregation, school, or community. Reemphasize that no home is immune from AIDS and write this "slogan" above the collage. Conclude by stressing that just as the participants cooperated to build the models and the collage, cooperation is needed by people in all parts of the world regarding AIDS education, treatment, and prevention.

Art

PURPOSE To research information on epidemics throughout history and to report the findings through a mural project.

PREPARATION *Materials*

- Shelf paper or newsprint roll, white
- Markers or crayons
- Tape
- Scissors
- Resource materials on epidemics
- World map

Advance Preparation

- Cut seven pieces of paper to the desired length
- Hang the world map
- Invite a speaker or obtain a video on epidemics

PROCEDURE AIDS is an epidemic that is rapidly spreading throughout the entire world. AIDS, however, is not the only epidemic the world has ever seen. Major epidemics include the bubonic plague, smallpox, and yellow fever. Use this activity to research facts on major epidemics throughout history and to report on their causes, symptoms, transmission, effects, treatment, and prevention by portraying the information through a mural-making project.

Begin by defining the word "epidemic." Invite the group to offer ideas on its meaning.

Emphasize that an epidemic is an illness or disease that occurs at a significantly greater frequency than expected in a given population. Although not everyone gets the disease during an epidemic, more people than expected become sick. Not all epidemics are fatal. Causes, symptoms, transmission, effects, treatment, and prevention vary from epidemic to epidemic. Supply additional background information on epidemics by inviting a speaker, such as an epidemiologist or public-health nurse, to address the group, or show a video on the topic.

Explain that the students will have the opportunity to research and report on epidemics throughout history: what they were, how they developed, and how they are stopped. Assign specific topics to individuals or small groups. Explain to the students that their task is to gather information and to develop a mural depicting the data in various categories. Identify or discuss the resource materials that are available for the project. Include epidemics such as:

The Bubonic Plague

Also called "The Black Death," the worst incidence of bubonic plague ever recorded was the Great Plague in Europe in 1348–1349. One-fourth of the total population, about twenty-five million people, died. People contract bubonic plague from the bites of fleas that have acquired the infection from infected rats. Since living conditions were crowded and unsanitary, rats and fleas flourished. People who contracted the disease died in one to three days. There was no treatment and no cure.

Bubonic plague appeared in San Francisco in 1900. Since most cases were diagnosed among Chinese people, the San Francisco Board of Health believed Chinatown was the source of the disease. Overcrowded conditions in Chinatown promoted the spread of infected rats and their fleas. Once the animals were destroyed, the disease was stopped.

Smallpox

Although this serious disease is now under control because of the worldwide use of vaccine, it has brought about much death and disfiguration throughout history. Caused by a virus, smallpox is generally transmitted by close contact with an infected person, including contact with respiratory discharges or sores on the skin or materials contaminated by the victim. There were many smallpox epidemics before a vaccine was found in the early 1800s.

Yellow Fever

Yellow fever is caused by a virus transmitted by the bite of a mosquito. It has caused numerous deaths throughout recorded history in many areas of the world, primarily the United States and Spain. Today immunization controls the spread of this disease.

Polio

Although polio is considered a recent epidemic, human remains from 3700 B.C.E. indicate the disease. Polio is caused by a virus that invades the central nervous system, attacks motor cells, and results in paralysis. Paralysis of muscles for breathing and swallowing may threaten life. In 1954 Dr. Jonas Salk developed a vaccine to prevent polio, and in 1955 Albert Savin developed an oral vaccine. Currently, very few cases of polio are reported throughout the world.

Sexually Transmitted Diseases—STDs

In the United States alone, one in seven teenagers has a sexually transmitted disease (STD), which is transmitted during intimate sexual contact. One of the most common STDs, gonorrhea, causes death, sterility, or blindness; however, it can be treated with penicillin. STDs can be prevented by abstaining from sex, refraining from sex with an infected person, limiting the number of sex partners, and using condoms.

Acquired Immune Deficiency Syndrome—AIDS

Reaching epidemic proportions and affecting people in every country of the world, AIDS is caused by the human immunodeficiency virus (HIV). It is transmitted by the exchange of body fluids, generally through sexual contact or by sharing equipment used for injection of drugs. The AIDS virus attacks a person's immune system and damages the ability to fight other diseases. At present there is no vaccine or cure, and the disease is generally fatal.

Allow each group time to accumulate facts about the assigned epidemic. When the allotted time is up, or when enough information has been obtained, explain that each individual or small group will work to make a mural depicting data about the assigned epidemic. Distribute a length of newsprint or shelf paper and a variety of markers to each group. Instruct the participants to divide the paper into six sections and to write one of these words at the top of each part:

- Cause
- Symptoms
- Transmission
- Effects
- Treatment
- Prevention

The name of the epidemic should also be written on the paper. Tell the learners to report information on the epidemic they researched by drawing pictures and writing words and phrases for each of the categories. When the sheets are completed, tape the papers to the walls. After all participants have posted a sheet, invite the group to walk around the room looking at and learning from the murals. After a short time, invite each person to stand by his or her sheet on the wall. Take turns having people introduce themselves and tell at least one thing they learned about the specific epidemic. If a world map is available, group members should use it to show the rest of the class the location of their epidemic. When the groups have finished their presentations, invite the students to brainstorm as to how the information they learned about epidemics throughout history can be used to help fight the AIDS epidemic of today.

Banners/Textiles

PURPOSE To explore ways in which children around the world are affected by HIV/AIDS.

PREPARATION *Materials*

- Yarn
- Push pins or heavy tape
- Bulletin board or wall surface
- International statistics on children and AIDS
- List of countries of the world
- Paper
- Duplicating or photocopying equipment

Preparation

- Obtain a list of countries of the world from reference materials or from *Background Notes,* a publication of the United States Department of State, Washington, D.C.
- Reproduce a list of countries for each participant

PROCEDURE Children with HIV/AIDS is a world-wide concern. In almost every country, boys and girls under the age of thirteen are infected and affected by the human immunodeficiency virus. The World Health Organization estimates that nearly one million children throughout the world are infected with HIV. Ask the participants to names ways in which young people in this age group contract the virus. Supply factual information.

Most children under the age of thirteen become infected from their infected mothers during pregnancy or birth. The virus may also be passed to a baby by breast milk from an infected mother. Most babies born infected become sick and die before the age of three. Some children become infected with HIV from infected blood transfusions and certain blood products. Although most blood products are carefully screened before they are administered, many countries of the world do not have funds or equipment to take this precautionary step. In some developing nations, the virus is spread to children because medical equipment is reused without sterilization. Like adults, young people can become infected by sharing drug needles or syringes or by having sex with an infected person; children can also become infected through sexual abuse. Sometimes the virus is spread when youth share needles for tattoos, ear piercing, and "blood pacts." Like all documented AIDS cases, pediatric AIDS is transmitted through an intimate exchange of body fluids.

HIV/AIDS affects the world's children in other ways, too. Infected parents are often too sick to properly care for their children. There are also many orphans throughout the world whose caregivers have died from AIDS-related complications. In both cases, other people need to care for these young people.

Emphasize that children and AIDS is an international concern by engaging the participants in a simple activity involving a ball of yarn. This exercise will help the youth realize not only are they connected to people throughout the world but to the AIDS issue in numerous other ways. Begin by distributing or posting a list of the countries of the world. Ask the group to study the names of the nations for a designated amount of time, such as one or two minutes. Challenge the group to memorize as many country names as possible. Remove the list or collect the sheets.

Ask for a volunteer to begin this activity. Give that person a ball of yarn and ask him or her to complete the phrase: "The AIDS issue affects children in . . ." A response will be to name a country, such as "Kenya." Upon completing the phrase, the volunteer should hold the end of the yarn, call out the name of another participant, and throw the ball to him or her. This will begin to create a web. Continue this process until everyone has had an opportunity to speak several times and until a large web is formed. See how many different countries can be named. Supply prompts when needed. Begin the process again, asking the group to complete the phrase "The AIDS issue affects me personally . . ." A response may be, "Because God made all people in the world" or "So I'll learn more about how the virus is transmitted." Take turns responding to this phrase.

The resulting web of yarn symbolizes people's interdependence. Challenge the group to work together to bring the web to a wall to be hung as a wall hanging. Instruct them to stand up without letting go of their piece of yarn and to cooperatively move to the wall. Provide push pins or heavy tape to attach the yarn to the wall. Remember to keep the ends tight.

Remind the group that there have been no cases of young children getting HIV infection/AIDS from playing with other children who are infected with the virus. Challenge the participants to learn more about HIV/AIDS transmission and prevention in their own area and throughout the world.

Cartoons

PURPOSE   To explain viruses and to draw cartoons illustrating this topic.

PREPARATION   *Materials*

- *What's a Virus, Anyway?* by David Fassler and Kelly McQueen (Burlington, Vt.: Waterfront Books, 1990)
- Paper, pencils, and markers
- Scissors
- Tape or tacks

Advance Preparation

- Prepare a long, narrow strip of paper, 20" x 4" for each participant and draw lines to divide it into eight equal sections

PROCEDURE   "What's a virus, anyway? is a question children around the world are asking when they hear about the human immunodeficiency virus that causes acquired immune deficiency syndrome (AIDS). *What's a Virus, Anyway? The Kid's Book about AIDS* is a book that, in cartoon format, "explains AIDS in a sensitive manner, using words and concepts children can easily understand. It answers questions honestly and accurately, and encourages children to express their thoughts and concerns."[1]

Answering the question "What's a virus, anyway?" is essential to helping children, as well as people of all ages, understand HIV and AIDS. Use this activity to define the word "virus," to relate it to HIV and AIDS, and to provide an opportunity for the participants to draw cartoons about viruses to help them understand this concept.

Explain that a virus is a tiny organism. In fact, it is so small that 100,000 viruses could fit on the head of a pin. Viruses are invisible to the human eye and can only be seen under a high-powered electron microscope. This special instrument magnifies a virus to thousands of times its original size. A virus comes in many different shapes and sizes. Viruses cannot grow or reproduce without the help of living things. They grow best in a living cell. When a virus enters the body, it invades a cell and lives on the cell's protein. After viruses reproduce in a living cell, the host cell is destroyed. At that point the new viruses leave the dead cell and go after other cells. Now the body begins to show signs of disease. Diseases are groups of problems originated by bacteria, fungi, or viruses. Common symptoms caused by viruses are headaches, fever, colds, coughs, and vomiting. Other viruses trigger more serious diseases such a mumps, measles, chicken pox, polio, smallpox, and AIDS. The body's immune system often kills the viruses before or soon after they make a person sick. In the case of HIV, however, the virus attacks the body's immune system, the very system that protects the body from disease. HIV attacks the white blood cells, which are the body's main disease fighters. Since the white cells, actually the helper T-cells, are destroyed, other viruses, bacteria, and fungi can attack the body and cause it to develop a variety of life-threatening illnesses. Some viruses are easily transmitted, like the ones that cause colds and flu and are spread by coughing or sneezing. Others, like the one that causes AIDS, are much harder to catch. This virus is generally spread through sexual contact or intravenous drug use, when blood and body fluids are transmitted from an HIV-infected person to another individual.

If the book *What's a Virus, Anyway?* is available, show the participants the illustrations, which were drawn by children. Invite the group to make their own cartoons depicting various topics relating to viruses. Give each child a long, narrow strip of paper that has been divided into eight or more frames. Provide pencils and markers. Ask the students to use the cartoon format to illustrate each of the following themes in one of the sections of the paper.

- A picture of a virus
- 100,000 viruses on the head of a pin
- A virus magnified by an electron microscope
- A virus attacking a cell
- A white blood cell attacking a virus
- The human immunodeficiency virus
- HIV attacking a helper T-cell
- HIV multiplying in many cells

Encourage the children to supplement the list by drawing their own ideas in any of the frames. Pass out the strips of paper, pencils, and markers. Answer questions and clarify information related to viruses as the children work on their cartoon strips.

When the cartoon strips are completed, share the results by taping or tacking them to a wall or bulletin board. Take time to review the pictures together.

Creative Writing

PURPOSE   To use puzzle pieces as a method for researching and reporting information about the origins of AIDS.

PREPARATION   *Materials*

- Resource materials
- Paper and pens or pencils
- Blank jigsaw puzzle pieces

Advance Preparation

- Prepare jigsaw puzzles containing the desired number of pieces. Use one puzzle for the entire group or create a puzzle for each student. Blank jigsaw puzzles may be purchased, actual picture puzzles can be turned over so the blank, back side can be used, or shapes could be cut from manila file folders or poster board. Choose from the list provided and write one word associated with the origins of AIDS on each puzzle piece. Word choices include:

Africa
Green monkey
T-cells
Inadequate health care
Widespread disease
Wasting condition
Slim disease
Kaposi's sarcoma
Untreated venereal disease
Prostitution
Promiscuity
Zoonoses
1979-1981
University of California, Los Angeles
Dr. Robert Gallo
Dr. Luc Montagnier
Dr. Michael Gottlieb
Haiti
Immune system
Human immunodeficiency virus
1950s, 1960s, 1970s
Pneumocystis carinii
Centers for Disease Control
Sloan-Kettering Cancer Center, New York
Epidemiologists
Patient zero

Puzzling is a good word to use to describe the origins of AIDS. When and where and how AIDS really began will probably never be known for certain. Although theories abound, there are few facts to confirm the way in which the AIDS epidemic started. Many pieces of the puzzle exist; however, even when they are all put together, they only provide parts of the answer. Some evidence suggests that the virus originated in Africa, possibly with the green monkey, and was transmitted to humans when they ate raw monkey meat or were bitten by the animal. Quite possibly the virus was then transmitted to men, women, and children through the use of unsterilized medical equipment, from contaminated needles used for body decorations, and through sexual contact. Besides Africa, the country of Haiti is often mentioned as the place from which AIDS spread to the United States and to the rest of the world. The pieces of the Haiti part of the puzzle involve homosexual contact and widespread prostitution. Although HIV was identified by researchers in the United States and in France in the late 1970s and early 1980s, evidence points to the possibility that it was present, and even prevalent, in various countries of the world in the 1950s, 1960s, and early 1970s.

Assist students in learning more about the various parts of the story of the origin of AIDS by using individual or group puzzle pieces on which key words have been written. Help the learners connect the information by researching and reporting data about all or several of the parts of the puzzling story. If one puzzle is used for the entire group, distribute one or more pieces to each person. Invite the group to take turns adding their pieces to complete the puzzle. As each part is put into place, ask the student to share information on that part of the story of the origin of AIDS. Most likely, the details will be scanty at this point.

Researching the theories and facts about the origins of AIDS and reporting the information will help the students gain a better understanding of the various parts of the puzzle. Provide resource materials such as magazines, journals, newspapers, books, and encyclopedias. Show photographs and videos. Assign each student to write a report that includes all or many of the words written on the puzzle pieces. Different class members or groups may be given distinct reading assignments to provide a greater variety of research data for classroom discussion. Guide the learners as they explore these sources and gather materials. Furnish paper and pens or pencils and have the learners write their findings. Provide time for the learners to compile and complete their reports.

Add interest and involvement to the project by having the students report their information in creative ways. The puzzle pieces may be put together again, with each person supplying information gathered during the research activity.

Culinary Arts

PURPOSE   To learn about World AIDS Day and to hold a potluck dinner to share food and information from countries and cultures affected by the epidemic.

PREPARATION   *Materials*

- World AIDS Day information
- Invitations to World AIDS Day potluck
- Ethnic cookbooks and recipes and ingredients
- Utensils and equipment

Advance Preparation

- Secure a place to hold the potluck dinner
- Obtain information on ethnic foods and recipes
- Organize the food for the dinner
- Arrange for set-up and clean-up
- Invite speakers
- Acquire World AIDS Day Resource Booklet from: American Association for World Health, 1129 20th Street, NW, Suite 400, Washington, D.C. 20036-5883

PROCEDURE   As of 1994, more than 718,000 AIDS cases have been reported to the World Health Organization (WHO) from 168 countries and territories around the world. WHO estimates that, when underdiagnosis, underreporting, and delays in reporting are taken into account, the true global figure of AIDS cases is closer to 2.5 million worldwide. AIDS is an international issue.

World AIDS Day, observed annually on December 1, is the only international day of coordinated action against AIDS. It serves to strengthen the global effort to meet the challenge of the AIDS pandemic which continues to spread in all regions of the world. World AIDS Day aims to stimulate discussion and action among people not regularly confronted by AIDS and to enhance community support for HIV/AIDS programs.

The World AIDS Day program began at the World Summit of Health Ministers on Programmes for AIDS Prevention in London in January, 1988. Delegates from over 140 nations declared 1988 a year of communication about AIDS. The WHO proposed that the year-long effort should culminate in World AIDS Day on December 1, 1988. Since then, World AIDS Day has received the support of the World Health Assembly, the United Nations, governments, communities, and individuals around the world. Activities for World AIDS Day are coordinated by the WHO's Global Programme on AIDS. The Pan American Health Organization (PAHO), based in Washington, D.C., is WHO's regional office for the Americas. Also located in Washington, D.C., the American Association for World Health serves as the United States Committee for WHO and PAHO. In addition, the U.S. Department of Health and Human Services assists with coordinating activities for World AIDS Day and National AIDS Awareness Day, also observed December 1.

Share the history of World AIDS Day and teach that AIDS is a worldwide epidemic by holding an international smorgasbord. Plan an ethnic potluck dinner to be held on World AIDS Day, December 1. Tasting the cuisine of various countries encourages an appreciation for and an understanding of the people who live in different places. Sharing a meal also provides an opportunity for people to talk with one another about AIDS issues.

Distribute invitations to those who will participate in the event. Organize and arrange food for the dinner. For the greatest variety, serve samples of items from all over the world. Sources of ethnic recipes are available at libraries.

Invite guests from the countries represented by the foods to share the meal as well as to bring information that may help the young people understand the scope of AIDS cases and treatment in their nations and the effect of the epidemic on the people who live in these places. Conclude the event by encouraging the participants to strengthen the worldwide effort to stop AIDS by getting involved in programs in their own communities.

Dance

PURPOSE   To discuss United States immigration laws and to use a circle dance to illustrate this theme.

PREPARATION   *Materials*

- Information on current immigration laws
- Tape of soft music, music from other cultures, and tape player

Advance Preparation

- Obtain information on current U.S. immigration laws. Sources include: recent world almanac; U.S. Code; Federal Code of Regulations; Yearly Statistical Abstracts of the United States; Immigration and Naturalization Service of the United States Department of Justice

PROCEDURE   The word "immigration" means to come into a new country, especially to settle there. Every year thousands of people from other countries come to the United States with the intent of making it their new home. The United States has immigration laws which specify how many and what types of people from various nations may enter the country with the purpose of becoming U.S. citizens. This process is administered by the United States Immigration and Naturalization Services, a division of the U.S. Department of Justice. Preference is given to spouses and family members of persons living in the United States, professionals, persons with advanced degrees, and people with certain types of employment skills.

In 1993 the United States Senate voted to prevent people infected with HIV from immigrating to the U.S. Although President Clinton was in favor of reversing this decision, the Senate vote turned the policy into a law, and any change would require an act of Congress. In approving the amendment, the Senate said people with HIV could come to the country to attend conferences, to vacation, or to get medical treatment, but they could not remain permanently. Some senators said medical costs could range upward of $100,000 per person with AIDS and that the United States' resources should not be used to pay for foreigners with an expensive and fatal illness.

Research and report on current U.S. laws on admitting people into the county who are infected with the AIDS virus. Information is available from the sources listed in "Advance Preparation," above. Discuss the laws with the participants and ask them to voice their opinions on this decision.

Invite the group to illustrate immigration laws through dance. Ask the students to hold hands and form a circle. Leave three or four children out of the circle. Turn on a tape of music and invite the children in the circle to move to an easy dance step such as:

One step in, bend at the knee
One step out, bend at the knee
One step to the right, bend at the knee

One step in, bend at the knee
One step back, bend at the knee
One step to the right, bend at the knee, and so on

Tell the dancers to always hold hands. Remind them that if they drop hands it would permit the "left-out" children to take a hand and join the circle.

Put on music from another culture and encourage the students to do the same dance holding hands for the first round and dropping hands for the second, thus giving the left-out children a chance to step into the circle. Continue the process, holding hands for the third round, which now includes all the children, dropping hands for the fourth, and so on.

Talk about how behavior and attitude invites people in or keeps them out. Remind the group that the Christian's response should always be one of inviting people into the circle.

Drama/Clown/Mime

PURPOSE To help students learn the stages of AIDS by listening to a reading of letters written by persons infected and affected by the disease.

PREPARATION *Materials*

- Letter One, Letter Two, Letter Three
- Three envelopes and paper
- Duplicating or photocopying equipment
- Spotlight

Advance Preparation

- Copy each of the three letters onto separate sheets of paper. Place each letter in an envelope
- Arrange for two people to play the parts

PROCEDURE From the time a person is infected with the human immunodeficiency virus to the time when the individual is diagnosed with AIDS, many different stages of the disease are exhibited. In this activity letters are used in first-person dramatic readings to explain the stages of AIDS. These monologues emphasize that AIDS can happen anywhere and to anyone. Two participants or leaders are needed to present the information. The person on stage plays the role of a mother or father and the person off stage depicts the part of a daughter or son. The first two letters are read by the child who is off stage and is not seen by the audience. During these readings, the parent on stage holds each letter, pretending to read it. The third letter is read by the parent on stage. It would be effective to have the parent lighted by a single spotlight which goes on before each reading and off at the conclusion of each presentation.

Review the stages of AIDS with the participants before and/or after the dramatic presentations.

Stage One: Shows No Symptoms

Many HIV-infected people look and act healthy. They do not display any of the symptoms usually associated with AIDS. Doctors can only tell that they are infected by checking their blood for the presence of HIV antibodies. Although these people appear to be well, they are carriers of the virus that causes AIDS and are capable of spreading the disease to other people.

Stage Two: Mild Flu-like Symptoms

HIV-infected persons often develop flu-like symptoms that last for months. These symptoms may range from mild to severe and include chills, fever, rapid weight loss, severe fatigue, swollen glands, persistent diarrhea, and extreme susceptibility to infections.

Stage Three: AIDS

People in the third stage of HIV infection are those actually diagnosed as having AIDS.

People with AIDS may have white spots in the mouth and pink or purple spots on the skin. People with AIDS have trouble fighting diseases, especially a rare form of pneumonia and certain kinds of cancer. It is these diseases, not HIV itself, that eventually cause death.

Letter One

Dear Mother and Father,

I am sorry for the delay in writing to you. I realize it has been months since my last letter. Our time here is so busy, as you can well imagine. I often find myself very tired.

The other volunteers in my region are fine people. We have become family to one another in a very short time. It is good to have that closeness. It helps in lifting my spirits.

There is so much work to be done here. The poverty is more than I ever imagined it could be. Children hunger for the simple needs of life. I hold them in my arms and I remember both of you holding and loving me. The mothers are trying so hard to keep their children safe from all the pain and disease. Tears come easily for me.

The camps are so cramped. But, I feel as if I belong here. I have come to learn that poverty has many meanings. It is found in many faces. I have also come to realize that I will never come to a full experience of their poverty knowing what awaits me back "home" in North America. If I had any romantic notions about working with the poor in hopes of changing things, they're long gone. Poverty is painful and ugly. It speaks of death. Yet, in all of this the poor have been challenging, inspiring, warm, insightful, caring, and humbling. This has been a blessing.

There are days when I find it very difficult, and I miss you so much. Then I look at the faces of the children and I realize that I have been given a great deal more than I could ever give. That is the mystery of the Kingdom of God: the more you give, the more you are given.

I will close my letter for now. I love you very much and will write again soon. Let us keep one another in prayer.

Love,
Your daughter
Ann

Letter Two

Dear Folks,

Again, I begin my letter with an apology. I am sorry it has been so long since my last letter to you. You understand.

Work here continues to be hard but rewarding. Every day there is something new to be done and to learn. It takes me a while at times. There are not enough hours in the day.

Many children have died over the past few months. The reasons for the deaths are still unclear. Medical supplies and staff are rather slim. Only five of our volunteers are doctors or nurses. The come early to examine the people, and we do the rest. They do what they can to diagnose, but follow-up and medication is next to nonexistent. Still, their help is so needed.

For myself, I have not been feeling well for the past several weeks. The doctors think it's a form of stomach flu or a parasite from the water. I have had persistent diarrhea for more than two weeks. I have been given an anti-diarrhea medication, but it does not help much. Severe headaches come and go and when they do I find a cot or hammock and lie still for awhile. As a result of the diarrhea I have not been eating as I should, therefore I have lost some weight. If this continues I may need to come back to the States for proper medical care and treatment. What a gift to know that I have that option. There are so few options for the people here.

I will not seal this letter, but rather I will write again at the end of the week to let you know how I am feeling.

It is now late Friday night. I have been overcome with severe fatigue. The diarrhea continues and I have weakened extremely. The lay missionary office in the States is arranging for my flight home. It may be awhile before that can happen. Travel from here is not easy.

You will be informed with a phone call about my arrival. I am sure it will happen before you get this letter. Know of my love for both of you.

Peace,
Ann

Letter Three

My Dear Child,

I sit here next to your bed. This awful disease has consumed your body. You have failed rapidly. Today I called the hospice to say I thought it was going to be the day. They reassured me we had done all that we could do to make you comfortable. I put that lambs wool under you and the "doughnut" to ease your bedsore. AIDS tears at your body! You have fought one pneumonia after another and I'm afraid this one will overcome you. The nurse from the hospice said it will be soon. I can feel the end near. I would welcome it. Yes, a mother can say that.

When you came back home to us, you had already reached the terminal stages of AIDS. Perhaps we did not do enough and more could have been done. I will continue to do for you whatever I can, my child. I will keep you clean and comfortable until the end. I will soothe your face with warm water and witch hazel and clean the sores in your mouth with lemon swabs. It is OK to leave us and to go home to God. It is 2:30 a.m. I will try to sleep a little.

6:30 a.m. Slept till now on the floor next to Ann.

At the end of the day, keeping watch with Ann, it came. Ann breathed her last at 6:49 p.m. We were all there watching and waiting.

We called Cathy, her primary-care nurse. While waiting for her to come, we sat with Ann.

"Now . . . at the hour of" Ann's death, her father put his right hand on his daughter's head, his fingers buried in her hair. Her sister closed Ann's eyes and mouth. I rested one hand on Ann's chest over her heart. We waited until Cathy came; and at 7:24 p.m., she pronounced our daughter dead. Ann had given so much to so many. And now, with all her beauty, we give her back to God.

Forever yours,
Mom

Conclude the dramatic readings by asking and answering questions about the stages of HIV/AIDS.

Games

PURPOSE	To use a board game to help the learners identify the symptoms of AIDS.
PREPARATION	***Materials***

- Poster board
- Markers, pens, and index cards
- Dice
- Diagram or models of body parts

Advance Preparation

- Write the symptoms of AIDS on individual index cards.

Brain: The AIDS virus can affect the brain. In adults it causes dementia, the loss of memory and muscle control. In children it stops the brain from growing. Fever is often the first sign that something is wrong with the body. The body's temperature is regulated by complex brain mechanisms. Fever may cause chills or sweating.

Mouth: Thrush is a thick white fungus that coats the mouth and tongue. It makes eating difficult and can spread to the esophagus, the tube down which food travels to the stomach.

Lungs: Most AIDS patients develop a lung disease, pneumocystis carinii pneumonia, also known as PCP. The symptoms are fever, a day cough, and breathlessness.

Intestines: Persistent diarrhea lasting for many weeks is a common symptom. This is not just a brief attack but a long-term condition.

Stomach: Many symptoms prevent the patient from eating and digesting food properly which results in severe weight loss.

Lymph Glands: Painless, hard lumps form in the glands in the neck, under the arms, or in the groin. They are often one of the first signs of AIDS, but swollen glands may also be caused by many other conditions.

Eyes: Cytomegalovirus (CMV) causes blindness in about 25 percent of AIDS patients.

Skin: Blister-like sores are found on the neck, back, and face. They are very painful and persistent if not treated. Blotches on the skin, usually purplish in color, are symptoms of Kaposi's sarcoma (KS), a tumor that affects some persons with AIDS. They look very unpleasant but are not painful. A person with AIDS will suffer easy bruising or bleeding.

Other Symptoms: Severe fatigue. Partial or total paralysis.

- Make a game board by using markers to draw a large horseshoe shape on the poster board. Divide the board into twenty squares. Label the first square "Start" and the last square "Finish." Write the heading words from the symptom cards onto the square, staggering them throughout the game board. For example, two squares from start write the word "skin." Three squares from skin write brain, and so forth. Do this until all headings are used, repeating them a number of times.

PROCEDURE

People with AIDS display a variety of symptoms. Tell the students that they will learn about these symptoms by playing a board game. Before beginning the game, teach or review the symptoms of AIDS. Use a diagram or models of various body parts and provide information on the AIDS symptoms associated with them.

Show the group the board game and explain the procedure for playing it. Invite the students to take turns throwing one die and, beginning at the start position, moving according to the number indicated on the playing piece. As the students land on the heading words they are given the corresponding card and the opportunity to read the information silently to learn about the symptoms. The card is returned to the leader and the game continues with the next player. Once a student lands on a square for which they have already read the card, he or she has the opportunity to tell a symptom to everyone. If their information and knowledge of the symptoms are correct, they get another turn. The first player to reach the finish mark wins. Repeat the game as long as the students are interested in playing it.

Music

PURPOSE

To use song and gesture as a way of praying for people throughout the world who are living with HIV/AIDS.

PREPARATION

Materials

- Music to "Kum Ba Ya" and accompaniment (optional)

PROCEDURE

Hum the chorus of the familiar African American song "Kum Ba Ya" and ask the students to "Name That Tune." Explain that "Kum Ba Ya" means "Come By Here." When people sing the words, they are actually requesting God's presence in a variety of situations. Tell the group that they will be singing "Kum Ba Ya" and adding simple gestures as a prayer for persons in countries throughout the world who are living with AIDS. Teach or review the chorus together. It goes:

Kum ba ya, my Lord.
Kum ba ya.
Kum ba ya, my Lord.
Kum ba ya.
Kum ba ya, my Lord.
Kum by ya.
O, Lord, kum ba ya.

Once the tune is familiar, add gestures to illustrate the words, such as:

Kum ba ya (roll arms in front of body, extend arms forward, holding palms of hands upward)
My Lord (touch chest with palm of right hand, then make a capital "L" with right thumb and index finger and bring down across chest from left shoulder to waist)

Practice the chorus with the gestures. Name some of the themes that will be used for the verses, such as praying, crying, needy, giving, loving, asking, and dying. Ask the children to identify people infected and affected by AIDS who may find themselves in some of these situations. For example:

Praying—Teen who goes for HIV testing
Needy—Young adult addicted to drugs
Crying—Wife who learns husband is infected
Giving—Mother caring for infected child
Loving—Foster parents with AIDS babies
Asking—Elementary student who hears about AIDS on TV
Dying—Person suffering from PCP

Continue praying and singing, adding verses and gestures like:

Someone's praying—Fold hands in front of chest;
Someone's needy—Stretch hands over head
Someone's crying—Wipe tears from eyes
Someone's giving—Stretch hands in a giving manner
Someone's loving—Cross arms over chest
Someone's asking—Bring palms of hands away from mouth
Someone's dying—Bow head

Invite the children to suggest themes and gestures and create additional verses for the song.

Photography

PURPOSE   To create a collage of photographs reflecting the fact that all people in the world are affected by AIDS.

PREPARATION   *Materials*

- Newspapers, magazines, and calendars
- Poster board
- Scissors
- Glue
- World map

Advance Preparation

- Attach the world map to poster board to make it more rigid

PROCEDURE   All types of people in every country of the world are affected by the AIDS epidemic. Mothers in Malaysia as well as Mozambique care for HIV-infected babies. Teachers from

Turkey to Tanzania teach their students prevention methods. Health-care workers in Haiti as well as Holland counsel individuals who come for testing. Illustrate the "Many Faces of AIDS" by using a world map as the background and attaching a collage of pictures of people to it.

Show the participants a world map. Ask them to name the countries that are affected by HIV infection. Be sure that the group understands that AIDS is a worldwide epidemic. People in every country are affected by it. Question the children about the types of people that are affected by the disease. Are any groups exempt? Develop a list of categories of people, such as mothers, fathers, teachers, health-care workers, doctors, neighbors, bus drivers, babies, children, store clerks, police officers, firefighters, and others that are infected and affected by AIDS in every nation of the earth. Talk about ways in which various groups of people are involved in the epidemic. For example, store clerks wait on people with HIV infection, firefighters rescue infected people from dangerous situations, and doctors treat people with various stages of the disease.

Invite the group to create a collage depicting the "Many Faces of AIDS." Provide newspapers, magazines, calendars, and other materials containing photographs of people from around the world. Tell the children to find pictures representing individuals and groups from various countries or to find photos symbolizing different categories of people. Instruct the children to cut out the pictures and to arrange them on the world map. Illustrations may be organized by countries or by categories. Glue the pictures in place. Cut out letters to spell the name of the place or the type of people, such as "Poland" for a country name, or "Pediatrician" for a category title. Glue the words at the top of the pictures. Also cut out letters to spell the words "The Many Faces of AIDS" and attach them to the top of the poster.

Encourage discussion on ways in which AIDS touches everyone.

Puppetry

PURPOSE   To use body puppets to learn how the immune system functions.

PREPARATION   *Materials*

- Brown paper grocery bags and plastic bags
- Rubber bands, medium (two per puppet)
- Stapler and staples
- Markers
- Construction paper
- Glue
- Scissors
- Yarn

PROCEDURE   Every person's defense against germs such as viruses, fungi, and bacteria is the immune system. This complicated system of cells located throughout the body has the task of keeping an individual well. When a person becomes infected with the human immunodeficiency virus his or her immune system is attacked, disabled, and destroyed. Without an immune system, the body falls prey to any infective agent it encounters. Since people with HIV or AIDS have little or no defense system, this means that they have more colds and minor infections as well as a higher incidence of fatal conditions such as pneumonia and certain cancers. These are the most common causes of death among persons with AIDS.

Learn how the immune system works and what happens to it when a person has HIV or AIDS. Since the immune system is a vital part of every person's body, make body puppets and use them with the puppet show provided to impart this information. Body puppets are worn, rather than held. The characters needed for the puppet show include:

Narrator
Germ
G-Cell

P-Cells One and Two
T-Cells One and Two
Helper T-Cells One and Two

Adapt the number of characters to fit the needs of the group. More or fewer "Cells" can be added or subtracted depending on the number of participants. When using body puppets to present the script, no puppet stage is needed. The puppeteers, wearing the body puppets, are in full view of the audience.

Follow these easy directions to construct the body puppets from large brown grocery bags. Start with a full-size brown paper grocery bag. The bottom flap of the bag will become the puppet's head and the remainder will be the body. Pick a full sheet of construction paper and glue it to the body portion of the bag (to cover up any writing on the bag). Using a marker, write the name of the character on the body. Make a face on the flap. Decorate the character with marker and additional construction paper. Make a neck strap by cutting a 30" piece of yarn. Staple the center of the yarn to the middle of the top of the bag. For arms, cut two 18" x 2" strips from a plastic bag. Tie a rubber band to the end of each piece of plastic. Staple the other end of each arm strip to the paper bag, just below the flap. To wear and work the puppet, tie the yarn around the neck, and slip the rubber bands over the wrists. The puppeteer's motions and movements manipulate the puppet.

Assign characters and place the supplies within sharing distance of the students. Encourage the group as they work and answer any questions about the process or the project.

Allow time to practice the puppet show. Lines may be memorized, read off of a script or overhead projector, or recited by others as the puppeteers act them out. Present the story for many groups.

Puppet Script[2]

NARRATOR: Knowing about the body's immune system is one way of learning more about HIV and AIDS. The body's immune system is what helps to keep a person healthy.

GERM: Yeah! Germs like me are all around. There are so many germs in the world, this puppet show could go on forever if we all appeared.

NARRATOR: Well you're not going to appear. In fact, this puppet show is about making you disappear. Today we want to talk about the cells from the immune system that protect the body from germs.

G-CELL: Like me. Cells from your immune system are all over your body.

P-CELL: Not just in your blood.

T-CELL ONE: Our job is to protect you from sickness and disease.

HELPER T-CELL ONE: Protecting your body is a big job, so we divide up the work. Each kind of cell does a different kind of job.

G-CELL: I'm a granulocyte. I fight the group of germs called bacteria and the diseases they cause, like strep throat. I defend the body by surrounding bacteria and eating it.

P-CELL ONE: I'm a phagocyte, but you can call me a P-cell.

GERM: Forget the big names. What do you do?

P-CELL TWO: We fight any kind of germ anywhere in the body.

B-CELL ONE: May I talk next? I'm a B-cell.

NARRATOR: That's just your nickname. Tell us your real name,

B-CELL ONE: B-lymphocyte. Most of the time all we do is hang around in lymph nodes.

B-CELL TWO: But when a germ gets inside of a person's body, and we hear about it—

GERM: Then what?

B-CELL TWO: We do something really amazing!

B-CELL ONE: We change into completely different cells called plasma cells.

B-CELL TWO: We make sticky things called antibodies that float around in the blood.

B-CELL ONE: Antibodies stick to any germs they get near.

B-CELL TWO: Antibodies tell other white blood cells to get bad germs.

T-CELL ONE: It's time to hear my story. All of you are important, but I'm the most important kind of cell in the immune system.

GERM: Big deal. Who are you?

T-CELL ONE: I'm a T-cell or T-lymphocyte. T-cells and B-cells are produced in the bone marrow. We mature in the thymus gland, that's why we're called "T."

T-CELL TWO: We do best at fighting germs like viruses and funguses.

GERM: Oh, oh! I'm one of them!

T-CELL ONE: We're the ones that tell B-lymphocytes to turn into plasma cells.

T-CELL TWO: We send chemical orders to other cells telling them where the trouble is and what to do when they get there.

T-CELL ONE: We also kill cells that have germs hiding inside them.

HELPER T-CELL ONE: I'm a special kind of T-cell called a helper T-cell.

HELPER T-CELL TWO: Me, too! Our main job is helping all the other immune cells get their jobs done.

T-CELL TWO: Some T-cells have the job of remembering every germ that's ever been inside a person's body.

GERM: Sure. Sure.

T-CELL ONE: T-cells are the smartest cells in the immune system.

T-CELL TWO: No offense to the rest of you. You're important, too.

T-CELL ONE: We may be smart, but we had to learn all we know.

T-CELL TWO: Right, like how to tell the difference between cells that are part of a person's body and cells that aren't.

T-CELL ONE: Everyone's cells look different to us T-Cells.

T-CELL TWO: There's more to the story. Each person's cells have special markers, or labels, on them.

T-CELL ONE: These labels are called antigens.

T-CELL TWO: Every cell in a person's body has an antigen label on it, and many cells have more than one.

HELPER T-CELL ONE: I have at least three antigen labels. One says I'm a T-cell, another says I'm a helper, and the third says I belong to a specific person.

HELPER T-CELL TWO: The first two antigens are found on everybody's helper T-cells, but the last one is unique to each person.

HELPER T-CELL ONE: When a cell from a person's immune system sees another cell with their antigens on it, it leaves that cell alone.

HELPER T-CELL TWO: But when it sees a cell with someone else's antigens on it, or something else's antigens on it, like a germ's . . .

GERM: Ouch!

HELPER T-CELL TWO: The immune system does everything it can to destroy the strange cell and protect the body from harm.

HELPER T-CELL ONE: When all the parts of the immune system are working right and working together, people are pretty well protected against germs.

HELPER T-CELL TWO: Even sneaky germs, the ones that try to hide from the immune system by going inside cells, are almost always found and destroyed.

HELPER T-CELL ONE: Sneaky germs get found out because they make the cell they live in sick and sick cells don't look like healthy cells.

HELPER T-CELL TWO: Sick cells have different antigen labels on them, antigens made by the germ inside them.

GERM: Well at least no one has mentioned me yet.

HELPER T-CELL ONE: The immune system can be disrupted or impaired for many reasons.

G-CELL: Genetic defects.

P-CELL: Nutritional deficiencies.

T-CELL ONE: Infections caused by certain viruses, fungi, and bacteria.

HELPER T-CELL ONE: Certain treatments for cancer, such as irradiation and chemotherapy.

T-CELL TWO: Severe burns, traumas to the body, and sometimes surgery.

T-CELL ONE: Immune deficiency leaves the body open to infections that it could otherwise fight off.

NARRATOR: That's especially true with the human immunodeficiency virus, or HIV.

GERM: Stop the name calling.

T-CELL TWO: HIV causes AIDS.

HELPER T-CELL ONE: Helper T-cells are the one's the HIV virus attacks.

HELPER T-CELL TWO: When HIV infected blood, semen, or other body fluids from one person enter the body of another person, the Helper T-cells can become infected with HIV.

HELPER T-CELL ONE: The virus can stay in the cell for a long time without causing any damage.

HELPER T-CELL TWO: HIV can hide quietly for weeks, months, or even ten or more years.

HELPER T-CELL ONE: Sometimes a signal is received by the AIDS virus to start reproducing itself. Scientists don't know why.

HELPER T-CELL TWO: When we become too crowded with HIV we burst, and we're destroyed.

HELPER T-CELL ONE: That's bad, but the worst part is that the HIV is free to hunt for and destroy more of us.

HELPER T-CELL TWO: Then the body's in trouble. As more and more of us are destroyed, it becomes harder and harder for the body to fight germs.

HELPER T-CELL ONE: People with AIDS can get many diseases like a type of pneumonia and a kind of cancer.

GERM: These people know too much. I'm finding a new home.

NARRATOR: And, there's something else that everyone should know. Know how HIV is transmitted and how it can be prevented.

ALL CELLS: Good idea!

GERM: NOT!

Storytelling

PURPOSE To use the folk tale "The Blind Men and the Elephant" to focus on the role of perception in decision making.

PREPARATION *Materials*

- Folktale, "The Blind Men and the Elephant"[3]

PROCEDURE Folk tales are stories that provide the oral and written traditions of people around the world. Many folk tales convey themes, such as cooperation, sharing, and problem solving, which can be used to address numerous issues, including AIDS. "The Blind Men and the Elephant," a folk tale from India, is an excellent story to use to study the concept of perception and to stress the point that people need complete, rather than partial, information when making decisions. As six blind men attempt to discover what an elephant is like, each person forms a different impression. The man who only touched the ear thought an elephant resembled a fan and the one who felt the trunk thought it must look like a snake. Each man believed that his own perception was completely correct. Each person, however, only had partial information on which to base his decision.

Memorize and recite the tale "The Blind Men and the Elephant."

The Blind Men and the Elephant

There were six blind people. They heard that the king was visiting the next village, riding on an elephant. None of them had ever encountered an elephant. "An elephant!" they said. "I wonder what an elephant is like?"

They went to find out. Each of them went alone. The first held the elephant's trunk. The second a tusk. The third, an ear. The fourth, a leg. The fifth, the stomach. The sixth, the tail. Then they went home, each of them sure that he now knew exactly what the elephant looked like.

They began to tell one another. "Oh, it's a fantastic elephant," said the first, "so slow and soft, long and strong." "No," said the one who had felt the tusk. "It's quite short and very hard." "You're both wrong," said the third, who had felt the ear. "The elephant is flat and thick like a big leaf." "Oh, no," said the fourth, who had felt the leg, "It's like a tree."

And the other two joined in, too—"It's like a wall." "It's like a rope" They argued and argued, and their argument grew very bitter. They began to fight.

Then someone came up who could see. "You are all right," said this person with sight. "All the parts together are the elephant."

After the story, help the children realize that the way people perceive things often influences their reaction or response to a situation. People bring their own experiences, needs, values, and feelings to the occurrence.

Follow the story by asking questions such as:

- Do people in the approximately 170 countries of the world perceive one another differently?
- Are decisions related to world issues sometimes based on complete or incomplete information, facts, and details? Give examples.
- How does this folk tale relate to the issue of HIV/AIDS?
- Do people sometimes make decisions based on all or part of the information about the subject? Give examples. Is this true in just a few countries or in all nations?

Another folktale from India that stresses an important point also involves an elephant. "The Elephant's Way" emphasizes the theme of cooperation, which is an essential component of nations working together to discover an effective treatment for HIV infection. "The Elephant's Way" has been produced as a video and uses beautiful shadow and rod puppets as the storytellers. It is available from Church World Service, P.O. Box 968, Elkhart, Indiana 46516 (telephone: 219-264-3102).

Show the class "The Elephant's Way" as another example of a folk tale with an important message.

1. David Fassler and Kelly McQueen, *What's a Virus, Anyway? The Kid's Book about AIDS* (Burlington, Vt.: Waterfront Books, 1990).
2. Lynn S. Baker, *You and HIV: A Day at a Time* (Philadelphia: W. B. Saunders, 1991). The puppet show is based on information in this book and was adapted by permission.
3. Maria Leach, "The Blind Men and the Elephant," in *Noodles, Nitwits, and Numskulls* (Cleveland, Ohio: William Collings, 1961).

CHAPTER 3
Nation

Activities in this chapter touch on many themes and topics—including "The NAMES Project," transmission, and prevention—and should be used to empower children with the information and insights they need to address the issues of AIDS in the nation.

Architecture

PURPOSE To build awareness of the HIV/AIDS-related work of various federal government departments, agencies, offices, and organizations.

PREPARATION *Materials*

- Bricks
- Acrylic paints and paint brushes
- Trims
- Shellac or spray acrylic
- Felt
- Glue
- Scissors
- Permanent markers
- Resource materials on federal government departments, offices, agencies, and organizations that have HIV/AIDS involvement

Advance Preparation

- Clean the bricks and dry them thoroughly. At least one brick is needed for each participant.
- Using a permanent marker, write on each brick a different acronym representing a federal government department, agency, office, or organization that has HIV/AIDS involvement. Suggestions include:

ACTU—AIDS Clinical Trials Unit
ADAMHA—Alcohol, Drug Abuse, and Mental Health Administration
BHCDA—Bureau of Health Care Delivery and Assistance
CBO—Congressional Budget Office
CDC—Centers for Disease Control
CID—Center for Infectious Diseases
DHHS—Department of Health and Human Services
DOED—Department of Education
FDA—Food and Drug Administration
GPO—Government Printing Office
HCFA—Health Care Financing Administration
IHPO—International Health Program Office
NAPO—National AIDS Program Office
NIAAA—National Institute on Alcoholism and Alcohol Abuse
NCI—National Cancer Institute
NIH—National Institutes of Health

OMH—Office of Minority Health
PAHO—Pan American Health Organization
PHS—Public Health Service
SSA—Social Security Administration

PROCEDURE Show the participants a brick and ask them to brainstorm about its uses. Most likely, someone will mention that bricks are basic building materials. Challenge the group to name ways in which bricks are used in connection with the theme "HIV/AIDS and the Nation." One answer is that there are numerous federal government departments, agencies, offices, and organizations that are involved in funding HIV/AIDS-related programs, finding a vaccine or cure for the virus, and furnishing educational information about the infection and its resulting disease. For example the Justice Department tests and treats prisoners; the Veterans Affairs Department cares for HIV-infected veterans; the State Department oversees compliance with HIV screening for immigrants and travelers; the Labor Department monitors workplaces for practices that could expose workers to the virus.

Direct the group's attention to the bricks that were prepared in advance. Note that each brick has different letters of the alphabet written on it. These letters are called acronyms. An acronym is a word formed from the first letters of several words, for example, CDC stands for Centers for Disease Control. Tell the group that each person will have the opportunity to select a brick and to learn more about the governmental agency represented by the letters. Resource materials may be provided for this purpose or time could be given for the research to be done outside of class, with a report to be given at the next meeting. Ask each person to select a brick and to figure out the organization represented by the letters, the purpose of that particular federal agency, what the office has to do with HIV/AIDS, and the group's annual budget for HIV/AIDS-related spending. Allow time for this part of the project.

Once the information is gathered, tell the students that they will report their findings on the bricks. Invite each person to paint or write words, pictures, and designs on five sides of the brick. They are to include the words represented by the acronym and information about the HIV/AIDS-related work of the organization. For example, using the acronym CDC, the words "Centers for Disease Control" would be written on the brick. Because the CDC is located in Atlanta, Georgia, this information might also be listed. Since the CDC is a large complex of buildings, a series of structures could be drawn on one side of the brick. Words related to the CDC's purpose should convey that it is a federally funded research facility whose job is to track down and monitor diseases in the United States and, in cooperation with international health organizations, throughout the world.

Provide supplies such as permanent markers, acrylic paints, paint brushes, and trims. Once the bricks are completed, cover them with acrylic spray or paint the surfaces with several coats of shellac. This part of the process should be done with adult supervision and in a well-ventilated place.

Provide scissors, felt, and glue. Tell each person to cut felt to fit the bottom of his or her brick and to glue it in place. This will prevent the brick from scratching the furniture or the floor.

Invite the learners to share information about the federal department, organization, agency or office they researched. Ask each person to take a turn to show his or her brick and to discuss the facts and figures drawn and written on it. After the report, tell each student to place the brick on a table. Use the individual pieces to create one large building or structure. Remind the group that it will take the cooperation of numerous agencies to conquer the HIV/AIDS epidemic. Despite the competition for funds and recognition, all of these organizations must work together. Also emphasize that the students have only researched a fraction of the federal organizations that relate to various aspects of HIV/AIDS, and that besides federal agencies there are many other national institutions that are connected to the disease. These include the national headquarters of religious denominations, the pharmaceutical industry, and federally funded hospital facilities and universities.

If bricks are not available for this activity, use other materials such as Lego blocks, pieces of wood, shoe boxes that have been covered with paper or paint, match boxes, or even sugar cubes.

Art

PURPOSE
To educate participants about treatment options and treatment processes for persons living with HIV/AIDS.

PREPARATION
Materials

- Sponges
- Scissors
- Tempera paints—various colors
- Poster board or butcher paper
- Styrofoam meat trays
- Tape
- Alphabet letter patterns (optional)
- Information on HIV/AIDS treatment options

Advance Preparation

- Cut 2" or 3" letters of the alphabet from sponges. A number of sets may be helpful. A toy printing set may be used in place of cutting the letters.

PROCEDURE
Everyone wants to stamp out HIV/AIDS. Although there is currently no cure for the virus that causes AIDS, there is hope for persons living with the infection and the disease. Long-term survival is becoming a greater reality with the development of new medical treatments. There is a great deal that people can do to create the conditions for medicines to work and to increase their quality of life, as well as their length of life. Use this activity to discuss treatment options for people living with HIV/AIDS and to design a creative method for helping the students remember this information.

Scientists in the United States, as well as around the world, are working to produce a vaccine to protect people against infection with HIV. Vaccines are the way people are protected from many viral diseases. Vaccines contain some part of the virus but in an incomplete or weakened form that cannot cause disease. This gives the body a chance to mount an immune reaction to the virus components without the danger of actually contracting the disease. If the virus invades a vaccinated person's body, the immune system is ready to ward it off. Making a vaccine against HIV poses considerable problems because of the complicated nature of the virus itself. But, scientists continue to work hard to discover and develop an anti-HIV vaccine.

In the meantime, there are a number of treatments that people living with HIV/AIDS are taking in the hope of increasing the quality as well as the length of their life. Some of these treatments are:

Medical and drug treatment. Drugs such as AZT (azidothymide) are no cure for AIDS, but they slow the production and infection rate of the HIV virus.
Spiritual. Spiritual treatment such as prayer and meditation has been a help to many persons with AIDS. The use of positive imagery and guided meditation as healing therapies has proven to be wholesome for many people living with the virus. Reconnecting with the sacred has given strength to those dying from AIDS.
Lifestyle. Healthful living has served as a treatment to many persons with AIDS. Eating healthful foods and exercising on a regular basis has been essential. Getting proper rest and work time is a help to those fighting the HIV virus.
Prevention. Prevention is the best treatment.

Depending on the age and interest of the group, supply information about specific drugs and additional treatment options and procedures.

Use an art activity as a way to reinforce the measures a person living with HIV/AIDS can take to improve the length and quality of life. Also use this activity to stress that everyone must work to "Stamp Out AIDS!"

On a full sheet of poster board or a long piece of butcher paper, print the word "AIDS" in large capital letters. Tell the group that they will have the opportunity to work together to "stamp out AIDS." Each person will create a rubber stamp from sponge letters of the alphabet. Each word will represent a different treatment possibility or process for controlling HIV/AIDS. Invite each person to choose a word to use for the activity, such as:

AZT
Meditation
Assertiveness
Support
Information
Education
Yoga
Diet
Exercise
"N O"
Prevention
Commitment
Dreams
Responsibility
Adjustments

Once the words are selected, prepare the painting and printing supplies. Place a sponge on a styrofoam meat tray and pour one color of tempera paint over it. Prepare several sponges in this manner, using a different color of paint on each. Show the students the sponge letters which were prepared in advance. Tell the group to choose or create the letters of the words that they will use for the activity. Demonstrate how to dip a letter onto a paint-filled sponge pad and to press it onto the poster board containing the word "AIDS." Tell the group that they are to work together to stamp out the word "AIDS" by covering it with their treatment options. Display the poster in a prominent place.

Remind the participants that everyone must work together to stamp out AIDS.

Banners/Textiles

PURPOSE To impart information about the NAMES Project AIDS Memorial Quilt and to teach the importance of remembering those who have died of AIDS.

PREPARATION *Materials*

- Items related to the NAMES Project AIDS Memorial Quilt

PROCEDURE *Out of something terrible*
There is something beautiful.
Colorful and beautiful
Symbolizing hope.
Out of something terrible
There is something beautiful.
Powerful and beautiful
People found a way to cope.[1]

These phrases, and those that follow, describe the NAMES Project AIDS Memorial Quilt. The Quilt is a living memorial to all those who have died of AIDS.

Out of something terrible
There is something beautiful.
Something very beautiful
Out of something very bad.
Out of something terrible.
There is something beautiful.
Something very beautiful

Out of something sad.
Out of something terrible
There is something colorful.
Colorful and beautiful
Out of something very bad.
Out of something negative
There is something positive.
Positively beautiful
Beautiful and plain.
Out of something pitiful
There is something powerful.
Beautiful and powerful
Something to relieve the pain.

The Quilt actually began out of pain and frustration. People were dying and little was being done to stop it. On February 20, 1987, in San Francisco, California, Cleve Jones went out into his backyard carrying spray paint, stencils, a sheet, and twelve years of memories of Marvin Feldman. He created the first panel. By the time he finished, his grief was replaced with a feeling that he had completed something. He also started something: The NAMES Project AIDS Memorial Quilt.

In the spring of 1987, Jones organized and met with six other people in an empty San Francisco storefront. Though strangers, they shared a common bond. Each person told a story of a friend, lover, or family member who had died of AIDS. And each came with the hope of creating something that would serve as a lasting symbol of love and remembrance to those who had died. Starting with sewing needles, thread, and a few scraps of fabric, their special tribute soon took the shape of a quilt. Response was immediate and widespread. People in the cities most affected by the epidemic—New York, Los Angeles, and San Francisco—sent Quilt panels to the San Francisco workshop in memory of their loved ones. As awareness of the Quilt grew, so did participation. Thousands of individuals and groups from all over the United States and many other countries began to send panels to be included in the Quilt.

On October 11, 1987, the NAMES Project Foundation displayed the Quilt for the first time on the Capitol Mall in Washington, D.C. It covered a space just larger than two football fields and included 1,920 panels. Half a million people visited the Quilt that weekend. The overwhelming response to the Quilt during this inaugural display led to a four-month, twenty-city, national tour in the spring of 1988. Local panels were added to the Quilt in each city, tripling its size to more than 6,000 panels by the end of the tour. In October, 1988, the Quilt returned to Washington, D.C., for a second showing. At this time 8,288 panels were displayed on the Ellipse in front of the White House. In October, 1992, over 20,000 panels were displayed on fifteen acres in Washington, D.C., and hundreds more were contributed to be added to the Quilt in memory of loved ones who had died of AIDS.

Goals of the NAMES Project are to illustrate the enormity of the AIDS epidemic by showing the humanity behind the statistics, to provide a positive and creative means of expression for those whose lives have been touched by the epidemic, and to raise vital funds and encourage support for people living with HIV/AIDS and for their loved ones.

Share the story of the NAMES Project AIDS Memorial Quilt with the participants. Talk to the group about the Quilt, take them to see an actual exhibit of the panels, or show them items related the topic. Merchandise available from the NAMES Project Foundation includes posters, cards, books, videocassettes, clothing, buttons, pins, and notecards. Show videocassettes such as *We Bring a Quilt*, a 30-minute documentary that chronicles the historic weekend in October, 1988, when the NAMES Project AIDS Memorial Quilt returned for a second time to Washington, D.C., or *Common Threads: Stories from the Quilt*, a 79-minute portrait of the first decade of the AIDS epidemic in America. The film tells the story of five individuals with AIDS—all of whom are now commemorated in the Quilt. Books about the Quilt include *The Quilt: Stories from the Names Project, A Promise to Remember*, and *The NAMES Project Book of Letters. Quilt: A Musical Celebration*, a recent play, is a collage of stories for, from, and about the NAMES Project AIDS Memorial Quilt. The production examines one 32-piece block of the Quilt in song and story.

Tell the group the process for creating a panel for the NAMES Project AIDS Memorial Quilt. There are several steps to follow:

1. Design the panel. Include the name of the person and additional information, such as the dates of birth and death and hometown.

2. Choose the materials. Durability is a crucial factor when choosing material, as the Quilt is folded and unfolded many times. A medium-weight, nonstretch fabric such as cotton works best. The finished panel must be 3' x 6', the size of a grave. When cutting the fabric, leave an extra 2" to 3" on each side for a hem.

3. Construct the panel using one or more of the following techniques:

   Applique—Sew fabric letters and small mementos onto background fabric. Do not use glue, as it will not last.

   Paint—Brush on textile paint or color-fast dye, or use an indelible ink pen. Puffy paint should not be used; it is too sticky.

   Stencil—Trace the design onto the fabric with a pencil, lift the stencil, then use a brush to apply textile paint.

   Collage—Although a variety of materials can be added to panels, items such as glass and sequins should be avoided because they will tear the material. Bulky objects should also be avoided. The best way to include photos or letters is to photocopy them onto iron-on transfers, iron them onto 100% cotton fabric, and sew that fabric to the panel.

4. Write a one-or two-page letter about the person who is remembered in the panel. The letter might include a favorite memory and a photograph of the person.

5. Include the name(s), address(es), and phone number(s) of the people who made the panel. Also indicate the cities where this panel should be displayed. The full name of the person memorialized on the panel is requested, although not required.

6. If possible, send a financial contribution to defray the cost of preserving and displaying the Quilt.

7. Pack everything carefully, and send it to: The NAMES Project Foundation, 310 Townsend Street, Suite 310, San Francisco, Calif. 94107. Telephone: 415-882-5500.

Explain to the group that individual pieces are sewn together to form a block consisting of 32 panels. The blocks are displayed in a grid, with plastic walkways between each section. Volunteers unfold the blocks in a beautiful, ritualistic ceremony at the beginning of each exhibit of the Quilt, and the names of the persons memorialized on the panels are read during the entire display.

Challenge the participants to become involved with the NAMES Project by visiting an exhibit of the panels, making a quilt square for a family member or friend who has died of AIDS, contributing funds to the project, volunteering at a Quilt workshop, or finding additional information about the Quilt.

Conclude by reminding the participants that most memorials are monuments made of stone or metal and are stationary, rigid, and cold. The Quilt is different. It is soft, colorful, emotional, personal, warm, and vulnerable. It needs to be cared for, folded and unfolded, and protected. It needs people to care for it, just as real people need others to care for them—especially those who are infected and affected by AIDS. Remind the group that the Quilt illustrates that no person is a statistic. Every life has its own fabric, its own colors, its own soul.

Cartoons

PURPOSE   To create awareness of cartoon strips and comics that address homosexuality and HIV/AIDS themes.

Materials

- Magazines, newspapers, and comic books addressing national issues
- Paper and pens
- Envelopes and stamps

Advance Preparation

- Obtain the addresses of comic book publishers and syndicated cartoon strip artists from reference materials at a library.

PROCEDURE   Ask the children to name their favorite comic strips. Inquire if any of these ever address issues related to HIV/AIDS. Suggest that *Family Circus* spotlights the theme of communication among family members, *Peanuts* often centers on self-esteem or cooperation, and *Doonesbury* is intended to be a political satire. State that recent comic books and comic strips have addressed a topic associated with HIV/AIDS: homosexuality.

Explain that the word "homosexual" refers to a person who is more sexually attracted to people of the same sex than to people of the opposite sex and/or prefers to practice sexual behaviors with people of the same sex. Men who are orientated this way are often called "gay." Women homosexuals are usually called "lesbians." It is estimated that one in ten persons is homosexual. Also explain that "heterosexual" refers to a person who is more sexually attracted to people of the opposite sex, and "bisexual" refers to people who are attracted to and/or practice sexual behaviors with both sexes.

Sexual feelings and emotions are complex; no one really knows why people are drawn to others. Some people think that sexual orientation may be present even in early childhood. Because of the prejudice against homosexual people, some homosexuals do not feel they can act on their real feelings or be very open about their sexual identity. Other homosexual people feel it is important for them to be open and honest about who they really are, even though they may face prejudice.

Address the theme of homosexuality by sharing recent comic books and strips with the group. In 1992 Marvel Comics character Northstar admitted that he is homosexual in *Alpha Flight*, issue 106. Furthermore, Northstar adopts an orphaned baby who tests HIV positive. In this issue there is also a stranger whose son has died of AIDS. In 1991, the Pied Piper, a character in DC Comics *Flash* series, said he is gay. In March, 1993, artist Lynn Johnson's strip "For Better or for Worse" began a series in which Lawrence, a seventeen-year-old friend of Mike Patterson, reveals he is gay. Mixed reactions from readers poured into newspapers as the strip continued for several weeks. If any of these strips are available, share them with the group.

While AIDS is by no means confined to the gay community, the truth remains that of the reported cases in the U.S., especially during the early years of the epidemic, a significant majority have been homosexual or bisexual males. Because of this, many people, including Christians, have responded with fear. Many gay people face widespread social discrimination, alienation, and even brutality. If the church is to minister effectively amidst the AIDS crisis it must deal with its attitudes about homosexuals and homosexuality. This is a complex and complicated issue. Christians must be in touch with the realities of AIDS and with the biblical teachings of the compassion of Christ.

One way to address serious subjects is through the cartoons. If possible, show the book *Comic Relief*[2] which contains drawings from the Cartoonists' Thanksgiving Day Hunger project. In 1986, many cartoon strips and editorial drawings employed a hunger theme. Another year on Thanksgiving Day the cartoonists addressed the topic of homelessness. Invite the participants to write comic book publishers and cartoonists to ask them to incorporate the theme of HIV/AIDS into this medium. Emphasize that information on transmission and prevention, as well as compassion and concern, can reach many people who read the comics. Provide paper, pens, envelopes, stamps, and addresses if the group is willing to become involved in this project. Share the results of the letters as they are received. Challenge the participants to watch for HIV/AIDS-related themes in the comics and to show them to the group.

Creative Writing

PURPOSE To teach the history of the AIDS epidemic by reading and writing quatrain poetry.

PREPARATION *Materials*

- Paper and pens or pencils
- Definition of the quatrain form of poetry
- Resources on the history of the AIDS epidemic
- Chalkboard or newsprint
- Chalk or markers

PROCEDURE Quatrains are four-line poems that follow any of four different rhyme patterns: AABB, ABAB, ABBA, ABCB. When quatrains are combined to form longer poems, each group of four lines is called a stanza. Stanzas are the paragraphs of poetry. Quatrains are used in ballads to tell a tale, most often a sad story. The following quatrain was written to present the chronology of the AIDS epidemic. Read it to the participants and use it as a springboard for individual and small-group research and reports, through quatrain poems, on the history of AIDS.

1981

The Centers For Disease Control
    Known as the CDC
Reports a disease not very old
    AIDS: it can hurt you and me.

A New York Times article announced
    "Rare cancer seen in Homosexuals"
    Not a concern for Heterosexuals.
The gay community is being denounced.

1982

1,300 cases of AIDS have been reported.
The figures in my head are all contorted.
    More than 317 people are now dead.
    AIDS is an epidemic, the CDC has said.

1983

The first AIDS discrimination suit;
Will the PWA [person with AIDS] get the boot?
    Sonnabend and Callen versus 49 West 12th
    The PWA is out due to his health.

1984

They have isolated the infectious agent
    Scientist prove conclusively.
The agent believed to cause AIDS
    Human Immunodeficiency Virus, HIV.

89,920 cases of AIDS now
    Reported in the U.S.
3,665 are dead—how?
    From the infectious agent—I guess.

1985

20,470 cases of AIDS—WOW!
    Reported in the U.S.
8,161 are dead now
    From being HIV infected? Yes!

First minority agencies come into being;
  HIV antibody test is licensed, I read.
Screening of the blood supply is now helping.
  On the front page Rock Hudson is dead.

After reading some of these stanzas to the participants, invite them to write quatrains as a method of learning more about the history of the AIDS epidemic. Print the poetry patterns (AABB, ABAB, ABBA, ABCB) on a chalkboard or on newsprint so the students may refer to the formulas. Point out the resource materials available for the students' use. Distribute newsprint sheets and markers to each person or group. Guide the learners as they locate and list information about the history of AIDS. If the group is large, assign a different year to each person or group and compile information about the epidemic by combining the stanzas. Post the poems around the room and read the information together.

Culinary Arts

PURPOSE To discuss the importance of a healthy lifestyle as a factor in preventing HIV/AIDS.

PREPARATION *Materials*

- Butcher paper
- Pencils
- Scissors
- Markers
- Magazines and newspapers
- Glue

PROCEDURE Health habits are an important factor to consider when talking about HIV/AIDS. Scientists believe that poor health habits make a person more susceptible to both bacterial and viral infections. A healthy lifestyle keeps the body strong so that it is better able to resist infections, including AIDS. Persons infected with HIV also live longer once they improve their health habits. Since a healthful lifestyle is a key to preventing AIDS, use this activity to establish this basic concept.

Invite the children to name things that are involved in establishing and maintaining a healthy lifestyle. These include diet, nutrition, sleep, hygiene, fitness, risk, safety, drugs, alcohol, stress, and prevention. Talk about each part.

Diet/Nutrition

State that it is important to eat from all the food groups each day. Alert the students to eating disorders such as excessive dieting for cosmetic or competitive purposes.

Sleep

Everyone should get an adequate amount of sleep or rest. Although individual need for sleep may vary, the average person requires about eight hours of sleep each day.

Hygiene

Cleanliness is a powerful disease prevention method. Washing hands after using the toilet and before handling food or eating is a good hygiene habit to establish.

Fitness

Regular exercise is essential to overall wellness.

Risk Behavior

Accidents are the number one killer of children. Students need to understand the difference between healthy excitement and life-threatening behavior.

Drugs/Alcohol

Substance use and abuse lowers the functioning of the immune system. Injection of drugs puts individuals at risk for HIV infection in addition to drug addiction. The use of alcohol decreases a person's ability to think clearly and may lead to risky sexual or other behavior.

Stress

Depression, suicide, sleeping disorders, eating disorders, substance abuse, academic pressure, and family problems can be indicators of stress. Emphasize the importance of strong relationships with friends and/or family members as factors in stress reduction.

Prevention

Prevention includes proper immunization and regular check-ups with doctors and dentists.

Invite the learners to consider their own health lifestyles. Ask the students to make large body tracings to illustrate what they have been discussing. Cut a piece of butcher paper the length of each child. Pair the students, distribute pencils or markers, and instruct the partners to take turns tracing each other onto the paper. Tell each person to cut out his or her outline. Invite the children to use markers to fill in the tracings by writing or drawing information for each section of their lifestyle inventory: diet/nutrition, sleep, hygiene, fitness, risk/safety, drugs/alcohol, stress, and prevention. Headlines and pictures showing ways to stay healthy may be cut from old magazines and newspapers and added to the body tracings.

Hang the completed tracings around the room. Allow the students to share and describe their work.

Dance

PURPOSE   To explain the significance of the red ribbon and to use it in dance to make the simple statement: "Something needs to be done about AIDS."

PREPARATION   *Materials*

- Red and yellow ribbon
- Scissors
- Pins
- "That's What Friends Are For" cassette tape and cassette player
- Merchandise with "Red Ribbon" symbol
- "Red Ribbon" postage stamp
- Obtain merchandise with the "Red Ribbon" symbol. Mugs and buffet plates are available in the china section of several major department stores. Manufactured by Swid Powell, carrying the art of Freddie Leiba, profits from the sale of the dishes benefit DIFFA, Design Industries Foundation for AIDS.

PROCEDURE   Show the participants a piece of yellow ribbon and ask them to talk about its meaning. Yellow ribbons have been tied around trees and other places to show support for the military. Display a piece of red ribbon and ask someone to explain its significance. The Red Ribbon Project is a reminder that, after more than ten years, the fight against AIDS goes on. Point out that almost twice as many Americans have died from AIDS than from the Vietnam War and the Persian Gulf War combined. Sponsored by Visual AIDS, Broadway Cares, and Equity Fights AIDS, the simple red ribbon promotes compassion for those living with AIDS. The symbol also encourages active support for the many people and service organizations whose efforts assist persons with AIDS. It demonstrates backing for education and research leading to effective treatments, vaccines, or a cure. Show merchandise containing the red ribbon symbol.

Red ribbons were first worn at the Oscar, the Emmy, and the Tony award ceremonies. Some of the most recognizable names in the entertainment business pinned a red ribbon to their tuxedos or their sequined gowns. They did it because they knew that millions of people would be watching them and they wanted to say one simple thing: "Something must be done about AIDS." Now the Red Ribbon Project has become a grass-roots effort, and red pieces are worn by people everywhere.

Invite the group to make their own red ribbons to wear. Distribute a 6" length of red ribbon to each person. Instruct them to fold it at the top into an inverted "V" shape. Use a safety pin to attach it to clothing.

Show those gathered red ribbons of various widths and lengths and suggest that they use them to develop a dance to a song such as "That's What Friends Are For." This recording was made by Dionne Warwick, Elton John, Gladys Knight, and Stevie Wonder to benefit AIDS research. Distribute ribbons and encourage the participants to use them, individually and collectively, to create gestures and movements that interpret the message of the music. Encourage the children to think about the importance of friends, remembering friends, and how all people must do something about AIDS.

Drama/Clown/Mime

PURPOSE   To introduce participants to dramatic performances with HIV/AIDS themes.

PREPARATION   *Materials*

- Scripts on HIV/AIDS themes
- Cassette tapes of sound tracks and cassette player
- Programs from performances

PROCEDURE   Drama is a powerful tool for educating people about many topics. Whether a person is a member of an audience, a student reading a script for a classroom exercise, or a part of the cast or crew of a local or national production, many layers of learning take place during involvement in dramatic experiences. People are learning about HIV/AIDS through drama, too. Several plays that communicate a message related to HIV/AIDS have been written and performed in recent years, and more are in the process of being prepared and produced. These include:

- *Angels in America. Millennium Approaches.* Part of a 7fi-hour epic drama about HIV/AIDS by Tony Kushner, *Angels in America* has captivated Broadway audiences and won numerous theater awards.
- *Heart Strings: A Play in Three Acts. Heart Strings* is an upbeat show filled with beautiful music, dramatic dance, and dazzling production numbers. Musical selections, interspersed with the words of mothers and fathers, brothers and sisters, people living with AIDS, friends and caregivers, are performed by professional singers and dancers together with local musical groups, children, and volunteers. Generally staged in connection with an exhibit of the NAMES Project AIDS Memorial Quilt, *Heart Strings* is used as a fund raiser for AIDS research and service organizations.
- *Quilt. A Musical Celebration. Stories for, from, and about the NAMES Project AIDS Memorial Quilt. Quilt,* with lyrics by Jim Morgan and music by Michael Stockler, is based on a book by Jim Morgan, Merle Hubbard, and John Schak. *Quilt,* which premiered in October 1992, in Washington, D.C., is a collage of stories for, from, and about the NAMES Project AIDS Memorial Quilt. It examines one 32-piece block of the Quilt in song and story. Primarily about the lives of the people who created the panels, the production celebrates life in the face of death. *Quilt* is not a documentary. Although it is based on real people and real situations, creative license has been used and stories and events have been combined, shaped, or altered. For additional information, contact: Jim Morgan, 92 Horatio Street, #1S, New York, N.Y. 10014.
- *Songs of Love and Remembrance.* With music by Ronald Hirsch and lyrics from poems by Walt Whitman, Joyce Carol Oates, and others, *Songs of Love and Remembrance* is a play dedicated to those who have died of AIDS and their loved ones who survived them.

Throughout the 70-minute composition, themes depicting the conflicting emotions and ever-changing nature of love, the sorrow of loss, and the redemptive power of memory are conveyed in a musical production.

Help the participants become aware of opportunities to explore and experience the subject of HIV/AIDS through drama. Some ideas are listed below.

Attend a Performance

Arrange an outing to a performance of a play with an AIDS-related theme. Discuss the content of the show before and after the production.

Obtain a Script

Explore information about HIV/AIDS by reading portions of a script as part of a classroom activity. Obtain catalogs from drama publishers to discover titles and topics.

Stage a Show

Put on a play with an AIDS theme. Use the performance as an opportunity to educate the public about HIV/AIDS issues and to raise funds for an AIDS organization.

Listen to a Sound Track

Obtain a recording of the music to a show such as *Quilt*. Listen to the words and music and invite responses and reactions from the participants.

Watch a Video

View a performance that has been videotaped. Watch *Til Death Do Us Part* by the Everyday Youth Theater Company, Randall Building, Room 110, 1st & I Streets, SW, Washington, D.C. 20024; telephone 202-554-3893.

Talk about Theater Projects

Learn about theater projects that assist persons with AIDS. Season of Concern in Chicago raises money for organizations and members of the theater community who are fighting the disease. Money comes from cast members making donations in lieu of exchanging opening-night presents, from benefit performances, from cabaret shows, and from volunteer labor on the part of everyone involved in a production.

Regardless of the method used for conveying the information or the subject or script selected, use drama as a way to challenge the participants to learn about various aspects of HIV/AIDS.

Games

PURPOSE   To learn vocabulary associated with testing for HIV antibodies.

PREPARATION   *Materials*

- Word search game
- Pencils
- Reference materials on HIV antibody testing
- "Testing for HIV Infection" brochures

Advance Preparation

- Duplicate a copy of the word search game for each participant
- Obtain "Testing for HIV Infection" brochures from the American Red Cross

PROCEDURE   "Is there a test for AIDS?" is a commonly asked question. Unfortunately, the answer is " N o ."

```
A Y Q H C R A E S E R Z Y P C R E
N P O S I T I V E N T K C T A M V
T O L B N R E T S E W W A T N D I
I N C U B A T I O N P E R I O D T
B L G O Y E B C F G A H U X N S I
O C Y G S H I B M S G O C Z Y J S
D Q S P N T O K I N N E C L M G O
I U E W X Z L L S P I E A Y I Q P
E V I T A G E N F A L S M O T U E
S H C B A D E T N I E R J W Y I S
H S U H A R U A L E S E A R K B L
P P R E C A U T I O N S G Y T R A
T I F A S G D W T A U T S I O A F
S E I G E T A R T S O N I T T F X
B B Q T C T O A T T C C T M G A P
C F J E V I T A G E N E S L A F H
C O N F I D E N T I A L I T Y O W
```

Words

A. Antibodies
B. Negative
C. Western blot
D. Counseling
E. Accuracy
F. False positive
G. PCR
H. Precautions
I. Incubation period

Words

J. Positive
K. IFA
L. Strategies
M. False negative
N. Confidentiality
O. Research
P. Anonymity
Q. ELISA
R. Cost

Definitions/Descriptions

1. _____ Enzyme-linked immunosorbent assay, the easiest and most inexpensive test used to screen blood for antibodies to the HIV virus.
2. _____ Test results indicate the presence of antibodies to HIV. Also called reactive or seropositive.
3. _____ Plans to stay healthy and to manage HIV infection.
4. _____ Results indicate the person did not have HIV antibodies on the day the test was taken. Also referred to as nonreactive or seronegative.
5. _____ Time it takes for antibodies to HIV to develop, ranging from weeks or months to years.
6. _____ A person has the antibody, but tests negative.
7. _____ Polymerase Chain Reaction, a complex, new genetic test that multiplies the DNA in a blood sample so that minute amounts of HIV can be detected.
8. _____ New diagnostic tests are being developed and refined.
9. _____ Two or more tests are needed for a correct diagnosis.
10. _____ Personal information is recorded but test results cannot be revealed without written permission.
11. _____ Immunofluorescent Antibody, one of the tests conducted following a positive ELISA test to more accurately determine the presence of HIV infection.
12. _____ Methods to protect others from becoming infected with HIV disease.
13. _____ Help in making the decision to take the test and support in understanding the test results.
14. _____ A person does not have antibodies but tests positive.
15. _____ Substances naturally created by the immune system in response to viruses and other germs that enter the body.
16. _____ Name and test results are not recorded together, and there is no record that a person took the test.
17. _____ Some clinics and health departments offer free testing or request a small donation in exchange for their services. Private lab fees can range from free to expensive.
18. _____ Test performed after a positive ELISA to confirm results.

Answers

1. Q	5. I	9. E	13. D	17. R
2. J	6. M	10. N	14. F	18. C
3. L	7. G	11. K	15. A	
4. B	8. O	12. H	16. P	

There is, however, a test to determine whether a person has been infected with the virus that causes AIDS. Developed in mid-1985, the ELISA test became available as a way to screen donated blood and plasma for the presence of antibodies to HIV. A positive HIV antibody test indicates that a person has been infected with HIV and has HIV disease. It does not mean the person has AIDS, nor does it mean that he or she will necessarily develop AIDS. Early medical intervention and behavioral changes to strengthen the immune system can be beneficial in preventing the development of AIDS. A negative test result only means the person did not have HIV antibodies on the day the test was administered. Often it takes several weeks, months, or even years before antibodies to HIV show on a test. If negative test results are obtained, periodic retesting is essential. People should consider getting HIV/AIDS counseling and having an HIV antibody blood test if they have engaged in risky behaviors, especially those connected to having sex or sharing needles. People who have hemophilia or who received a blood transfusion between 1977 and the spring of 1985 may also be advised to get counseling and be tested. An important benefit of HIV antibody blood testing is the chance for early treatment for people with positive results. Early treatment can help people infected with HIV live longer and can make the quality of their lives better. Knowing the test results can also help HIV positive persons become more responsible in their relationships with others.

There are many words associated with testing for HIV antibodies. Study the vocabulary list with the participants and use the word search game as a way to help the students remember the terms and their meanings. For additional information on many of the words, refer to the Glossary at the back of the book. An additional resource is the American Red Cross brochure "Testing for HIV Infection." After a thorough discussion on HIV testing, pass out photocopies of the word search puzzle and pencils. Instruct the group to match each word with the statement that best defines or describes it. Then ask them to locate the term in the puzzle and circle it. Words may be hidden horizontally, vertically, or diagonally, forward or backward.

Music

PURPOSE To introduce participants to music that relates to the AIDS epidemic.

PREPARATION *Materials*

- Selected recordings and record, cassette, or CD player

PROCEDURE What do current musical recordings have to do with AIDS? The answer is: A lot! In response to the AIDS epidemic, recording artists, composers, writers, technicians, actors, and actresses are using music to make a point: Something has to be done about AIDS. Many recordings by popular artists are not only good listening but also potentially life saving. Profits from several recordings and performances benefit AIDS research and AIDS service organizations. Other music imparts a message of care and compassion or important educational information through lyrics. Introduce the participants to the variety of music that has been written and performed in response to the AIDS epidemic. Listen to several recordings and discuss ways in which music impacts persons infected and affected by HIV/AIDS. For example, funds are collected, awareness is raised, and action is prompted. Many titles of popular music, musical dramas, and classical recordings are provided. Begin with this list, but also have the group contact record stores and recording companies to research additional titles and themes.

Popular Music—Albums

Red, Hot and Blue and *Red, Hot and Dance* were recorded at a benefit for AIDS and contain the songs of Cole Porter. Artists include K. D. Lang, U2, Neneh Cherry, Sinead O'Connor, Annie Lennox, Lisa Stansfield, and Neville Brothers.

For Our Children presents songs for children and families by artists such as Paula Abdul, Bruce Springsteen, Barbra Streisand, Little Richard, Bob Dylan, and Sting. All proceeds of this Disney production benefit the Pediatric AIDS Foundation.

Five Live, by George Michael and Queen with Lisa Stansfield, is a mini-album produced as a fund-raising project for the Mercury Phoenix Trust, an AIDS relief fund established in the name of the late Queen lead singer Freddie Mercury, who died of AIDS related complications in 1991. The album was released simultaneously with the video *The Freddie Mercury Tribute Concert*, another fund raiser for the trust, featuring Guns 'N Roses, Metallica, Roger Daltrey, Def Leppard, Extreme, Liza Minnelli, and others. Both the video and the album were recorded in 1992 at London's Wembley Stadium.

Popular Music—Singles

Elton John's "The Last Song," from the album *The One*, emphasizes the relationship of a father and a son. Elton John has promised to donate all of the proceeds from every single he releases to AIDS research and service organizations for the rest of his career.

"That's What Friends Are for" by Dionne & Friends (Dionne Warwick, Elton John, Gladys Knight, and Stevie Wonder) has almost become the "theme song" of the AIDS epidemic.

Other recordings include: "We're All in This Together," by Patti Austin; "Healing Power of Love" and "Love Don't Need a Reason," by Michael Callan; "We'll Be Back in the High Life Again," Nell Carter (Nell's brother, a physician in Chicago, died of AIDS); "This Time," by Neil Diamond; "Get on Your Feet," by Gloria Estefan; "I Think about You" and "You Can't Judge a Book by Its Cover," by Patti LaBelle; and "Some People's Lives," by Bette Middler.

Music from Broadway Shows

Some music with messages that can be related to AIDS themes include: "No More," from *Into the Woods*; "Will You Join in Our Crusade," from *Les Miserables*; "Children Will Listen," by Stephen Sondheim; and "There's Me," from *Starlight Express*.

Musical Drama

Quilt: A Musical Celebration, with lyrics by Jim Morgan and music by Michael Stockler, was inspired by the NAMES Project AIDS Memorial Quilt. The play tells the stories of two dozen people who died or are dying of AIDS.

Musical Benefits

Many recording artists have lent their names and donated their time to fighting AIDS. *Red, Hot, and Blue* was originally a concert to benefit AIDS research. On June 4, 1992, the "AIDS Quilt Songbook," held at Alice Tully Hall in New York City, brought together the work of eighteen poets and eighteen composers in a much publicized benefit for the AIDS Resource Center, an organization that provides shelter for homeless persons with AIDS. Many of the songs were settings of poems from the powerful anthology *Poets for Life*.

Classical Music

"Symphony No. 1," by John Corigliano, and "Song of the Helix," by Bryan Shuler, were special compositions written for symphony orchestra performances given to benefit various organizations combating the AIDS epidemic. Encourage the participants to be aware of products and performances that support this cause.

Suggest that members of your group write to thank the artists who are supporting AIDS causes.

Photography

PURPOSE To research and report on the lives of nationally known entertainers who are HIV infected and who have died of AIDS.

PREPARATION *Materials*

- Newspapers, periodicals, and books
- Camera and slide film
- Tape recorder and cassette tape

- Costumes and props
- Projector and screen
- Newsprint and marker or chalkboard and chalk

PROCEDURE No segment of society has been spared the tragedy of AIDS. Female, male, straight, gay, minority, white, white-collar, blue-collar—every community is at risk. But the entertainment community in particular has been devastated by the AIDS crisis, and even a short list of those lost to the disease can shock the most informed individual into stunned silence. Use this activity to review the lives and accomplishments of several nationally known entertainers whose lives have been lost to AIDS or who are currently infected or battling the disease.

Distribute a sheet of paper and a pen or pencil to each participant. Ask them to spend two minutes compiling a list of professions within the entertainment field. Time the activity, announcing the beginning and the end. Occupations might include directors, choreographers, dancers, singers, song writers, lyricists, rock stars, actors, technicians, producers, authors, set designers, painters, costumers, musicians, and sports figures. Review the list together, compiling one list with many headings. Record each category on a separate sheet of newsprint, a column on a chalkboard, or on one long, horizontal sheet of paper that has been taped to the wall. Review each category and name well-known persons in it. For example:

CHOREOGRAPHER: Michael Bennett (*A Chorus Line*)
LYRICIST: Howard Ashman (*Beauty and the Beast*)
SONGWRITER: Peter Allen
ROCK STAR: Freddie Mercury
ACTOR: Rock Hudson
PIANIST: Liberace
DANCER: Alvin Ailey
TENNIS STAR: Arthur Ashe
CHILDREN'S ARTIST: Arthur Lobel (*Frog and Toad*)
BASKETBALL STAR: Magic Johnson

Invite the students to research the lives and contributions of several of these people and to present the information in the form of a slide show. Data can be gathered by reviewing back issues of newspapers and periodicals found at the library. Books have been written about many of these people, too—*The Courage of Magic Johnson: From Boyhood Dreams to Superstar to His Toughest Challenge*, by Peter F. Pascarelli (New York: Bantam Books, 1992), is one example. Materials may be gathered in advance, or time should be allotted for this part of the project. Determine individual or small group assignments. Instruct the group to locate one or more pictures of the people they are studying, as well as the facts.

Once the information is accumulated, make a slide show to tell each person's story. Photographs of the person may be copied onto slide film. A more involving and interesting option is to have the participants act out the story of the person's life and photograph it. Divide the story into scenes, choose props and costumes, and assign and practice parts. Tape record the story while the students read it. Play back the recording and have the costumed actors take their poses. Snap pictures of each scene. At the next session, set up the projector and screen and show the visualized story to the pupils. Present it for other groups as well.

Make the group aware that there is an annual "Day Without Art," generally observed on World AIDS Day. Throughout the country thousands of arts institutions, galleries, organizations, theaters, studios, and radio and television stations commemorate all those who have died and will die of AIDS. The day, originally established by Visual AIDS and Broadway Cares—AIDS support and resource organizations of the entertainment community—is intended to help people stop to think about their reaction and response to the AIDS epidemic. It is more than a political statement; it is an acknowledgment of the needs of caregivers and persons with AIDS. In some places, paintings are shrouded, theater lights are dimmed, music is silenced, and stages are bared.

Conclude the activity by reminding the young people how much richer people's lives are because of the people they remembered and many others like them. Consider how much more each individual had to give had he or she lived. Now think of all those beyond the entertainment field who have been silenced by AIDS: educators, scientists, clergy, doctors, and the list goes on. Challenge the participants to continue spreading the story that something must be done about AIDS.

Puppetry

PURPOSE To make and use an envelope puppet to explore ways in which letters can be used to express opinions and to obtain information about AIDS-related issues.

PREPARATION *Materials*

- Envelopes, any size
- Markers
- Glue
- Scissors
- Yarn
- Fabric, construction paper, or plastic bags
- Addresses of national officials
- Paper and pens
- Resource materials on HIV/AIDS

Advance Preparation

- Obtain the names and addresses of national leaders, such as: the President of the United States, The White House, 1600 Pennsylvania Avenue, Washington, D.C. 20501; Senator (name), United States Senate, Washington, D.C. 20510; Representative (name), U.S. House of Representatives, Washington, D.C. 20515

PROCEDURE Local, national, and international leaders make many important decisions pertaining to HIV/AIDS-related issues. Presidents, governors, mayors, senators, representatives, and councilpersons need to know how concerned citizens, of all ages, feel about these topics. Letters are an effective way for people to express opinions, to ask for information, and to suggest action on critical matters. Letters to elected and appointed officials can express views, raise questions, and suggest alternatives on the many topics effecting the lives of thousands of people infected and affected by AIDS.

Envelopes can carry mail to national leaders, but they can also be used in other educational and entertaining ways. Turn envelopes into puppets and use them to encourage people to write letters to their elected and appointed officials, to distribute envelopes and address lists to interested participants, to instruct people about the way a bill becomes a law, to provide suggestions for writing to a member of congress, or to give a summary of federal AIDS legislation.

Begin by constructing envelope puppets according to these easy directions. Choose an envelope to make into a person or a character puppet. Tuck the flap in and place one hand inside the envelope. The thumb should touch the bottom corner and four fingers should extend toward the top corner. Use the other hand to press on the bottom crease, between the thumb and the fingers, and bring the two lower corners of the envelope together. This will form a moveable mouth. Use markers or scraps of construction paper to add eyes and a nose to the face. Make hair by cutting strips of yarn and gluing them to the top of the head. Create a costume by cutting a piece of fabric, construction paper, or plastic bag and gluing it to the edges of the envelope.

After everyone has made a puppet, form small groups and instruct each team to use their characters to address national topics and themes related to AIDS. Group One might prepare a presentation on "How a Bill Becomes a Law," including ways in which letters influence the process. Group Two could address "Suggestions for Writing to a Member of Congress." Group Three's topic might be a "Summary of Federal AIDS Legislation."[3] Supply background information and resource materials to each group. For example:

How a Bill Becomes Law

A bill may start in either the House of Representatives or the Senate, but must be passed by both houses. It may also begin simultaneously in both houses. Below is given a description of the typical procedures for considering a bill in the House of Representatives. Note that there are many times, both before and during the process, when letters would influence decisions.

1. Introduction. It is "dropped into the hopper," a box on the clerk's desk, by a House member.
2. Committee Assignment. The bill is assigned to the committee that has jurisdiction over that type of legislation.
3. Public Hearings. The committee holds public hearings. People are asked to testify or to send experts to Washington.
4. Committee Action. Not all bills make it out of committee. If there is interest in the bill, it may stay the same or be amended and then voted on. If the vote is favorable, the bill goes to the full House.
5. House Vote. The bill is debated, amended, and voted on. If it passes, it is sent to the Senate.
6. The Senate Committee. The committee holds its own public hearings, amends the bill, and sends it to the full Senate.
7. Senate Vote. The full Senate debates the bill, amends it and votes on it. If it passes, it goes to the Conference Committee.
8. Conference Committee. If the House and Senate versions of the bill are not identical, conferees from the House and Senate are appointed to resolve the differences. Then the House and Senate each need to vote on the final bill.
9. President Signs Bill. Within ten days the president must veto or sign the bill. If he does neither, the bill automatically becomes law.

Suggestions for Writing to a Member of Congress

Recommended forms of salutation are: Dear Senator _____ or Dear Representative _____. When writing to the chair of a committee or the speaker of the House or the majority leader of the Senate, it is proper to address them as: Dear Mr. Chairman/Dear Madam Chair/or Dear Mr. Speaker/or Dear Mr. Leader.

Selected Guidelines on writing a letter: Use personal or business stationery with a correct return address. Confine each letter to one topic or piece of legislation. Because of the volume of correspondence received by members of Congress, it is not unusual for different staff to be assigned to reply to specific issues.

Keep the letter brief. Making the point in one page is ideal. State the purpose clearly within the first paragraph. Be specific about the action you want the member to take. If you want information, ask for it. If you want the member to vote a certain way or to co-sponsor legislation, be specific and direct.

Summary of Federal AIDS Legislation

1982. Under the stewardship of Rep. William Natcher of Kentucky, the first federal funds, in the amount of $5.6 million, are allocated to AIDS research.

1984. Under the sponsorship of Rep. Edward Roybal of California, the first targeted federal funds are made available to community-based AIDS organizations, in the amount of $150,000.

1985. Congress approves major increase in research funds to accelerate the National Institutes of Health AIDS research effort.

1986. Congress adds $47 million to the budget to create a network of AIDS research units—later to become the AIDS Clinical Trial Group.

1987. The first "Helms Amendment," introduced by Sen. Jesse Helms (Republican, North Carolina), passes overwhelmingly—in the Senate by 94 to 2. Attached to an appropriations bill, this amendment prohibited federal funding of AIDS education efforts that "encourage or promote homosexual sexual activity."

Congress provides $30 million to assist poor Americans in the purchase of expensive AIDS drugs, at that time limited to the newly approved AZT.

1988. The Health Omnibus Programs Extension (HOPE) Act, sponsored by Senator Edward Kennedy (Democrat, Massachusetts) and Rep. Henry Waxman (Democrat, California), establishes AIDS prevention and research programs.

1989. Another "Helms Amendment" to an appropriations bill adds HIV to the immigration list of excludable illnesses, barring people with HIV from entering the country.

1990. The Americans with Disability Act, prohibiting discrimination against people with disabilities, including those with HIV, becomes law.
The Ryan White Comprehensive AIDS Resources Act (CARE), sponsored by Senators Kennedy and Orrin Hatch (Republican, Utah), provides disaster relief to cities and states hard hit by AIDS.

The AIDS Housing Opportunities Act, passed as part of the Cranston-Gonzalez Affordable Housing Act, authorizes $156 million to expand housing options for people with HIV-related illnesses. The 1990 Immigration Reform Act essentially reverses the 1989 Helms Amendment, by charging the Secretary of Health and Human Services with formulating a new immigration list of excludable illnesses.

1991. The Secretary of Health and Human Services proposes removing HIV as an excludable illness for immigration purposes. Months later the administration reverses this decision with new provisions that allow for continued testing for HIV, assessing potential cost of HIV treatment, and then determining whether the "alien is likely to become a public charge."

Current Information

Using the library or other sources, such as the National Minority AIDS Council, obtain current information on legislation related to HIV/AIDS.

After the groups have prepared their stories and scripts, provide opportunities for them to present their puppet performances for one another and for additional audiences.

Storytelling

PURPOSE To create a shape book of the United States to help children explore the AIDS epidemic on a national level.

PREPARATION *Materials*

- White drawing paper
- Cardboard
- Scissors
- Patterns of the United States, 5" x 7"
- Markers and pencils
- Hole punch
- Yarn or string

Advance Preparation

- Cut 5" x 7" cardboard patterns of the United States
- Obtain current statistics on the categories of AIDS cases in the United States. For up-to-date information on HIV/AIDS, recorded messages are provided by the Centers for Disease Control (CDC) at 404-332-4570.

PROCEDURE Remind the students that all types of people—babies, children, teenagers, middle-aged, and elderly people—become HIV infected. Males and females as well as rich, poor, educated, and illiterate people die of AIDS. Talk about some of the statistics that have been reported on a national level. Call the CDC information number 404-332-4570 and include the most current information for each category:

Total reported AIDS cases:
_____Adolescents and adults
_____Children under 13

Total AIDS deaths:
_____Adolescents and adults
_____Children under 13

AIDS cases by age categories:
_____Under 5
_____5–12
_____13–19
_____20–24
_____25–29
_____30–34
_____35–39
_____40–44
_____45–49
_____50–54
_____55–59
_____60–64
_____65 and over

AIDS cases by ethnic orgins:
_____White, not Hispanic
_____Black, not Hispanic
_____Hispanic
_____Asian Pacific Islander
_____Native American
_____Unknown

Tell the participants that they will be making shape books to depict the fact that everyone in the U.S. is affected by AIDS. Pass out white drawing paper, map patterns, pencils, and markers. Ask the young people to trace the pattern of the United States on several pieces of paper. These will serve as the pages of the book. Punch two holes at the top and string the pages together. Invite the students to use the markers to draw pictures of people on the pages of their books. Encourage drawings of people of different ethnic origins and of all ages, shapes, and sizes. The sketches could be created in chronological order with page 1 showing a baby, page 2 a young child, and so forth. Or the drawings may be included in the shape book in random order. Review the statistics that were mentioned at the beginning of the activity. Ask each person to include some of this information on the last page of the book. Encourage the participants to share their shape books with one another.

1. Jim Morgan, Michael Stockler, Merle Hubbard, and John Schak, *Quilt: A Musical Celebration: Stories for, from, and about the NAMES Project AIDS Memorial Quilt* (New York: Morgan, Stockler, Hubbard, Schak, 1992). Performance rights and publication, Music Theatre International, New York, New York.
2. *Comic Relief: Drawings from the Cartoonists' Thanksgiving Day Hunger Project* (New York: Henry Holt, 1986).
3. National Minority AIDS Council, *Public Policy Primer* (Washington, D.C.: National Minority AIDS Council, n.d.). Adapted with permission.

CHAPTER 4
State

Activities in this chapter are intended to provide information about HIV/AIDS-related programs and problems that are common in many states. Suggestions are offered for prompting positive attitudes toward affected and infected persons, networking with groups throughout the state, and addressing the facts related to the topic.

Architecture

PURPOSE To learn how states are responding to the AIDS crisis in the area of housing.

PREPARATION *Materials*

- Paper and pens
- Envelopes and postage stamps
- White contact paper
- Permanent markers
- Scissors or paper cutter
- Architect's tools: drawing board, straight edge, triangle, templates
- Blueprint

Advance Preparation

- Cut contact paper into rectangles the size of bumper stickers
- Obtain names and addresses of state departments connected with housing issues

PROCEDURE Explore the issue of equal housing for all people. Introduce the subject by explaining that an architect is a person who designs buildings and supervises their construction. Architects often draw blueprints, or plans, for buildings. Blueprints serve as guides for construction workers who build structures to the exact specifications on the plans. Show the group a sample blueprint. Architects use specific tools to do their work, such as drawing boards, straight edges (often called T-squares), templates, and triangles. Tell the students that they will have the opportunity to use these tools later in the activity. State laws and policies are like blueprints. They tell the citizens of the state, as well as other states, what they can and cannot do. Investigate specific state laws regarding housing, especially for persons with AIDS.

Is there equal housing for all people? Is there equal housing for persons infected with HIV or for those living with AIDS? Tell the students that several states have tried to pass laws preventing persons with AIDS from obtaining access to housing. Invite the group to learn more about the laws and policies of their own state regarding this issue. Brainstorm with the students about places where health policies and housing regulations are made on the state level. Such places may include the state capitol, state department of health, state department of housing, and so forth.

As a group, write a letter to those in authority on the state level. Share with them the need for information regarding care and housing for persons living with AIDS. Ask about policies and housing regulations to learn if the state has fair and equal housing laws for all people. After obtaining this data, review the information with the group. Use this information to make bumper stickers advocating for equal housing for all people, even persons with HIV/AIDS.

Show the group how to use the architects' basic drafting tools. Then, using only these, create bumper stickers with slogans that might address the state's efforts, or lack thereof, in addressing this disease. Distribute precut contact paper and permanent markers to each person. Guide the group as they create their bumper stickers. Once the projects are completed, ask the participants to share their work. Encourage the students to ask family and friends to display the bumper stickers as a way of advocating for equal housing for all people.

Art

PURPOSE To learn that hotlines provide information and assistance about many AIDS-related topics.

PREPARATION *Materials*

- Chalkboard and chalk or newsprint and marker
- Paper and pens or pencils
- Poster board or index cards ("hot" colors)
- Stencil paper, lightweight cardboard, or plastic pattern sheets
- Stencil knife or sharp-pointed scissors
- Paints: acrylic, tempera, or fabric
- Shallow containers
- Stencil brushes
- Telephone pattern, optional
- Paper towels
- Cardboard or cutting board
- Pins or tape

Advance Preparation

- Write on the board "Who Would You Contact to Obtain Current Information about AIDS?"
- Prepare telephone pattern

PROCEDURE Hotlines are a service offered by agencies and groups to provide assistance and information about specific topics. Use this activity to acquaint the participants with the variety of Hotlines associated with the HIV/AIDS pandemic. Encourage participation by all the learners and stimulate their interest in the coming lesson by inviting them to answer a question that has been written on the board in advance. The question is: "Who would you contact to obtain current information about AIDS?"

Invite the class to stand and to form groups of three. Tell the class members to be seated as soon as they have formed a group of three. Direct attention to the question that has been written on the board and read it to the group. Tell the pupils that each person in the group will have one minute to suggest answers to this question; that at the end of the first minute, time will be called, and the conversation will move to the next person who will have one minute to respond; and that this process will be repeated for the third person. Remind the groups that there are many answers to this question. Distribute paper and pens or pencils to one person in each group so answers may be recorded. Give the groups a starting signal and encourage them to come up with as many answers as possible to the question.

When the three minutes are up, ask each group to share several of their answers. Write the ideas on a piece of newsprint or on a chalkboard so everyone may see and remember them. After everyone has had a turn to report, concentrate on hotlines as a way of obtaining current information about AIDS. If someone has mentioned this idea, call attention to it on the list or introduce the information.

Explain that hotlines are telephone lines operated by organizations and groups to provide help and to answer questions about specific topics. Some hotlines have people who answer the calls; others play recorded messages. Hotlines are a helpful ways for people to get the facts specific to their individual needs. Hotlines also refer callers to additional resources, both people and places.

Tell the group that there is a National AIDS Hotline. Write the number on the board: 1-

800-342-2437. This is a toll-free call and the phone is answered 24 hours a day, seven days a week. The people at the hotline have a database (a computerized pool of information) of names and phone numbers for every area of the country. When the caller tells the hotline operator where they live and the type of information they need, the operator can supply the numbers to call. This can include information on HIV counseling or testing centers, speakers for groups, and drug treatment centers. Note that telephone numbers that begin with 1-800 are toll-free. The call does not cost money and the numbers will not appear on the phone bill.

Every state has an AIDS hotline. Many of these phone lines are toll free, however they can only be called from within that state. Mention that several agencies have national AIDS hotlines. These include the Centers for Disease Control, drug prevention agencies, and sexually transmitted disease treatment centers.

Invite the students to become involved in a project that will help people become more aware of and use AIDS hotline numbers. Suggest that they make wallet-size cards with these important numbers written on them.

Pass out paper and pencils and ask each person to draw a simple outline of a telephone on it. Patterns may be provided and the students may draw around them. Distribute the materials needed for the pupils to draw or trace the numbers onto lightweight cardboard, plastic pattern sheets, or commercial stencil paper. Before beginning the next step, protect the work area, such as table tops or desks, with heavy cardboard or cutting boards. Give each learner a craft knife or sharp scissors and tell them to carefully cut out the phone shape. Save the inside and outside of the stencil pattern.

Distribute pieces of poster board or index cards to each person. Use "hot"-colored paper, if possible, to connect with the "hotline" theme. Tell each learner to place the stencil on the left-hand side of the paper and to secure it with tape or pins. If the inside piece of the stencil is used, place the piece down and brush away from the edges of the object. If the outside, or frame piece, is used, brush from the cut edge toward the center of the open shape.

Set the paint supplies within easy reach of the students. If fabric paint is used, follow package directions; if acrylic or tempera is used, be sure the paint is of thick-cream consistency. The paint should not be watery or applied heavily. Demonstrate how to stencil paint the paper. Dip the stiff brush into the paint, tap excess paint onto a paper towel and tap gently, but firmly, to apply the paint through the stencil opening onto the cloth. Make the edges of the design clean and definite, not irregular. Guide the children as they paint their designs. Allow time for the paint to dry thoroughly. The children may wish to create several cards.

Ask the painters to clean their brushes. These should dry completely before reusing. The stencils should be cleaned with damp paper towels to avoid paint build-up.

Provide pens or markers and tell the group to write several hotline numbers on their cards. Include the National AIDS Hotline number and the number for the state in which the children live. Invite the group to share their stenciled "hotline" cards with many people. Remind them that hotlines are one of many ways in which people receive information about HIV/AIDS.

Banners/Textiles

PURPOSE To create banners using slogans and symbols that promote positive attitudes for the fight against AIDS.

PREPARATION *Materials*

- Muslin, 100% cotton
- Bamboo poles, two per banner
- Pencils
- Beeswax or paraffin
- Pan, coffee can, or electric skillet, for heating wax
- Paint brushes, various widths
- Dye and wide container
- Water

- Brown paper grocery bags
- Scissors
- Iron
- Tacks

Advance Preparation

- Prepare banner background(s) to desired size. Be sure to include borders wide enough to attach to the poles
- Research positive slogans that are being used in the fight against AIDS
- Obtain addresses for state buildings and state officials

PROCEDURE Banners, with and without words, communicate powerful messages. Invite the participants to make individual or group banners that promote positive attitudes toward persons infected and affected by HIV/AIDS. Explain that the banners are to contain slogans and symbols that address statewide issues regarding AIDS. Brainstorm some of these matters as well as messages that can address them. For example, prejudice might be confronted with words such as "Hate Is Not a Family Value," discrimination with "Fight AIDS Not Persons with AIDS," and self-esteem with "Remember Their Names." "All One People," "Love One Another," and "Shalom" are appropriate phrases, too. Scripture calls for justice, and banners can embody God's call in a bold, creative, festive manner. Use verses such as Amos 5:24, Micah 6:8, and Matthew 25:35, 36.

Explain that if every state in the nation worked on promoting positive attitudes toward people with AIDS, the country would be further ahead in the fight against this disease. Discuss places in the state where banners could be displayed. Public buildings that house government offices and officials would be great places for banner exhibits. List several of these, such as the capitol building, governor's residence, and state colleges and universities. The projects may also be used in statewide parades and processions and at conferences and conventions.

Explain that batik, an Indonesian method of layering wax and dyes, will be used to create the banners. Decide if each person will make a banner or if one or more will be made cooperatively. Demonstrate the construction process.

Sketch with pencil all letters or artwork that will appear on the muslin cloth. In addition to words, include drawings and positive symbols such as hearts, peace signs, smiley faces, candles, and "I love you" in sign language.

Mix one-half beeswax and one-half melted paraffin in a container with an opening wider than the widest brush that will be used to apply the mixture. When melting beeswax and paraffin, use low heat only, as the wax is flammable at high temperatures. Controlling the heat is easier when using an electric skillet with various temperature settings.

Apply the wax mixture within the pencil sketches on the cloth with whichever size paint brush is most appropriate for the degree of detail in the design. Let the wax harden for a brief time. Wrinkle the piece into a ball shape until the wax begins to crack slightly, then carefully open the cloth.

Gently slide the cloth into a wide container of cold or warm water dye solution. Do not use a dye solution that requires boiling the water or the wax will melt. After totally saturating the cloth with the dye solution, remove it and clip it to a clothesline to air dry. Do not wring the cloth. Newspaper should cover the floor in this area.

At this time, provide supplies for the individual or group projects. Allow time for the students to apply the wax and dye to their banner backgrounds. Carefully supervise this procedure.

While the cloth is drying, gather the group and explain the next step of the process to them. Place the dry cloth between sheets of brown paper or split brown grocery bags. Iron the paper with a warm iron until the wax is absorbed into the paper. Remove the brown paper. Tack or tie the banner to poles. When the banners have dried, help the learners complete this step of the project. Depending on the age of the participants, the ironing should be done, or carefully supervised, by an adult. Use these few minutes with each individual as a time to talk about the slogan and symbol on his or her banner. Encourage the young people to proclaim these positive messages with their lives as well as with their words.

Once the banners are completed, display them locally as well as statewide. Note that people who see them may respond and grow in their interest and involvement in AIDS issues and causes.

Cartoons

PURPOSE To make and use mix-and-match blocks to emphasize that all persons are affected by HIV/AIDS and to stress ways in which the infection is transmitted and prevented.

PREPARATION *Materials*

- Index cards
- Markers
- Square wooden blocks or cardboard cartons
- Permanent markers
- Tempera paints and brushes

Preparation

- Prepare index cards containing HIV/AIDS-related jobs and job descriptions. Write one job title per card and the job description on a separate card. Possibilities include:

  Advertising executive: Writes copy and takes photographs for a poster about AIDS prevention
  Bus driver: Drives a person with AIDS to a clinic appointment
  Clergyperson: Reads scripture and prays with a patient
  Construction worker: Builds group home for persons with AIDS
  Counselor: Meets with persons before and after HIV testing
  Dietician: Develops nutritional plans and pointers
  Disease control specialist: Finds people who have had sex with or shared needles with individuals who have tested positive for HIV
  Doctor: Plans tests and treatments for persons with AIDS
  Lawyer: Advocates for rights for HIV-infected persons
  Mortician: Plans and arranges funerals
  Nurse: Implements treatment procedures
  Police officer: Arrests persons for illegal drug and sexual activities
  Politician: Introduces bills regarding spending for HIV/AIDS
  Principal: Makes decisions about classroom curriculum content
  Reporter: Researches and reports data on HIV/AIDS
  Researcher: Analyzes data and checks experiments
  Social worker: Matches people with needs with agencies that provide services
  Student: Learns facts about transmission and prevention
  Teacher: Plans lessons on prevention themes
  Volunteer: Stuffs envelopes for a fund-raising event

PROCEDURE Disease control specialists and dieticians; police officers and politicians; reverends and researchers—everyone in a state is affected by HIV/AIDS. Demonstrate this concept by making and using mix-and-match blocks portraying a variety of people. Introduce the activity by helping the participants think about various individuals in a state who are affected by HIV/AIDS. Distribute the cards containing job titles and job descriptions to the group. Explain that each student holding a card that lists a job title is to find the person with a card containing the corresponding job description. For example, the person who received the card with the word "doctor" will find the player who has a card describing one HIV/AIDS-related facet of a doctor's work. State that some descriptions may fit more than one category; however, by the time everyone has found a partner, the best matches will be made by the process of elimination. Allow time for the students to talk to one another and to make matches. Take turns reading each job and its corresponding description.

Invite the group to make mix-and-match blocks depicting people who are affected by HIV/AIDS. Explain that individuals or groups will draw the persons they choose on three separate blocks. One block will contain the head, the second the upper body and arms, and the third the lower body and feet. Each person or group will draw six different people, one on each of the four sides, the top, and the bottom of the block. Arrange the learners in the work areas and ask each person or group to select six different people to depict.

Indicate the location of the supplies for the project. Distribute three large wooden or cardboard play blocks or three square cardboard cartons per person. If there are words or designs on the blocks, have the students cover them with paint or paper. Supply paper, glue, and scissors, or paint and brushes, for this purpose. Remind the group that they are to draw six different heads on the first block, one on each side. On the second block, they will illustrate six upper bodies and arms, and on the third square, six lower bodies and legs. Suggest that they vary the clothing on each drawing to correspond to the person's profession. If small blocks are used, permanent markers may be appropriate for the project; however, if large cartons are employed, paint will cover the surface more efficiently and effectively. Allow time for the artists to design and draw the people.

Once the blocks are completed, invite the students to take turns matching the correct sides to make the whole character or to mix them up and make imaginary characters. Tell stories of how these people are affected by HIV/AIDS.

Continue the activity by using three blocks and writing words related to HIV/AIDS transmission and prevention on them. On one side of the first block, write a category of transmission/prevention, for example, IV drug use. On the second block, write a method of transmission, such as sharing needles. On the third, write a prevention method related to IV drug use, such as "Don't share needles" or "Bleach needles." Create one or more sets of blocks following this theme and use them to teach important information about HIV transmission and prevention.

Creative Writing

PURPOSE   To report statewide AIDS issues and statistics in the form of poetry patterns.

PREPARATION   *Materials*

- Paper, pens, and markers
- Scissors
- Map of the United States
- Tape or tacks

Advance Preparation

- Obtain HIV/AIDS statistics for each state

PROCEDURE   Poetry patterns are poems, which do not have to rhyme, written in the shape of the poem's main idea. Use this unique creative writing style to compose verses about statewide AIDS issues or to report AIDS statistics for a particular place.

Ask the group to guess the number of reported HIV-infected persons in their state and the percentage of those infected who have AIDS. Supply the information gathered in advance. Begin this project by having each person write a shape poem that records the number or percentage of HIV/AIDS cases or relates to an HIV/AIDS-related issue in his or her own state. For example:

In the shape of the state of New York, write:

New York State has the largest number of AIDS cases in the country.

In the shape of the state of California, write:

Two California metropolitan areas are in the top ten cities with reported AIDS cases.

Provide resource materials, paper, pens, and markers, and guide the group in this creative writing activity. The verse may be repeated as many times as necessary to complete the shape.

Show the group a map of the United States. Invite them to guess the ten states and the ten cities with the largest number of reported AIDS cases. Supply the correct information as needed. As a group project, challenge the participants to create a bulletin-board map of the United States composed of poems shaped as individual states. Direct each person to research issues and numbers for several assigned states and to report the information by writing a shape poem for each of them. Cut each shape out of the paper and form the map of the nation by taping or tacking the poetry patterns to a bulletin board.

Culinary Arts

PURPOSE To play a game of Jeopardy to teach participants food safety advice for persons with AIDS.

PREPARATION *Materials*

- Poster board, construction paper, or chalkboard
- Markers or chalk
- Tape or tacks
- Timer
- "Eating Defensively: Food Safety Advice for Persons with AIDS" brochures[1]

Advance Preparation

- Write the Jeopardy answers on poster board, construction paper, or chalkboard
- Write the Jeopardy questions on separate pieces of paper

PROCEDURE Even though state and local health departments issue food sanitation guidelines to ensure cleanliness, hygiene, and proper processing, packaging, and preparation, many food-related illnesses result when people do not eat defensively. "It must have been something I ate!" is a phrase often uttered by people following a bout of nausea, upset stomach, cramps, diarrhea, or vomiting. Food poisoning, an illness caused by eating food on which harmful bacteria have grown, can cause ailments ranging from mild to severe and even life-threatening. Ordinarily the human body is well equipped to deal with this type of bacteria, but people with weakened immune systems, such as people with HIV or AIDS, may be at far greater risk of serious illness. People with weakened immune systems are also more susceptible to contracting any food-borne illnesses. Their infirmities can be more difficult to treat and can come back again and again. As a result, their immune systems become even weaker, often hastening the progression of HIV infection and sometimes proving fatal for persons with AIDS. HIV-infected persons can put their lives in "jeopardy" because of the food they purchase, prepare, and eat. Play a game of "Jeopardy" to help the participants learn more about food safety advice for persons with AIDS.

In the game of Jeopardy the answer is revealed and the question must be supplied. Individuals or groups may play the game together. Indicate the location of the game board and that one answer at a time will be revealed. The first individual or team will have one minute to state the question. If they provide the correct question, they will be given ten points. If they cannot come up with the question, the other player or team will have a turn to attempt it. Rotate teams after each question. The game ends when all questions are answered or when a pre-determined number of points are reached.

Discuss any of the questions and answers that need clarification. Remind the group that all people should eat defensively; however, this is especially important for people in high-risk groups, especially persons who are HIV infected. Not being aware of the hazards and not taking appropriate steps to reduce the risk of food poisoning can be life-threatening to these people. Challenge the students to spread the message that people should not play "Jeopardy" with food!

Jeopardy Answers

1. Nausea, upset stomach, cramps, diarrhea, and vomiting.
2. The cause of food poisoning.
3. The system of the human body that deals with bacteria and viruses.
4. Bacteria commonly found in raw or undercooked poultry, unpasteurized milk, and nonchlorinated water.
5. Bacteria that can cause meningitis, an inflammation of the membranes covering the spinal cord and brain, or encephalitis, an inflammation of the brain itself.
6. Bacteria contained in uncooked eggs.
7. Includes the words pasteurized, sell by, or best used by.
8. Unwrapped food and torn plastic wrap.
9. Keeping shelves, counter tops, refrigerators, freezers, utensils, sponges, and towels clean.
10. Preferred food preparation surface because it is easier to clean and sanitize.
11. Soap and hot water used after handling one food and before handling another.
12. 140 degrees Fahrenheit.
13. 165 degrees Fahrenheit.
14. Used instead of shell eggs when making home made ice cream, eggnog, and mayonnaise.
15. Required after the microwave cooking time to ensure that a proper temperature is reached throughout the food.
16. State and local health department regulations to ensure cleanliness and good hygiene in restaurants.
17. Thoroughly cooked food.
18. Avoid this type of salad because it contains raw eggs.
19. Oysters on the half shell, raw clams, sushi, sashimi, lightly steamed mussels, and snails.
20. Boil this liquid before drinking it when traveling abroad.
21. Boil it, cook it, peel it, or forget it.
22. Rest and fluids.
23. The agency to which incidents of food poisoning should be reported.

Jeopardy Questions

1. What are symptoms of food poisoning?
2. What is bacteria?
3. What is the immune system?
4. What is Campylobacter?
5. What is Listeria?
6. What is Salmonella?
7. What are food labels?
8. What is improper packaging?
9. What are ways to prevent bacterial contamination of food at home?
10. What are plastic cutting boards?
11. What is hand washing?
12. What is the minimum cooking temperature necessary to kill bacteria?
13. What is the minimum cooking temperature for reheating leftovers or heating partially cooked foods?
14. What are pasteurized eggs?
15. What is standing time?
16. What are sanitation guidelines?
17. What is well done?
18. What is caesar salad?
19. What are seafoods to avoid?
20. What is water?
21. What are food guidelines to follow when eating abroad?
22. What are treatments for food poisoning?
23. What is the local health department or the Food and Drug Administration?

Dance

PURPOSE To help children learn by experience that all people, though unique, must be treated without bias.

PREPARATION *Materials*

- Script for "Biasburg"
- Construction paper or fabric
- Scissors
- Tape or pins

Advance Preparation

- Find a person to narrate the story as it is presented, or prerecord the script onto a cassette tape to be used during the acting
- Assign the parts of the Wise Magus, the Blockies, and the Roundies
- Cut circles and squares from construction paper or fabric. Attach square shapes to the clothing or costumes of the Blockies and round shapes to the clothing or costumes of the Roundies
- Practice the story

PROCEDURE "Biasburg" is the story of two groups of people who live in the same town. Although they are similar in many ways, the "Roundies" are covered with circles and the "Blockies" are covered with squares. Because the members of each group look different, there is much anxiety and apprehension between them. Although "Biasburg" is only a story, its message is a common statewide theme. People in the cities and those in the countryside often look at the other group with mistrust and misgiving. Unfortunately, this is especially true in situations concerning AIDS. Misinformation and misunderstanding promote prejudice and paranoia. Anxiety and apprehension levels are high between people who are different because of a certain disease, a sexual orientation, or a problem such as drug abuse.

Use this story to help the participants explore and express some of their own biases regarding the differences between people. Guide the discussion before and after the acting to examine biases that are held on a statewide level. Include issues such as medical care, housing needs, legal services, and employment opportunities. Encourage each person in the group to realize and remember that he or she has a role and a responsibility to promote understanding among people.

Turn the tale into a dance activity. Invite one or more people to narrate the story. The words may be read during the performance or be pre-recorded. Instruct the people who are playing the parts of the Wise Magus, the Blockies, and the Roundies to interpret the narration nonverbally as the words are spoken. Be sure everyone in the group has a part to play in the project. Simple costume pieces, such as circles and squares made from construction paper or fabric, will add to the effect.

Biasburg[2]

Once upon a time in a place not too far away there existed a burg brimming with biases. The town was called Biasburg. Two types of critters lived in the village: a Roundy and a Blocky. Overall Roundies and Blockies looked the same. Both had two eyes, no hair, and huge mouths. However, one difference existed. Roundies had small circles on their skin. Blockies had small squares on their skin. They had them everywhere: on their eyelids, on their toes, on their bottoms, and on their noses. The contrast between circles and squares stripped a sense of companionship from the critters. Roundies differed from Blockies, and Blockies differed from Roundies. The villagers of Biasburg resented each other's variations.

Sordid suspicions arose in the city. Roundies raised rumors about Blockies. Blockies blabbed scandals about Roundies. Roundies remarked that Blockies were sharply mean and edgy. Blockies buzzed that Roundies were bursting with arrogance. Roundies and Blockies chattered, clattered, yipped, yapped, yammered, yakked, gibbered and jabbered about each other. Soon no one knew lowly lies from simple truths. Yet, everyone in Biasburg knew that Roundies and Blockies differed and acted as if that were all that mattered.

One day an elderly magician ambled into Biasburg. His long shimmering silver robe glistened in the sun's rays. The robe draped over his square shoulders and fluttered at this feet. A long pointed hat cast a shadow upon the magician's rounded face. His dark skinned hand clasped a shiny, smooth old oak rod. The elderly enchanter with the pointed hat and rounded rod was known throughout the land as the Wise Magus.

The Wise Magus viewed the village. He watched the two-eyed, no-haired, huge-mouthed critters scamper and scoot from site to site. The circles and squares blurred together in the scurry and scuttle. The Magus enjoyed the visual variety. The circled, squared sight delighted the elderly enchanter.

Strolling through the streets, the Magus surveyed Biasburg and the incredibly created critters. He noticed their eyes and observed the grimacing glares in their stares. The circled critters smiled at circled critters and frowned at squared critters. The squared critters grinned at squared critters and scowled at circled critters. The bizarre scene bewildered the elderly enchanter.

A Roundy walked toward the Magus. Abruptly, the circled critter halted and stood silently. Neither squares nor circles appeared on the man's dark skin. The Roundy did not know whether to grimace or grin, or perhaps both.

So, the critter quizzed, "Who are you?"

"I am known as the Wise Magus."

Immediately, the critter skedaddled from sight. The magician gently grinned and continued his stroll.

Some time later a hushed voice whispered, "Mr. Magus, come this way, please."

The Wise Magus turned and found a Roundy peering around a wall. The Magus followed the critter to a large hut. The door opened, and they entered. The oval room was dotted with Roundies. Roundies packed themselves into the room to meet the Wise Magus. As he entered, smiles passed from face to face throughout the room.

A confident critter stepped forward and announced, "You are the Wise Magus, and we welcome you to Biasburg. We are the Roundies. Creatures from land to land know you and the help you offer towns in need. Can you help us?"

The Wise Magus replied, "First, I must know what you desire."

The confident critter explained, "Biasburg is plagued with Blockies. I am sure you saw the nasty mean things. They are edgy and sharply mean. We try and try to civilize them to circled ways. They refuse to change. Roundies are soft in character without sharp edges. We grow tired of Blockies. Not to be rude, but we are tired of the cubes."

An approving uproar filled the room. Whoops and howls bounced from wall to wall. Anticipation swept through the room as Roundies waited for the Magus' reply.

The Magus replied with a light grin, "I will help. However, I can only point the way. Roundies and Blockies must complete the journey which may lay ahead."

A yipping, yowling yea shook the room. The confident critter remarked in the clamor, "I knew you would help.

Slowly the clatter quieted. The confident critter said, "What we desire most of all is sameness. Make us all the same—so there is no difference between a Blocky and a Roundy."

The Wise Magus slowly closed his eyes. With his hands clasped in fists, the sorcerer raised his arms above his head. The skies darkened darker than ever before. The Magus said, "Alla-Rallo-Wat." There was a crack of thunder. Then everything appeared the same.

Roundies burst from the oval room. Running faster than fast, the confident critter broke from the group. He darted through alleys and dashed through the streets. He zipped to all four corners of the town. Slowly, his brow formed a frustrated frown. Blocky after Blocky appeared in Biasburg. Perplexed and puzzled, the critter ran faster than faster than fast. Still, only Blockies appeared.

Slowly, his legs slowed to a lag. He ran and then walked until his legs only dragged. He looked north and then south, east and then west. "What happened," he shrieked, "What happened, I say." He raised his arm to wipe the sweat from his brow. In the corner of his eye, the critter saw a square. He screeched, "Not to be rude, but I'm tired of cubes." So the Roundy covered his eyes with his hands. A moment passed, and then his mouth dropped. "What's happening . . ." screamed the critter. "What's happening to me?" He looked at his hands, his arms, and his toes. He even crossed his eyes to look at his nose. He found squares on his skin and not a circle was around.

Energy swirled into his draggy, lagging legs. Again, the critter zoomingly zipped across Biasburg. A Roundy could not be found. Racing up and down streets, he passed houses and huts. Roundies could not be found. So he scurried downtown. Roundies could not be found. He looked in the town square. He circled city blocks. Roundies could not be found. Instead, Blockies were everywhere: in houses, in huts, up streets, down sidewalks, and in every corner of town. Not a Roundy was around.

Finally, the critter came upon the sorcerer with the shimmering silver robe. He scowled and glared. Being a critter of Biasburg, he had a huge mouth. Opening his mouth wide, he yelled louder than loud, "What did you do?"

The Magus grinned softly and replied, "You asked to look the same and asked nothing more."

"But I wanted Blockies to be Roundies. Not Roundies to be Blockies. Look at my town, there is not a difference around. I cannot tell Roundies from Blockies. What do you have to say?"

"Who I am right now is unique and special," replied the Wise Magus. "Smiles, frowns, ups, and downs alter me little by little. New faces and new places add layers of character to me. To live a full, rounded life, I celebrate who I am today, appreciate who I was yesterday, and anticipate the me of tomorrow. There are differences, my friend. You differ from me, and I differ from you. You differ from Blockies and Roundies, too. Just as I differ from day to day, you and I differ in little and big ways. Sameness is an illusion in your mind. For we can never be one of a kind."

The Roundy with squares on his skin did not understand. The critter distrusted differences. Biases blocked other views from his mind.

Elsewhere in Biasburg, Blockies and square-skinned Roundies bumped into each other. Instead of grimacing glares, surprise filled their eyes. Everyone's skin looked the same. So, they smiled and shared with one another. Some giggled, some chuckled, and some snorted when they laughed. Some limped. Some skipped. Some wheezed. Some coughed, and some sneezed. Their differences laid beyond squares and circles. They still talked and shared. Biasburg still brimmed with many biases. It takes more than a day to break biased beliefs.

Evening began in Biasburg. The sun's rays turned orange and red. Purple clouds crawled across the sky. The assorted colors danced up and down the Wise Magus' sparkling robe. The dark skinned magician viewed the village and thought, "We all have differences. Biases build around anything. For this town, it is circles and squares. Biases build because of nose sizes, sickness or health, hair color, or amount of wealth. If only we extended friendship's hand, even to those we do not understand.

Drama/Clown/Mime

PURPOSE To use role play to address issues of discrimination related to HIV/AIDS.

PREPARATION *Materials*

- Paper
- Stencils (optional)
- Scissors

Advance Preparation

- Cut out the individual letters of the word "DISCRIMINATION"

PROCEDURE Role play, a dramatic method, is intended to enable a person to experience the feelings of another individual or group. Use role play to help the participants address instances of discrimination associated with HIV and AIDS.

As the students arrive, hand each person a letter of the word "DISCRIMINATION." Randomly distribute the letters without any hint of the theme of the class. Instruct the group to work together to spell one word with the letters. Provide encouragement and assistance as needed. When the pupils have spelled the word "discrimination," ask them what it means. List the answers, and supply accurate information as needed. A simple definition for the word is "to make distinctions in treatment, or to show partiality or prejudice." Ask the class to think of situations where discrimination has been shown in their state or in other states in the nation. Answers could include the Japanese concentration camps in California during World War II and segregation in the South during the Martin Luther King, Jr., era. Focus the group's attention on discrimination as it relates to the topic of HIV and AIDS. Ask if HIV-infected persons are discriminated against? What about people with AIDS? Challenge the group to name instances of discrimination throughout their state. Answers should include the areas of housing, jobs, legal assistance, medical treatment, education, and much more. Challenge the class to explore several of these situations by role playing them.

Explain that role play is a dramatic method in which a person puts himself or herself into the "shoes" of another individual. Role play is intended to enable a person to experience the feelings of others. Decide on a situation to role play. For example, consider the case of a person who has lost his or her job because of HIV infection. Pose questions for the children to ponder, such as what might have happened before this situation? After?

Decide on the characters in the scene and ask for volunteers. Briefly review the situation. Do not offer suggestions for playing the roles; rather, help each person clarify his or her part by asking questions.

When the people playing the roles are ready, spontaneously enact the situation. Have the rest of the group watch. After several minutes, or when a climax is reached, or when the players run out of dialogue, stop the action. Discuss the situation. Help group members attempt to understand how the people in the scene felt and why. Repeat the scene with new people playing the roles, or choose a new situation to illustrate through this drama technique.

Remind the group to be aware of instances of discrimination and to work to end these occurrences through teaching, trust, and tolerance.

Games

PURPOSE   To design and play a game to help learners see how the AIDS virus cannot be spread.

PREPARATION   *Materials*

- Chalkboard and chalk or newsprint and markers
- Paper and pens or pencils
- Red ribbon
- Scissors
- Bingo sheet master

Advance Preparation

- Duplicate a Bingo sheet for each participant

PROCEDURE   Regardless where they live—Alabama to Alaska, California to Connecticut, and Michigan to Maine—children need to learn the same message: AIDS cannot be spread by casual contact. Since there is so much misinformation about the ways in which AIDS can be contracted, play a game to provide the facts. Begin by brainstorming ways that the AIDS virus cannot be spread from one person to another. Write a list on a chalkboard or on a piece of newsprint, discussing each idea as needed. Twenty-five possibilities are listed below. Provide ideas from this list to supplement the children's suggestions.

Hugging
Holding hands
Swimming

Sharing a soda
Riding in a car
Riding the school bus
Sitting in a classroom
Going to the same church
Mosquitos
Using a bathroom
Eating in a restaurant
Talking on a phone
Using the same towel
Dancing
Playing a game
Having slumber parties
Borrowing a book
Licking an ice cream cone
Kissing on the cheek
Sneezes
Drinking from the same water fountain
Tears
Sharing headsets
Money
Door knobs

Try an unusual game of Bingo. Distribute copies of the blank game board and pens or pencils to all participants. Instruct them to write one word or phrase in each square as it is read from the list they compiled. Explain that each participant should put the words in his or her own order, so that each board is unique. As the students write on their game boards, the leader should write each word or phrase on a separate small slip of paper. Deposit the slips into a container from which they will be drawn randomly as play takes place. When all participants are ready, place game markers, which could be small pieces of red ribbon, within sharing distance of each person. Play begins when the leader draws a word out of the container and reads it aloud. Each player covers the space containing that word or phrase with a marker. Play continues until one person has five spaces covered in a row vertically, horizontally, or diagonally. Repeat the game as time and interest allow.

This lesson could also be taught with a game of Win, Lose, or Draw. On slips of paper, write ways in which AIDS cannot be contracted. Allow the young people to take turns selecting a slip of paper and drawing the information named on it on a chalkboard or a piece of newsprint. The rest of the participants will attempt to guess what is being drawn.

Music

PURPOSE	To use music in an activity to explore every person's need for love.
PREPARATION	*Materials*

- Song books and hymn books
- Magazine pictures
- Scissors
- Markers or pens
- Glue
- Cardboard

PROCEDURE   Leslie. Louise. Lester. Luis. Lincoln. Livonia. Long Beach. Lubbock. It could be anyone, in any city, in any state. Regardless of the person or the place where they live, everyone needs to love and to be loved. Persons infected and affected by AIDS are no exception. In fact, love is essential for HIV-infected individuals. Sharing a message of God's love can be done in many ways. Music in an inviting, involving method to use to help people explore the theme of love. Use familiar songs in hymn books and children's song books to create a group activity.

Select magazine pictures that depict positive, exciting images of love. Choose one picture for each group of five children. Glue the picture to a cardboard surface to strengthen it. Cut each picture into five pieces. On the back of the five pieces from one picture, write the name of a familiar song with the theme of love. Repeat this process with a different song for each picture used. Songs to use include:

> For God So Loved the World
> Love in Any Language
> Love Makes the World Go Round
> They'll Know We Are Christians by Our Love
> What the World Needs Now Is Love

Look in the index of song or hymn books for additional songs with the theme of "love."

Randomly distribute one puzzle piece to each child. Instruct the participants to sing the song on the back of the puzzle piece while moving around the room attempting to locate others who are singing the same song. If the children do not know the words, instruct them to keep repeating the title written on the puzzle sheet. When the five children find one another, tell them to form a group and complete the puzzle. If the children do not know one another, each should introduce him or herself. Invite each group, in turn, to share their song. Use the completed puzzles to form a bulletin board display. Guide the group in a discussion of specific ways to show love to people with AIDS.

Photography

PURPOSE   To make a video report on ways in which departments, agencies, and organizations in a state are involved in AIDS prevention education.

PREPARATION   *Materials*

- Video equipment and video tape
- Pens, writing paper, envelopes, and postage stamps

Advance Preparation

- Obtain the addresses for state agencies, departments, and organizations, such as: department of health; department of education; Boy Scouts of America; Girls Scouts of America; Camp Fire; denominational offices; AIDS organizations

PROCEDURE   Make a "live" news report to document ways in which your state is addressing issues related to HIV/AIDS, especially prevention. Guide the students in writing letters to be sent to the departments, agencies, and organizations that educate others about HIV/AIDS. Provide the required supplies. Lead the children in asking their contacts to send information on various topics. Suggest questions such as: What is being done to provide schools with current AIDS education? Is there a packaged curriculum just for AIDS awareness and education? Do groups provide educational materials on AIDS for various age levels? Is there a statewide AIDS education organization? Are there current statistics on the state level of AIDS cases and deaths? How are groups across the state encouraging safe-sex awareness? Does the state department of health provide names and telephone numbers of clinics that provide free HIV testing? How are drug-related issues being addressed? How is the "Just Say No" program getting attention on the state level? Is drug-related AIDS an important issue throughout the state? Many additional concerns may be raised in the letters.

Once the information is gathered, allow the students to research and discuss the findings and to compare it to what may be happening on the local level. Invite groups of students to report their data by dramatizing a mock "News Report." Set up a news station with the young people as the news team. Using the video equipment, tape the report to share with local individuals and groups. A possible format for the students to follow should be drawn up ahead of time. From the information gathered, what should they report? Who will view the "News Report"? Include persons and organizations such as the PTA, the board of education, principals and teachers, parents, pastors, health-care providers, other classmates, and so forth.

A sample script for the project is given below.

ANCHOR PERSON: As the HIV/AIDS epidemic continues to grow, more people are in danger of getting the AIDS virus, HIV, through sex and IV drug use. In some cities in the United States, AIDS is already the leading killer of young heterosexual people. Because AIDS will be with us a long time, it is important to know the facts and how to prevent HIV infection, which can lead to AIDS. When people know the facts, they can take steps to protect themselves and the people they care about. Today we have several reporters who will share information on various aspects of the statewide campaign for AIDS prevention.

1. [Name], what needs to be known about HIV infection and AIDS?
   Report

2. [Name], how does the state provide AIDS education?
   Report

3. [Name], how many women and children have become infected with the AIDS virus? How?
   Report

4. [Name], where can a person go to be tested? What is involved in the testing process?
   Report

Continue asking and answering questions as time allows. Once the video is completed, make arrangements to show it to as many people as possible.

Puppetry

PURPOSE   To create bottle puppets to learn that bleach is a substance that helps control the transmission of the AIDS virus.

PREPARATION   *Materials*

- Bleach bottles
- Felt
- Fabric scraps
- Yarn, fake fur, or polyfil stuffing

- Scissors
- Glue
- Paper towel tubes
- Duct tape
- Rickrack, ribbon, buttons

Advance Preparation

- Clean the bottles and remove the labels

PROCEDURE   Drug use is a critical issue in every state. Drugs are a factor in a state's crime statistics since property is stolen to support drug habits; in traffic fatality counts since many automobile accidents are caused by drivers who are using drugs; and in financial support because tax and insurance dollars are needed to pay the medical bills of people with drug-induced ill-nesses. There are also many ways in which drug use is involved in the spread of the AIDS virus. It is estimated that users of intravenous drugs make up 25 percent of the cases of AIDS in the U.S. Although drug-related issues are big problems to tackle and will take time to correct, an immediate solution when addressing drugs and AIDS is to teach children how a simple substance, bleach, can help to prevent the spread of the HIV virus.

Hold up a bottle of bleach and ask the participants to state its use. Most people will respond that it is used as a cleaning product, particularly when washing clothes. Indicate that the group will be learning how bleach also helps to control the transmission of the human immunodeficiency virus, or HIV. Comment that the class will be turning bleach bottles into puppets that will be used as tools to help educate others about HIV transmission and pre-vention.

Ask a volunteer to explain ways in which drugs are associated with the spread of the AIDS virus. Supply the correct information, as needed. People who inject intravenous drugs risk getting the AIDS virus if they share needles. It is estimated that nearly one-fourth of the peo-ple who have been infected acquired the virus through needle sharing. As people inject drugs into their veins, minute amounts of their blood may be drawn into the needle and syringe. If the person is infected, this blood may contain HIV. When another person uses the same nee-dle, the virus in the blood may be transmitted to this second user. Because people can carry and transmit HIV without exhibiting any symptoms, sharing needles is never safe. One use of a contaminated needle may be all it takes to become infected with HIV for a lifetime.

The use of recreational drugs, such as PCP (angel dust), cocaine, and crack, legal drugs prescribed for another person, and alcohol are involved in the spread of the AIDS virus. Both drugs and alcohol affect a person's judgment. Because of the influence of these sub-stances a person may take dangerous risks or avoid protecting him or herself from HIV infection.

Note, too, that it is never safe to use or play with needles found in trash or other places. No one can be sure that the needles were not used by an infected person.

Talk about ways in which bleach is associated with IV drug use and AIDS. Bleach kills the AIDS virus that gets into used needles and syringes. If a person is injecting drugs, it is extremely important to spread the message that sharing needles can also spread the AIDS virus. The AIDS virus can, however, be killed by proper cleaning of needles, syringes, and other drug-related implements before and after each use.

Bleach is also used to clean up spills of blood and body fluids. Spills should be flooded with a solution composed of ten parts bleach to one part water. Precautionary procedures are described the chapters "Community" and "School."

Tell the students that used bleach bottles can be recycled into puppets by adding low-cost or no-cost materials. Make a puppet person or character and employ it to talk about the uses of bleach as they relate to HIV/AIDS.

Pick a bottle. Turn it upside down and decide if the side with the handle will be turned toward the front or the back. If it is to be the front, the handle becomes the puppet's nose. Place a paper towel tube on the pouring spout of the bottle to serve as the rod by which the puppet is operated. Use duct tape to secure the two pieces together.

Form the face by cutting eyes and a mouth from felt scraps. Glue them in place.

Eyebrows, eyelashes, and cheeks may be added.

Make hair from yarn, fake fur, or polyfil stuffing. Glue it to the top of the puppet head.

Choose a large square of fabric for the costume. Cut a small hole in the center of the material and slide the paper tube through it. Tape the fabric to the neck of the puppet. Add contrasting pieces of cloth and trims to complete the costume.

Discuss ways in which the bleach bottle puppets can be used to help people learn more about the transmission and prevention of the AIDS virus, particularly as it relates to drugs. Obtain statistics on drug use and AIDS cases in the state and include this information as part of the presentation.

Storytelling

PURPOSE To use news stories to learn the importance of keeping informed on AIDS issues.

PREPARATION *Materials*

- Newspapers, magazines, and journals
- Scissors
- Bulletin board
- Tacks or pins
- Construction paper

Advance Preparation

- Prepare a current events bulletin board with headings such as: Statistics, Civil Rights, Economics, Research and New Developments, Government, People, Health

PROCEDURE New information about HIV/AIDS appears almost daily. It may be reports about a new treatment, government legislation, or stories of people infected or affected by the disease. Ask the participants to name ways in which they learn about AIDS. Responses may include radio, television, newspapers, magazines, journals, books, comics, video tapes, pamphlets, brochures, and more. Ask the learners to share reasons why it is so important to stay informed about AIDS issues. Answers include making intelligent decisions, helping other people, and adjusting personal actions and attitudes. Tell the students that to stay informed about the AIDS epidemic they must have access to the frequent changes in information. One way to do this is to search newspapers, magazines, and journals for stories. These types of publications keep people informed about critical issues. Invite the group to create a current events bulletin board using articles from newspapers and other printed materials in their own community and in cities throughout their state and other states.

Direct each person or group to locate articles on the following topics, such as:

Statistics—Reports on the number of reported HIV/AIDS cases in the community, state, nation, and world
Civil Rights—Stories on housing and employment
Economics—Articles on fund raisers for AIDS organizations
Research and New Developments—Details on treatment and studies
Government—Columns on legal decisions and policy statements
People—Features on persons working for AIDS causes
Health—Suggestions on wellness and lifestyle

Show the students the bulletin board that has been prepared with these categories. Tell the group that they are to find articles for each theme, read them, cut them out, and post them in the appropriate section of the bulletin board. Distribute newspapers and publications to individuals or groups. Place scissors and tacks or pins within sharing distance of the participants.

After the group has had time to complete the project, ask individuals to share the news reports they located about AIDS issues. Talk about one article from each category.

Extend the project by encouraging the students to continue looking for articles and to bring them to hang on the bulletin board. Also suggest that the learners obtain newspapers from other cities within their state and others states within the United States. These are available at news stands, at book stores, and by writing the publishers. Articles on various topics will be available from numerous sources. Compare and contrast the information obtained from different publications. Remind the group that gathering information on a topic, such as AIDS, is a lifelong process, not just a one-time activity.

1. U.S. Public Health Service, Food and Drug Administration, *Eating Defensively: Food Safety Advice for Persons with AIDS* (Washington, D.C.: Department of Health and Human Services, 1990).
2. Tim Chartier, "Biasburg," Kalamazoo, Mich., 1993. Used with permission.

CHAPTER 5
Community

Children with HIV/AIDS and protection of health-care workers are only two of the issues connected with the theme "Community." Besides issues, concepts to consider include cooperation, communication, and conflict resolution. These themes and topics, and many others, are addressed in creative ways through the activities in this chapter.

Architecture

PURPOSE   To construct bag buildings and to learn about workplace issues involving HIV/AIDS.

PREPARATION   *Materials*

- Brown paper grocery bags
- Markers
- Items listed in "Advance Preparation"
- Paper and pencils
- Construction paper
- Tempera paint and paint brushes
- Crayons
- Magazines
- Scissors
- Glue
- Stapler and staples
- Tape
- Miscellaneous materials such as egg cartons, cardboard tubes, packaging materials, etc.
- Rocks or stones

Advance Preparation

- Prepare one grocery bag for each letter of the word "EMPLOYMENT." Number the bags 1-10 in large numerals. Do not write letters on the bags at this time. In each bag, place a common item that has the same first letter as a corresponding letter of the word. Each item must relate to a place of employment. For example:

  1. E—Envelope
  2. M—Money
  3. P—Plunger
  4. L—Level
  5. O—Oil can
  6. Y—Yarn
  7. M—Mittens
  8. E—Egg (plastic)
  9. N—Newspaper
  10. T—Teddy bear

PROCEDURE   HIV/AIDS touches all areas of life, including the workplace. Before long, almost everyone will know someone who is infected with HIV. In many instances, these acquaintances will be co-workers. Young children may hear their caregivers discussing employer policies regarding

AIDS. Older youth may work with a person who is infected. People who provide services such as school staff members, food service employees, and park department personnel may have friends or family touched by the epidemic or may be directly affected themselves. Engage the participants in thinking about workplace issues connected with HIV/AIDS. Begin with a guessing game involving objects associated with various professions. These have been placed in brown paper bags which will then be used to build a community of places where people work. Suggestions for discussing principles for the workplace will be offered to guide the conversation throughout the activity.

Introduce the theme of employment by playing a game with the brown paper bags that were prepared in advance. Place the bags in numerical order (see above) on a table or ledge. Tell the group that, when combined, the first letters of the items in each bag will spell out a word. Challenge them to identify each object by reaching into the bag and feeling it. No peeking allowed! Distribute paper and pencils. Ask the participants to number their paper 1 to 10 vertically. Instruct them to write the name of the object by its corresponding number on their sheet. Give the learners five minutes to explore the bags and then gather as a group. It is not necessary to do the bags in order as long as each word is written next to the appropriate number.

When time is up, stand near the row of bags. Beginning with bag number one, ask what item it contained. Allow the students to answer and then hold up the object. Write the letter on the bag. Continue until each object and letter are revealed. Read the word "Employment" together. Tell the group that they will look at each object again and name a workplace where it might be used. For example:

1. E—Envelope—Office
2. M—Money—Bank
3. P—Plunger—Plumbing company
4. L—Level—Construction company
5. O—Oil can—Automobile repair shop
6. Y—Yarn—Fabric shop
7. M—Mittens—Department store
8. E—Egg (plastic)—Grocery store
9. N—Newspaper—Newspaper office
10. T—Teddy bear—Day-care center

Tell the group that they will be using these bags, and others, to create a "model" community. Each building will represent a place where people work. Ask each student or group of students to pick a place to make. The young people do not need to be limited to the locations associated with the objects. Ask them to name additional places of employment. These may include libraries, restaurants, hospitals, as well as pizza restaurants, skating rinks, and movie theaters, plus many more.

Show the supplies and provide each individual or team with a stack of brown paper bags. Encourage them to use the materials to construct their buildings. Suggest basics like doors and windows and details such as signs and shingles. Provide the basic directions for constructing a bag building.[1]

Open one bag and stand it upright on the floor. Place a weight such as pebbles, rocks, or other object inside the bag. Open a second bag and turn it upside down. Slip the second bag down over the first bag. Glue together. This is the basic building structure. For a taller building, open a third bag and slip the open end over the second bag a few inches. Glue them together. For even taller buildings, additional bags can be added in this manner. Horizontal bags can be added to the basic vertical structure for a rambling building. Make a 4" slit in all four corners of another bag; fold and crease the flaps of the narrow sides. Turn the bag horizontally and slide the open end of the bag onto one of the vertical bags. Glue all four flaps to the vertical bag.

Embellish the basic building structures. Here are several suggestions:

- Color brick, stone, wood, or aluminum siding designs on the bag.
- Make windows and doors by cutting holes in the bags. Plastic food wrap or report covers can be taped in place as windows.

- Cover bags with aluminum foil for a slick modern building.
- Cut out pictures from magazines that can be glued to the bag structure to add interest.
- Add details such as chimneys, towers, etc. from miscellaneous materials.

At a designated time, ask everyone to help clean up. Then assemble the box buildings as a community. Invite each architect to share something about his or her building, the type of work that takes place there, and the people who are employed in it.

Tell the participants to be seated. Ask the group if any of these workplaces are touched by HIV/AIDS. Request examples. Most people infected with HIV are active members of the workforce. Is the workplace safe? What if an employee has AIDS? What facts should employees and employers know about AIDS? How can they obtain this information? Brainstorm a list of ways in which workplaces can address HIV/AIDS issues. Use the *Ten Principles for the Workplace*[2] as a guide for discussion:

1. People with AIDS or HIV infection are entitled to the same rights and opportunities as people with other serious or life-threatening illnesses.
2. Employment policies must, at a minimum, comply with federal, state, and local laws and regulations.
3. Employment policies should be based on the scientific and epidemiological evidence that people with AIDS or HIV infection do not pose a risk of transmission of the virus to coworkers through ordinary workplace contact.
4. The highest levels of management should unequivocally endorse nondiscriminatory employment policies and educational programs about AIDS.
5. Employers should communicate their support of these policies to workers in simple, clear, and unambiguous terms.
6. Employers should provide employees with sensitive, accurate, and up-to-date education about risk reductions in their personal lives.
7. Employers have a duty to protect the confidentiality of employees' medical information.
8. To prevent work disruption and rejection by coworkers of an employee with AIDS or HIV infection, employers should undertake education for all employees before such an incident occurs and as needed thereafter.
9. Employers should not require HIV screening as part of general pre-employment or workplace physical examinations.
10. In those special occupational settings where there may be a potential risk of exposure to HIV infection, employers should provide specific, ongoing education and training, as well as the necessary equipment, to reinforce appropriate infection control procedures and to ensure that they are implemented.

At the conclusion of the session, gather around the bag buildings again. Compose individual or group prayers about the buildings, their functions, and the people who work in them. Share the prayers together.

Art

PURPOSE	To enable participants to draw their dreams of a world or community without HIV/AIDS.
PREPARATION	*Materials*

- Paper or paper bags
- Markers, crayons, or colored pencils
- Pencils
- Masking tape or push pins

PROCEDURE To a child, and even to many adults, a world without HIV/AIDS might seem like an unattainable goal. One way for a young person to contribute to a world without HIV/AIDS is to imagine what such a place would be like. Once conceptualized, the child can then begin to work toward that goal. The art activity "Draw Your Dream" provides an opportunity for students to visualize these concepts.

Arrange the participants into small groups and challenge each team to discuss their "dreams" of a world, nation, state, community, neighborhood, school, congregation, family, and person without HIV/AIDS. Be sure the students are familiar with the ways in which HIV is both transmitted and prevented. Assign each group a different concept to consider. Tell the groups to "dream" up answers to the question. There are no right and wrong responses. Something that seems totally impossible just might work! Fact, as well as fantasy, may be part of the solution. After ample time for discussion, ask each group to take a turn to report their responses. These could include:

> **World**: Divert some of the military budget to the fight against HIV/AIDS.
> **Nation**: There is an "AIDS CORPS" created similar to the Peace Corps or the Jobs Corps to address HIV/AIDS issues.
> **State**: State-supported colleges and universities devote more research time to HIV/AIDS.
> **Community**: HIV/AIDS programs are part of the agenda of every youth club.
> **Neighborhood**: People mount aggressive anti-drug campaigns.
> **School**: AIDS education is part of the curriculum.
> **Congregation**: People of faith offer care and compassion to infected and affected persons.
> **Family**: New ways of expressing love are shared between people.
> **Individual**: Self-esteem is developed.

Distribute large sheets of paper or paper bags and markers, crayons, or colored pencils and invite individuals to use one side of the paper to illustrate their ideas on one of these themes. Upon completion, tell the participants to turn the paper over and to draw their dream of a community without HIV/AIDS. Once the dreams are drawn, tape or tack them to bulletin boards or walls and encourage the students to explore one another's ideas.

Find a way to share the project with more people in the community. Ask permission to display the drawings in public places or at community events. Create a coloring book and sell it as a fund raiser for an AIDS service or research organization. Get creative and find a way to use the drawings as the basis of a billboard, ads on public transportation, murals on buildings, or paintings on the sides of buses.

Remind the students that dreams do become realities and that it is up to each person to strive to make it happen.

Banners/Textiles

PURPOSE   To weave a ribbon banner with colors symbolizing concern for community issues.

PREPARATION   *Materials*

- Ribbon (3/4" and 1" widths, various colors)
- Cardboard (3' x 5') or large wooden frame
- Heavy string or acrylic yarn
- Permanent markers
- Scissors
- Scotch tape
- Exacto knife
- Wooden slats, 1' long (optional)

Advance Preparation

- Prepare the cardboard base by using the exacto knife to cut 1" long slits into the top and bottom edges of the cardboard, approximately 1" apart. Run a continuous piece of heavy string or acrylic yarn through each slit, from one side to the other, being careful to maintain even tension. Cut the string and tape the ends securely to the back of the cardboard.

- Cut the ribbon into 6 1/2' to 8' lengths. (Note: Run a bead of glue along the ends to prevent unraveling.) Place these strips in a basket or box.

PROCEDURE   Ribbons of various colors are used in many ways as signs and symbols of concern for other people. For example:

> **Yellow Ribbon**: Signifies waiting for the return of a loved one, often serving in the military.
>
> **Red Ribbon**: Shows support for a Drug Free America. Also used to raise AIDS awareness.
>
> **Rainbow Ribbon**: Represents concern for the rights of gay men and lesbian women.
>
> **Purple Ribbon**: Shows support for the fight against urban violence in America.
>
> **Green Ribbon**: Signifies concern for the rain forests.
>
> **Blue Ribbon**: Represents child-abuse awareness.
>
> **Pink Ribbon**: Shows support for breast cancer research.

Weaving is an art form that blends individual elements into a single piece with a variety of textures and colorful designs. Weavings can be frameworks for a thoughtful, compassionate response to community issues. Show the group the ribbons of various colors and discuss how the colors symbolize community concerns. Invite the group to use the ribbons in a weaving. This project can help them visualize how their individual contributions can be combined to work to address community concerns, including AIDS.

Show the students the base, the cardboard or wooden frame prepared in advance, and explain that individually and collectively they will be weaving with ribbons to symbolize "weaving a new tomorrow" in their community.

Ask each participant to select a strip of ribbon from the ones cut in advance. Distribute permanent markers and have the group write on their strip one way they will work to address issues in their community. The color of the ribbon they use for their idea should correspond to the color that represents the issue they are writing about. The ideas could include distributing ribbons at a community gathering or tying ribbons around a tree in front of a community building to raise awareness of a certain cause.

Give all the members of the group an opportunity to read their ideas aloud and then to weave their ribbons into the base. Have the first participant take the ribbon and weave it over the first string and under the second, alternating in this way until the ribbon is woven from one edge to the other. Finish by folding both ends of the ribbon and weaving them under several strings on the back of the cardboard. The next participant should insert a ribbon next to the first ribbon, but weave it under the first string and over the second; finish the ends in the same way. Have the group continue to weave their ribbons in this manner until everyone has had a chance. Periodically place a row of wooden slats into the weaving to make it more stable. When the weaving is done, make sure all the ribbons are sufficiently tight, then place a long strip of scotch tape across each set of ribbon ends to secure them to the back of the cardboard.

As the weaving is being done, discuss how this project symbolizes each person's part in weaving a new tomorrow and how this becomes possible when many people work together on the same cause or issue. Display the woven piece in a prominent location or send it to the mayor or city council with an explanation of the project.

If the students are interested in creating individual weavings, provide the supplies and continue the project.

Cartoons

PURPOSE   To use cartoons to illustrate activities in which there is no risk of getting HIV/AIDS.

PREPARATION   *Materials*

- "No Risk Here" cartoons[3]
- Paper and markers

No Risk Here!

Hugging

Kisses

Mosquitoes

Sneezing or Coughing

Sharing
Silverware or a
Drink

Toilet Seats

- Duplicating or photocopying equipment
- Dictionary

Advance Preparation

- Duplicate two "No Risk Here" cartoons for each game

PROCEDURE   Look up the word "risk" in a dictionary. Read and explain its various meanings. "Risk" is a word that is frequently mentioned in connection with HIV/AIDS. In many cases, the organism that causes AIDS is passed from one person to another because they engage in risky behavior. These risks generally include having sexual contact with an infected individual or sharing needles and syringes used for injecting drugs with a person with HIV.

People with HIV infection are at high risk of becoming sick with minor and major illnesses. Since the AIDS virus attacks a person's immune system, it damages his or her ability to fight other diseases. Without a functioning immune system to ward off disease, a person becomes vulnerable to infection by bacteria, protozoa, fungi, viruses, and malignancies, which may cause life-threatening illnesses, such as pneumonia, meningitis, and cancer.

Risk, when linked with HIV/AIDS, is often mentioned in connection with groups of people, too. Babies born to HIV-infected mothers are at high risk for contracting the disease. People who cannot afford proper medical treatment are at risk of serious complications from the virus. Males and females, of all ages, are at risk of getting AIDS if they engage in unprotected sex or sex with multiple partners or if they inject drugs and share the works.

Unfortunately, however, many people think that they are at risk of contracting the AIDS virus if they have casual contact with an infected person. There is no known risk of infection in most of the situations people encounter in their daily lives. There is no evidence of transmission, or spread, of the AIDS virus by everyday contact even when people share telephones, towels, toilet seats, or touches. Use a game of Concentration to emphasize that the AIDS virus is not transmitted by casual contact.

Show the group the six "No Risk Here" cartoons. Discuss each of the situations that are illustrated: hugging, kisses, mosquitoes, sharing silverware or a drink, sneezing or coughing, and toilet seats. Talk about the fact that the AIDS virus is not transmitted through casual contact. Brainstorm a list of other ways in which the virus is not spread, such as: using someone else's pencil, being in the same room with an infected person, and shaking hands.

Tell the group that they will be using the cartoons as game pieces to play Concentration. Distribute two pages of each cartoon, together with markers, crayons, or colored pencils, and invite the participants to color the pages. If additional pieces for the game are required, pass out two sheets of paper for each theme. Tell the illustrators to draw two identical pictures of a situation, putting one on each sheet of paper. Make sure one side of each paper is left blank. Collect the pieces from each person. Shuffle them and lay them out, picture side down, in a tiled pattern on the floor or on a table. If there are a large number of participants, prepare two or more games. However, be sure to keep the pairs together within a given game. Instruct the players to take turns exposing the cards and attempting to make matches. Each player may turn two cards over during his or her turn. If they match, another turn may be taken. If they do not match, the cards are returned to a face-down position. Then the next person attempts to make a match by turning over two cards. The play continues until all pairs have been uncovered. When the game is over, use the pictures as a bulletin board display or use the papers to create two books which may be shared with other people.

Creative Writing

PURPOSE   To discover and develop public service announcements, PSAs, as a tool for raising community awareness about AIDS issues.

PREPARATION   *Materials*

- Paper and pens
- Typewriter or computer and printer

- Envelopes and stamps
- Cassette or video recording equipment (optional)
- Addresses for community radio and television stations
- Examples of AIDS-related public service announcements

Advance Preparation

- Obtain examples of public service announcements from the Centers for Disease Control

PROCEDURE Public service announcements, often called PSAs, are short notices that radio and television stations use to promote awareness of various topics and to publicize events. Public service announcements are free air time, and the Federal Communications Commission requires broadcasters to play a specific number of them in their daily programming. The most used public service announcements are 10, 30, or 60 seconds in length. A 10-second spot runs 25 to 30 words, a 30-second message is 65 to 75 words, and a 60-second PSA would be approximately 150 words. Although the PSA may be neatly handwritten or typed and mailed to the media, some stations prefer prerecorded material to which they can add their local call letters. Radio stations may use cassette tapes and television stations might appreciate video recordings.

Introduce the topic of public service announcements by asking if anyone knows what PSA means. Explain that PSAs are public service announcements that are aired on radio and television stations. PSAs communicate messages to the listening and viewing audiences about important information and upcoming events. Ask if anyone has ever seen or heard a PSA about AIDS. Challenge the participants to think of messages regarding AIDS awareness that should be communicated to their community. Develop a list of topics and themes such as transmission, prevention, educational opportunities, and special events. Show the group examples of the public service announcements available from the Centers for Disease Control. These include:

Television Advertising

Campus (30-second spot—English): This PSA relays the idea that even if individuals are tired of hearing about AIDS, they need to understand that they may be putting themselves at risk for HIV infection.

HIV Positives (30- and 60-second spots—English): The message of this PSA is that HIV infection and AIDS are not confined to easily identified groups of people; they can happen to individuals whose behavior makes them vulnerable.

Mirror (15-second spot—English and Spanish): This PSA communicates the message that all individuals should take a close look at their behavior to determine whether they are at risk for HIV infection and AIDS.

Radio Advertising

Ask Yourself (60-second spot—English and Spanish): The message of this PSA is that individuals who are vulnerable to HIV infection should consider counseling, testing, and early intervention.

No Difference (60-second spot—English and Spanish): This PSA sends the message that you cannot tell by looking at individuals whether they are infected with HIV.

Wonderful World (60-second spot—English): The message of this PSA is that HIV infection and AIDS can be prevented with an individual and collective commitment to fight the disease.

Invite the group to pick one or several topics and to write or record public service announcements to send to radio and television stations in the community. Regardless of where it will be used, there are simple guidelines to follow when furnishing a public service announcement. Prepare your PSA according to the following format:

Letterhead: Write the story on letterhead. Be sure it is double spaced and, preferably, typed.

Release date: In the top left corner of the page, type the date. Beneath it designate when the information is to be used. If it can be used as soon as possible, indicate that it is "For Immediate Release." If it must be held until a specific date indicate "For Release (date)." Also state the length of the item in seconds and words.

Contact Person: In the top right corner provide the name and phone number of a person to contact for additional information.

Headline: Using active verbs, write a short headline. Center and underline it on the page.

Text: Press releases are written in an inverted pyramid style. This means that the most significant facts should be stated first with each succeeding paragraph decreasing in importance. The opening paragraph needs to answer the five "W's": Who, What, When, Where, and Why.

Details: Be sure the information is accurate.

Additional Information: Provide additional or background information by attaching brochures and documents to the story. List the attachments on the bottom of the last page of the release.

Ending a page: If the article continues to a second page, write "more" on the bottom of page one. End the release with "30" or "###" in the center of the last page.

Thank you: After the PSA is used, send a thank-you letter stating appreciation for the coverage and acknowledging the results of the publicity.

Provide time for individuals, small groups, or the entire class to prepare public service announcements. If the PSAs are handwritten, arrange to have someone type them before they are mailed or delivered to the stations. If cassette or video recordings are to be part of the messages, make provisions to tape the required information. Once the messages have been completed, address envelopes and mail them to the media or take a field trip to deliver them to the stations.

In additional to PSAs, arrange an appearance on a radio or television talk show. Attempt to interest stations in doing remote broadcasts at the site of major events and in providing live news coverage to highlight specific programs.

Culinary Arts

PURPOSE   To provide food and to share it with community organizations that minister to persons with AIDS.

PREPARATION   *Materials*

- Resource materials
- Recipe(s) and ingredients
- Cooking utensils and equipment

Advance Preparation

- Research community AIDS-related projects to which food may be donated

PROCEDURE   There are many needs and opportunities for sharing food in a community. Help the learners identify food-related ministries that are specifically connected with persons with AIDS. Enable the participants to become aware of some of these through the use of speakers, audiovisual materials, newspaper articles, and field trips.

Challenge the group to get involved in a project to prepare or provide food for AIDS-related causes. Possibilities include:

- Holding a food drive for an AIDS ministry organization
- Collecting money and donating it to a food pantry
- Growing vegetables and giving them away
- Providing bags and asking people to fill them with food and other essential products such as bleach and return them to a designated site
- Serving holiday dinners

- Delivering meals on a daily basis
- Holding a regularly scheduled "coffee house" for persons with AIDS and their loved ones
- Making food and delivering it to people or places that serve persons with AIDS

As a group, choose a project and get involved. Some ideas would be to bake bread and bring it to an institution, to prepare and package muffins and share them with other people, or to make soup and serve it at a selected site. Use favorite recipes or some from books at the library.

Emphasize to the students that giving and sharing are two ways to show care and concern to people with special needs. Food ministries are only one way to demonstrate these important qualities.

Dance

PURPOSE To hold a dance-a-thon to highlight HIV/AIDS information and to raise funds for HIV/AIDS causes.

PREPARATION *Materials*

- Sponsor sheets
- Information on HIV/AIDS service and research organizations
- Music
- Equipment (record player, tape player, CD player, etc.)
- Snacks
- Notebooks and pens or pencils

Advance Preparation

- Prepare and distribute sponsor sheets to each participant
- Designate the organization to receive the collected funds
- Collect pledges for segments of dancing time
- Obtain music and equipment
- Enlist personnel to run the equipment, to lead dances, and to chaperon the event

PROCEDURE Although there are many ways to raise funds for AIDS service organizations and AIDS research, one idea that involves many people in a community is a marathon. Marathons can take the form of a walk-a-thon, a dance-a-thon, an aerobic-a-thon, and a rock-a-thon, among other ideas. City of Hope, a southern California-based medical center that provides care and treatment for patients with diseases including cancer and AIDS annually sponsors events called "Workout for Hope: Aerobics Against AIDS." Participants raise a minimum of $50 per person and also bring two cans of food, which serve as weights during the workout and are donated to local facilities where persons with AIDS live and receive medical attention. AIDS walks are held in many communities. Funds raised through these events benefit agencies providing AIDS care and services such as meals, housing, medical treatment, and education.

Invite the participants to get involved in a marathon to raise funds to support assistance to persons with AIDS. Determine if any events are currently held in the local community and, if possible, participate in one of them. As an alternative, or in addition to involvement in existing events, start one. Encourage the students to prepare and present a dance-a-thon for AIDS. Identify a date, time, and place. Begin on a Friday evening and run nonstop through Saturday night, or hold the event for a whole day. Secure leaders and guest or celebrity dancers for the event.

Preparations for the event must begin in several ways. If part of the purpose of the dance-a-thon is to raise funds for an AIDS ministry or service organization, prepare sponsor sheets and distribute them to the participants. Challenge the group to find people who will pledge money for each minute, half hour, or hour that they dance. Gather music from various sources. Secure the required equipment (tape player, CD player, etc.) and find people to run it. Distribute the equipment throughout the building, designating rooms for different age levels. Participants may be asked to bring a notebook and pen or pencil to record their dance times. They should also be told to bring pillows, sleeping bags, and snacks.

At the beginning of the dance-a-thon, gather the group and explain the policies and procedures. Each person must keep track in their notebooks of the amount of time danced. Encourage everyone to keep dancing until the time runs out, stopping only for snacks, meals, stretching, and bathroom breaks. If varying age groups are involved, assigned people to designated rooms.

At the conclusion of the event, instruct the participants to collect pledges and to return them to a designated person by a specific date.

Drama/Clown/Mime

PURPOSE   To write original plays addressing ethnic issues related to HIV/AIDS.

PREPARATION   *Materials*

- Paper and pens
- Index cards
- Resource material on ethnic groups and HIV/AIDS

Advance Preparation

- Obtain current data on distribution of HIV/AIDS cases by ethnic group by calling the Centers for Disease Control statistical information number (404-332-4570) and listening to the recorded message.
- Prepare five assignment cards, each containing four categories: ethnic group, age, gender, and transmission type. For example:

Card One

Ethnic Group: American Indian
Gender: Man
Age: 32
Transmission: Homosexual relations

Card Two

Ethnic Group: African American
Gender: Woman
Age: 46
Transmission: Blood transfusion

Card Three

Ethnic Group: Hispanic
Gender: Male
Age: 17
Transmission: Drug use

Card Four

Ethnic Group: Asian/Pacific Islander
Gender: Female
Age: 23
Transmission: Rape

Card Five

Ethnic Group: Caucasian
Gender: Either
Age: Pre-school child
Transmission: Mother to child transmission

PROCEDURE HIV/AIDS does not discriminate. All people, regardless of ethnic background, can become infected with the virus that causes the deadly disease. As the epidemic escalates, minority groups are the most adversely effected. Write the following statistics on a chalkboard or newsprint and ask the participants to match the correct ethnic category to each number:

47,835 (Hispanic)
569 (American Indian)
1,823 (Asian/Pacific Islander)
150,247 (Caucasian)
608 (ethnic origin unknown)
88,238 (African American)

Challenge the class to write original plays as a method of gaining knowledge about ways in which people of different ethnic backgrounds are effected by HIV/AIDS. Organize the participants into five groups. Distribute an assignment card to each team. Tell each group to work cooperatively to write an original play incorporating the data on their card. In each case, the person described on the card has just learned that he or she is infected with the HIV virus, and the individual is seeking to find sources of help in the community. Assistance could relate to education, medical supplies and equipment, legal needs, transportation, treatment options, housing, employment, and so forth.

Begin the playwriting project by offering simple guidelines for developing the theme. Suggest that the young people decide what characters are needed and how many scenes there will be. The next step is to determine the action that will take place in each scene. Once a person finds out that he or she is HIV positive, there are a number of steps to be taken:

1. Testing for HIV infection
2. Monitoring the immune system
3. Treating with anti-HIV agents for halting immune decline
4. Preventing opportunistic infections
5. Planning alternative choices in case first therapies fail
6. Maintaining effective treatment combinations

Suggest that the students incorporate these stages into their plays. When these preparatory tasks have been accomplished, tell the groups to write the dialogue. Pass out paper and pencils and allow time for the pupils to work on their plays. Make resource and statistical information available. Offer assistance and encouragement where needed. Stress that each group must determine the community response for a person of the particular ethnic background listed on their card.

Once the scripts are written, provide an opportunity for each group to share their work. Discuss the options available, or unavailable, to people of different national origins. Find ways to present the productions to other audiences.

Games

PURPOSE To help students discover community support groups and services available to persons with HIV/AIDS.

PREPARATION *Materials*

- Paper and pens
- Newspapers
- Telephone directories
- Brochures

Advance Preparation

- Prepare scavenger hunt lists
- Arrange transportation for scavenger hunt

PROCEDURE In a scavenger hunt, a popular group game, individuals or teams are given a list of items to find and a designated time and area in which to locate them. This popular game is a good method to use to help young people learn more about community support groups and services available to people who have tested HIV positive and to individuals, family, and friends living with AIDS.

Ask the participants to name the types of services and support systems that HIV/AIDS-infected and affected people require. Answers could include: counseling, advocacy, housing, testing, and friendship. Also ask where people might go to fill these needs. Types of places might be: health departments, hospitals, hospices, youth centers, and discussion groups. Tell the learners that they will be going on a scavenger hunt to locate service and support groups available to persons with AIDS. Assign the individuals to teams. Indicate the procedure for the scavenger hunt. It could be played by using the telephone book and making phone calls, by looking through newspapers, magazines, and brochures and finding names of agencies, or by actually going to suggested sites. If the community is large, assign teams to different areas of the city so the reported information will be as broadly based as possible. Distribute the scavenger hunt lists and review them together so the learners understand what they are being asked to do. Sample items for the lists include:

- Find five congregations that offer support to persons with AIDS. List the names of the contact persons and the type of help available.
- Make a list of three organizations that offer advocacy programs. Services could include legal representation and legislative watch programs. Supply name of group, contact person, address, phone number, and list of services.
- Create a list of three youth service projects that are educating and supporting African American youth. Describe the programs offered.
- Find four organizations that supply basic needs, such as food, clothing, and shelter, to infected persons. Interview a worker at each location and write a short paragraph about the services provided.
- Bring brochures from three agencies that offer counseling services to persons and families living with AIDS.
- Go to a library and record the titles of ten books on AIDS-related subjects.
- Locate information about two organizations that offer support and services for children living with AIDS. Describe the programs provided.
- Record phone numbers and hours for three sites that provide HIV testing. Supply information on counseling, costs, and confidentiality.
- Find information about support groups for HIV/AIDS. Include groups that offer services for family members, friends, and caregivers of persons with HIV/AIDS.
- Discover five community resource groups that offer substance abuse and treatment services. Write a short report about them.

In addition to these suggestions, other possible investigations could include topics such as: advocacy, bereavement, coalitions, education, Hispanic services, holistic support, home care, hospice care, hospitals, hotlines, insurance, medical services, medical studies, parents, pets, spiritual help, teens, transportation, and women.

Before the groups begin the scavenger hunt, review the guidelines, such as time limit, locations, and so forth, and answer any questions that will clarify the procedure.

When the teams have finished the scavenger hunt, compare and compile answers so everyone can become more aware of the support and services available to persons infected and affected by HIV/AIDS.

Music

PURPOSE To write new words to a familiar tune to emphasize the importance of volunteers in various facets of AIDS ministry.

PREPARATION *Materials*

- Music to "Skip to My Lou" and accompaniment (optional)

- Overhead projector and acetate transparencies
- Fine-tip permanent markers

PROCEDURE   During the "America Responds to AIDS" campaign a helpful sheet was published entitled "How to Join the Community Response." It emphasizes that both adults and young people are vital members of the community team that provides HIV/AIDS education, reinforces safe behavior, and promotes healthful attitudes. It stresses that many communities have valuable resources to inform people about HIV infection and AIDS through organizations such as the American Red Cross, National Urban League, and boys' clubs and girls' clubs. Organizations that provide AIDS-related support and service rely heavily on the community for assistance. Most operate on shoestring budgets, with limited personnel, and depend on volunteers to spread their mission and ministry.

Emphasize the importance of volunteers who work for and with community AIDS organizations. Invite someone from an AIDS education or service organization, a community organization of people with AIDS, or the local health department to speak to the group and to share important ways people can volunteer their services to persons with AIDS. Direct services include offering help such as shopping, cooking, cleaning, and visiting. Many agencies welcome volunteers to answer phones, organize fund raisers, and make presentations.

Once the students learn about volunteer opportunities, invite them to compose new words to a familiar tune to stress the important role played by volunteers in the fight against AIDS. Tell the group that they will be writing new words to the tune "Skip to My Lou." Hum or play the tune so that everyone becomes familiar with it. Demonstrate a sample song, such as:

> *Bring a meal or answer the phone,*
> *Visit a person who lives alone.*
> *There are jobs that can be done*
> *By volunteers. Will you be one?*

Organize the participants into small groups and challenge each team to use the tune and to write words related to the theme of volunteers. Provide transparencies and fine-tip permanent markers so the groups may record their compositions. Once the groups have completed their assignments, take turns placing the words on the overhead projector and singing the new songs. Challenge the participants to volunteer to share their time and talents in some meaningful way.

Photography

PURPOSE   To use a photography project to look at the issue of women and AIDS.

PREPARATION   *Materials*

- Polaroid camera(s) and film
- Poster board
- Rubber cement
- Women's shoes (10 styles)
- Pens and index cards or paper
- Scissors

Advance Preparation

- Write true/false statements related to women and AIDS on separate index cards or pieces of paper. For example:

    Women are the fastest growing group being infected by the AIDS epidemic in the United States. [True]
    AIDS is one of the five leading causes of death among women between the ages of 15 and 44. [True]

Most women contract HIV infection through heterosexual contact and/or by using contaminated needles to inject drugs. [True]

Many infected women who are too ill to work cannot receive disability benefits. [True]

Women are often included in AIDS research only as possible infectors of children and men. [True]

Women can pass the AIDS virus to their unborn children. [True]

In major U.S. cities many HIV-infected women are African American and Hispanic. [True]

Human immunodeficiency virus can be transmitted to women who have graduated from college. [True]

AIDS does not discriminate between women who live in poverty and women with substantial incomes. [True]

AIDS is a leading cause of death for women ages 20 to 40 in Western Europe and sub-Saharan Africa. [True]

- Set ten different types of women's shoes on a table. Place one true/false question in or next to each of them.

PROCEDURE   It's true! As the HIV/AIDS epidemic continues to escalate, more and more women are in danger of acquiring the virus through sexual contact and use of injected drugs. In many cities of the United States as well as other regions of the world, AIDS is already one of the leading killers of young women. The World Health Organization predicts that within ten years as many as 80% of all AIDS cases will be transmitted heterosexually. Statistics show that a healthy woman who has sex with an infected man is fourteen times more likely to contract the AIDS virus than a healthy man who has sex with an infected woman.

Tell the group that they will be learning about women and AIDS. Begin by asking the participants to answer ten true/false questions related to the topic. Point out the women's shoes displayed in the room. Note the questions placed with the shoes. Distribute a piece of paper and a pen to each learner. Tell them to number the paper 1 through 10. Challenge the group to look at each shoe, to read the question, and to write the correct answer, "True" or "False," on their paper.

After the group has responded to the questions, review the answers, all of which are true. Provide additional information on these subjects. For example, many women who have AIDS today were drug users or were the sexual partners of drug users. Other women became infected by having sex with infected men who became infected by having sex with other infected men or women. Some women with AIDS were the sex partners of men who became infected from infected blood transfusions or blood products used for transfusion and to treat diseases such as hemophilia. Most of these women did not know that their sexual partners were infected. Even their partners may not have known that they were infected. Some women became infected with the AIDS virus through infected blood and certain blood products.

Continue the project by inviting the students to take photos of shoes that women in their community wear and to use the pictures to create a large poster or display, illustrating that HIV/AIDS infects females from many walks of life. The shoes will teach that AIDS does not discriminate and that all types of women can contract the virus. For example, take snapshots of shoes worn by a woman firefighter, nurse, dancer, ball player, police officer, farmer, mother, teacher, and so on. For instant results, use a Polaroid camera for this part of the project. Take a walk or provide transportation to various places in the community and photograph many different types of women's shoes. Explain the project to the subjects and ask permission to take the pictures.

Once the pictures are ready, mount them on a piece of poster board. Print the words "From Many Walks of Life" across the top of the poster. Take the project a step further by challenging the participants to write out the ways women can protect themselves against HIV/AIDS. Attach the papers to the shoe snapshots. Suggestions include:

Not injecting drugs
Not sharing drug needles or syringes

Not having sex
Having sex only with a partner who is not infected
Having protected sex

Display the poster in a place where many people will see it.

Puppetry

PURPOSE   To make and use tube puppets representing emergency and public safety workers to explain job-related risks and protection methods associated with HIV infection.

PREPARATION   *Materials*

- Paper tubes
- Felt
- Yarn or fake fur
- Fabric scraps
- Scissors
- Glue
- Craft sticks

PROCEDURE   Law enforcement workers, fire fighters, emergency medical service personnel, police officers, lifeguards, and rescue workers usually are the first professionals to arrive at the scene of an emergency situation. Most often assistance is provided without knowing the person or the person's medical history. Faced with job-related risks every day, emergency and public safety workers have concerns and questions about personal risk and HIV infection: Can I become infected with HIV on the job? Can I bring the virus home and infect loved ones? How can I protect myself and those I love?[4]

Ask the participants to name situations in which emergency and public safety workers might come into contact with HIV-infected persons. These include automobile accidents, explosions, drownings, emergency childbirth, and natural disasters. Also inquire why the emergency and public safety workers would not know that they were at risk of acquiring HIV infection. Explain that it is important to understand that people infected with HIV usually look and feel healthy and may not know for many years that they are carrying the virus. People who are infected remain infected for the rest of their lives and can pass the virus to others even if they don't have symptoms. When symptoms do appear, they can resemble those of many common illnesses, such as swollen glands, coughing, tiredness, fever, or diarrhea. These symptoms differ from person to person. Only a doctor and a blood test can tell if someone is infected with the AIDS virus. All emergency and public safety workers need to know how to prevent the spread of HIV in their personal lives. They need to treat everyone with the same standards of care, practice, and respect. They also need to follow the universal guidelines for infection control set by the U.S. Centers for Disease Control.

Relate to the participants that studies have shown that fewer than 1 percent of the workers who were accidentally stuck or cut with objects contaminated with HIV-infected blood or who had other direct exposure to blood become infected with HIV. Nearly all who do become HIV infected on the job are infected from needle sticks.

Help the pupils learn more about the risks and precautions related to HIV infection and emergency and public safety workers by making and using paper tube puppets. Let the puppet people represent many types of professions, such as ambulance drivers, police officers, nurses, doctors, and firefighters.

Demonstrate the procedure for making a tube puppet. Turn a paper towel tube, of any size, into a puppet. Form the puppet face by cutting a piece of felt and gluing it to the top one-third of the tube. Make facial features from felt scraps and glue them in place. Yarn or fake fur becomes hair and should be attached to the top of the tube. Glue a piece of felt around the remainder of the tube to serve as the costume. Layers of fabric in contrasting or complementary colors can be added as overgarments.

Make arms from strips of cloth or felt and glue them to the sides of the tube. Apply a craft stick to the inside back of the tube to serve as the rod by which the puppet is operated.

If felt is not available, use construction paper. The facial features may be drawn with markers. Substitute tissue or other types of papers for fabric to form the outer garments.

Provide the supplies and allow time for the group to construct their puppets. When the puppets are completed, use them to impart information about guidelines for protecting health-care workers to exposure to the AIDS virus. These include:

- Wear latex or vinyl gloves for contact with blood and other fluids requiring universal precautions. These substances include blood, semen, vaginal secretions, amniotic fluid, and fluid from the brain, spine, joints, chest, abdomen, and heart. Although these fluids are generally locked inside the body, when they are released because of injury they will usually be mixed with blood. Body fluids not requiring universal precautions unless visible blood is present are feces, nasal secretions, saliva, sputum, sweat, tears, urine, and vomit.
- When removing gloves, pull them off so that they are inside out, the contaminated side not exposed. Put them in a plastic bag or other container and dispose of them properly. Do not reuse gloves. Wear a new pair of gloves before handling another person.
- Wear protective eyewear when doing procedures which may result in splashes to the face.
- Dispose of needles and syringes in puncture-resistant containers without breaking or recapping the needle. Always dispose of needles immediately after use. Do not throw needles into regular trash.
- Wear protective clothing such as gowns or aprons to avoid spills of blood or body fluids onto uniforms or clothing.
- Wear a mask when conducting procedures.
- Wear gloves or a finger cot to cover a cut, abrasion, ulcer, rash, or skin infection on the hands.
- Wash the hands as soon as possible after contacting blood or body substances, touching objects that have been in contact with blood or body substances, or removing gloves.

Practice storytelling with the new puppets. Use these tools to share information about emergency and public safety workers and HIV/AIDS.

Storytelling

PURPOSE To emphasize that HIV-infected persons may be anywhere in the community and that a person carrying the virus cannot be identified by outward appearance.

PREPARATION *Materials*

- Poster board
- Scissors
- Markers or crayons
- Pencils and pens
- Magazines, newspapers, or catalogs
- Glue
- Paper punch
- Yarn
- String or ribbon

Advance Preparation

- Cut poster board into approximately 5" x 7" pieces

PROCEDURE Although there are many similarities among the people who live in a community, there are also many differences. Begin the activity by inviting the participants to name ways in which people are alike, regardless of where they live. Answers may include:

God made all people.
People have eyes.
Everyone needs to be loved.

Continue the discussion by asking the group to list ways in which people in various parts of a community are different. Generate ideas such as:

People speak different languages.
Religious practices may be different.
Skin colors vary from population to population.

In the course of the discussion point out that some people in the community are infected with HIV, the organism that causes AIDS. Ask the group if they can tell if someone is HIV infected by looking at the individual. The answer is "No." It is impossible to make this determination only on the basis of outward appearance. In fact, someone who is infected with HIV may look and feel healthy. They may not even know that they are infected. Sometimes it takes up to ten years for people with HIV to develop AIDS. The danger is that even if a person doesn't look or feel sick, he or she can infect others. By having unprotected sex or by sharing drug needles, as well as in other instances involving the transfer of body fluids, the virus can be unknowingly transmitted from one person to another.

Make story books to emphasize the fact that outward appearance is no indicator of whether or not a person is infected. Capitalizing on the popularity of the *Where's Waldo?* books, use the theme of "Who's Infected?" Ask the students to generate a list of places in the community where people gather. Answers may include:

Swimming pool
Zoo
Restaurant
Bus station
Grocery store
City park
Movie theater
Amusement park

Show the group two pictures of crowd scenes and ask them to tell which individuals in the scenes are HIV infected. It is impossible to tell.

Illustrate this theme by making accordion-folded books. Depict parts of the story on separate pages of the book. Choose several places that people in the community gather and include a page for each of them. For each book, choose as many pieces of poster board as there will be pages of the story. On each page, use markers, crayons, pens, or pencils to draw and write about the scene, or cut pictures and words from magazines, newspapers, and catalogs and glue them in place. Fill the page with as many people as possible. Create a cover. Punch three holes in the sides of each of the pages and the cover. Use yarn, string, or ribbon to lace the sheets together. Fold the book accordion style.

When the projects are completed, tell the students to trade books and to see how many different ways there are to illustrate this theme. Use the books to share this information with younger children, family members, and friends.

As a cooperative project, assign one location to each participant to illustrate on a separate page. Combine the sheets to make one book for the entire group.

1. Nancy Renfro, *Bags Are Big! A Paper Bag Craft Book* (Austin, Tex.: Nancy Renfro Studios, 1986), pp. 54–55. Adapted with permission.
2. Seventeenth General Synod, *Ten Principles for the Workplace* (Cleveland, Ohio: United Church of Christ, 1989).
3. Tim Chartier, "No Risk Here," Kalamazoo, Mich., 1993. Used with permission.
4. American Red Cross, "Emergency and Public Safety Workers and HIV/AIDS—A Duty to Respond" (Washington, D.C.: American Red Cross, 1989).

CHAPTER 6
Neighborhood

Using concrete, creative, and challenging methods, the activities for the theme "Neighborhood" are intended to help children understand facts and issues associated with AIDS. The learning experiences are designed to encourage people of all ages to respond with respect for those infected and affected by AIDS.

Architecture

PURPOSE   To explore local housing and care options for people living with AIDS.

PREPARATION   *Materials*

- Pencils and markers
- Newsprint
- Masking tape
- Bibles
- Information on housing options for persons with HIV/AIDS

PROCEDURE   One of the ways in which the AIDS epidemic has impacted local communities is in the area of housing. Because persons infected with HIV have particular needs, facilities as well as family and friends have had to adapt hospitals and homes to accommodate special situations. Learn more about local housing options for persons with HIV/AIDS through the use of this architecture-related activity.

Have the students count off and form groups of five or six. Provide each group with a large sheet of newsprint and a different color marker for each participant. Make a Bible available to each team as well.

Instruct the members of each group to work together to create a drawing of their dream house. Each participant can design his or her own living space in the house. Encourage the students to talk together about what would go into an ideal or dream home. How many rooms would it have? Would more than one bathroom be important? How many bedrooms? Challenge the groups to be as creative as possible in designing the homes. Remind the participants that each student may use only one marker for the project. The pupils may take turns sketching or they can draw at random whenever an idea comes to mind. Allow enough time for both designing the space and for sharing the plans. Once the task is completed, ask the students to look closely at their ideal homes. Whose color is seen the most? What rooms, if any, could be eliminated from the house? What might be added? How did the group decide what was important for the house? Ideally, how many people could live in this space?

Ask one member of each group to read aloud to their team the words of Psalm 84:3a, "Even the sparrow finds a home, and the swallow a nest for herself, where she may lay her young."

Reassemble the group and lead a discussion on the question: "Where do persons with AIDS live?" Allow the children time to respond. Ask if anyone knows of people in the area who are living with AIDS. Where do they reside? What kind of housing do they have?

Direct the students to research neighborhood housing and care options for persons with AIDS. List in the report such things as hospice and hospice home care; neighborhood group homes; church organizations; health-care clinics; hospitals; persons with AIDS who live alone and those who have moved in with family and friends. Ask questions such as: "How is care provided for people in each situation?" "Are some persons with AIDS in homeless shelters because they lost their own homes?" "Have some persons with AIDS moved back into the neighborhood, to be with family members and friends, after being gone for many years?"

Provide an opportunity for the students to do a follow-up report. Invite parents and other adults in the neighborhood to listen to the findings of the young people. Educate the adults on issues of housing and HIV/AIDS. Challenge people of all ages to suggest creative approaches to the housing and care concerns.

Now, ask the groups to redraw their ideal homes as if they were drawing it for a person or for persons living with AIDS. Share the results together.

Art

PURPOSE   To use socks to create wearable art projects that proclaim antidrug messages to the neighborhood.

PREPARATION   *Materials*

- Socks, two per person
- Cardboard
- Scissors
- Ribbons, trims, and buttons
- Fabric paints and brushes
- Permanent marking pens
- Needles and thread
- Iron

PROCEDURE   Gather the group in a circle. Pass a sock around the circle and ask each person to tell a way in which it could be used. Each participant should begin with the phrase, "I could use this sock to . . ." Group members may name such things as wear on a foot, make a puppet, wash a window, wipe a tear, or dust a table. If the group is enjoying the activity, allow each person two or more turns to name uses for a sock.

Challenge the group to think of ways in which something as simple as a sock could be used in connection with HIV/AIDS. Pass the sock around the circle again and ask each person to contribute an idea. Begin with the phrase "I could use socks . . . ." Ideas might include contributions to a care basket, protection for feet during a walk for AIDS, and projects for fund-raising activities. Tell the group that, although there are many ways socks could be used, today they will be decorating them with antidrug messages. When the socks are worn, they will be a statement to the people in the neighborhood that the wearers wish to say "no" to drugs.

Review ways in which drug use and HIV/AIDS are connected. Many drug users have acquired HIV infection from sharing needles, syringes, and other drug-related implements. Even the smallest amount of infected blood left in a used needle or syringe can contain live AIDS virus to be passed on to the next user of the dirty implements. Drug use also lessens a person's judgment, increasing the chances that the individual will take risks.

Discuss antidrug messages to place on the socks. Brainstorm a variety of responses, including:

- Say "no" to drugs
- Drugfree and proud
- The word "Drugs" inside the universal "No" symbol
- Drugs=AIDS=Death
- Don't do drugs
- I don't do it
- I'm special

Also talk about symbols that can be drawn on or attached to the socks. These could include a red ribbon, which is a symbol of the fight against drugs as well as the fight against AIDS; hearts to signify self-worth and self-respect; and flowers or leaves to represent growing up without using drugs.

Distribute a pair of socks to each person. Before embellishing them, designate a left and a right sock. Provide a variety of decorating materials. To attach ribbons and three-dimensional objects such as buttons to the socks, fold down the sock cuffs. Cut ribbon to the desired lengths and tie the pieces into bows. Using a threaded needle, tack a bow to each cuff, sewing through the top layer only. Trim the ends of the bows. Sew buttons to the socks in various places. If using paint or markers, cut strips of cardboard and place them inside the socks to absorb excess paint. Draw or write slogans and symbols on the socks. More than one coat of paint may be needed. Allow the surface to dry overnight. Set the paint by using an iron and pressing the cloth.

Once the socks are completed, invite the students to wear them as a visible symbol that they want to say "no" to drugs and to HIV/AIDS. Take time to look at everyone's designs and decorations. Provide the group with instructions for caring for their wearable art. Before washing, turn the socks so that buttons, ribbons, and drawings will be on the inside. Dry flat.

Banners/Textiles

PURPOSE To "Go Fly a Kite" for AIDS education or AIDS assistance.

PREPARATION *Materials*

- Paper grocery or lunch bags
- Balls of cotton string
- Sticks or wooden handles
- Tape
- Rulers
- Pencils and markers

PROCEDURE Although the words "Go Fly a Kite" usually have a negative connotation, they can easily be turned into a phrase with a positive perspective. "Go Fly a Kite" can also become the theme of a special event to help a neighborhood person who happens to have AIDS.

Gather the participants in a circle. Engage each person in a discussion by using a circle response method. State a question, such as "What's your response to the phrase 'Go Fly a Kite?' " Go around the circle, asking each person to contribute an idea. Assure the group that there are no right or wrong answers. Replies may range from "Go away" to "Fun." No one may speak a second time until all have spoken once. If the group is large, several small circles of learners may be used. Introduce a new phrase such as "I'd like to tell the AIDS virus to go fly a kite because . . ." Encourage a response from each person. Guide the group through the activity a third time, asking everyone to reply to the statement "How can a kite be used to help someone in the neighborhood with AIDS?" Possible answers include writing transmission and prevention statements on kites and flying them to educate people about HIV/AIDS; making and selling kites and donating the profit to AIDS organizations; sponsoring a kite-flying marathon as a fund raiser to help with a neighbor's AIDS-related medical bills and expenses. Choose a project and "Go Fly a Kite."

Teach the group to make a kite from a paper grocery or lunch bag. Provide bags, cotton string, sticks or wooden handles, tape, rulers, pencils, and markers to share. Direct each person to choose a bag and to cut off the bottom of it. Measure the length of the bottomless bag along the seam where it is glued. Make a mark one-third of the way down from the top. Put an "X" of tape over the mark. Measure 1/4" from each corner of the bag and put a dot there. Draw lines from the four dots to the "X" of tape. Cut along the lines on this side only. Be sure that the participants don't cut through both sides of the bag. Spread the wings, turn the bag over, and tape the wings to the body. Punch a hole in the tip of each wing and tape just above it. Draw and cut out a triangle near the bottom of the body and reinforce the corners with tape.

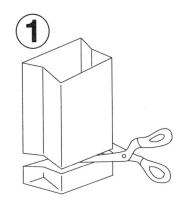

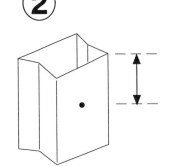

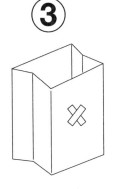

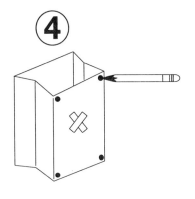

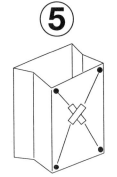

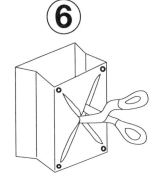

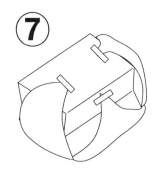

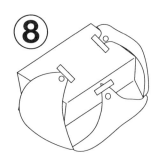

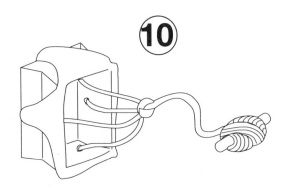

Tie a string 6' long through each hole, forming a bridle. Next tie on the flying line or ball of string to the center of the bridle. Instruct the group to roll the string onto a stick or wooden handle.

Tell the group to decorate the kites in ways that correspond to the selected project. For example, if the kites are to educate others about HIV/AIDS, pictures or words should be drawn or written on the paper. If the kites are to be sold, add interesting details and decorations. For use in a kite marathon, include the names of the owner and sponsors. Use the completed kites in a way that will tell HIV/AIDS to "Go Fly a Kite."

Cartoons

PURPOSE To make cartoon strips illustrating ways children can resist peer pressure in the neighborhood.

PREPARATION *Materials*

- "Peer Pressure" sheet
- Paper, markers, and pencils
- Duplicating equipment or photocopier
- Scrapbook or photo album
- Glue or tape
- Clock or timer

Advance Preparation

- Duplicate cartoon sheets

PROCEDURE Young people's decisions are often strongly influenced by pressure to conform with friends and acquaintances. Peer pressure can also cause young people to act on impulses rather than to think through their decisions. Use a cartoon activity to help youth consider the effects of peer pressure, especially as it relates to HIV/AIDS issues.

Tell the group that for the next two minutes they will be thinking about peer pressure. They will be participating in a "writing derby" and will have the opportunity to list words and phrases that come to mind when they reflect on the topic of peer pressure. For the first minute, they may record anything related to the theme. During the second minute, they are to write only words and phrases related to peer pressure and HIV/AIDS. When the starting time is announced, the group is to write continuously for the entire minute. If they are stuck, they are to write the words "peer pressure" until new thoughts and ideas surface. Time the group for sixty seconds. Call time and remind the students that for the next minute they will write words and phrases related to peer pressure and HIV/AIDS. Announce the starting and ending time. At the conclusion of the activity, ask for volunteers to share answers, especially those that relate to HIV/AIDS. Common themes might include trying drugs, experimenting with sex, and sampling alcohol.

Tell the class that each person will draw a cartoon to illustrate one real or fictitious peer-pressure situation. Assure them that it is all right to use stick people in the drawings. Show them how to make a bubble which is generally used in a cartoon to contain conversation.

Instruct the group to create the cartoon in three parts. The beginning illustrates how the situation started, the middle tells what happened, and the third indicates how it was resolved. Titles may also be written on the cartoons.

Hand out the sheets, pencils, and markers. As the students create the cartoons, talk to them individually about the many ways peer pressure takes place and encourage them to take responsibility for their own actions.

After the pupils have finished, compile a class book of the cartoons and leave it on display in the room. Remind the group that it is okay to act according to their best judgment, not according to what friends encourage them to do.

BEGINNING

MIDDLE

END

Creative Writing

PURPOSE
To identify positive and negative messages about AIDS that are conveyed in neighborhoods and to write alliterative poems using these themes.

PREPARATION
Materials

- Paper and pens
- Varied with additional activities

PROCEDURE
Numerous messages related to AIDS are communicated in neighborhoods. They may be found on billboards, written on buildings, and displayed through actions. Identify several of the positive and negative AIDS-related messages that are conveyed throughout a neighborhood. On the positive side, neighbors care for acquaintances with AIDS, congregations bring meals to families, and organizations sponsor fund-raising events. Negatively, drug dealers hang out at parks, people are afraid of others who are different, and schools turn away infected children.

Compose alliterative poems using the theme of AIDS in the neighborhood. Alliteration is the repetition of a sound in two or more neighboring words. It is also the repeated use of an accented syllable that has the same beginning, as in many common tongue twisters. Examples of some alliterative phrases are:

Don't do drugs.
Peer pressure produces problems
Caring congregations convey Christ's compassion
Friends forever
Educate everyone
AIDS Awareness

Or, try a tongue twister like:

Sally Smith's step-sister Sarah Swanson said students shouldn't share syringes

Alliterative poems may be written on paper, but they may also be shared in several other interesting and involving ways. Try a graffiti wall or door. Supplies needed include a long roll of paper, tape or tacks, markers, magazines, and glue. Cover a door with paper. Depending on the size of the group, one or both sides of the door may be used. Or attach a piece of paper to a wall or bulletin board. Provide markers or crayons and encourage the children to write their alliterative messages on the paper. Pictures may be drawn to illustrate the phrases, or photographs can be cut from magazines and newspapers and glued to the paper.

After obtaining permission, write the poems on the sidewalk. Make special sidewalk chalk to use for the project. For each stick, obtain 4-6 washed and dried eggshells, 1 teaspoon flour, and 1 teaspoon very hot tap water. Rocks, a small bowl, measuring spoons, and paper toweling will also be needed. Take the eggshells outside and smash them with a smooth rock. When they are powdery, throw away any large pieces and scoop the powdered shell into a small bowl or dish. Put the flour and water in another bowl, mix into a paste, then add 1 teaspoon of eggshell powder. Keep mashing until the mixture sticks together. Roll the dough into a chalk stick shape. Wrap it tightly with a strip of paper toweling. Let the chalk sticks dry for two or three days until they are very hard. Then use them on the sidewalk to write messages. Use the bottom of a shoe or the next hard rain as an eraser.

Send a living message by planting seeds in a particular shape. Choose a patch of soil. Write the message in the soil with a stick. Make large, clear letters. Shake the seeds into the grooves. Carefully cover the seeds with soil. Water the flower patch. Tend the soil, keep it weeded and watered, and watch the message grow.

Culinary Arts

PURPOSE
To have participants work cooperatively to plan and produce a meal.

PREPARATION   *Materials*

- Ingredients (see below for suggestions)
- Cooking supplies and equipment

PROCEDURE   Cooperation is essential in a neighborhood. It is also a key ingredient in addressing HIV/AIDS-related topics. Invite the participants to share a special lunch or snack to which everyone contributes an item and cooperates in the planning and preparation process.

Discuss some meals that could be made in this manner. These might be tacos where the tortillas are provided and cheese, lettuce, and tomato are purchased; rice with a variety of items such as chicken, celery, pineapple, and coconut on top; fruit salad for which each person brings an ingredient; broth or stock combined with various vegetables to make soup; waffles or pancakes with unusual toppings; or bread with several selections of spreads and condiments. *The More with Less Cookbook*[1] has detailed suggestions on how to build cooperative meals. In advance, assign each participant a specific item to bring for the meal. Prepare or purchase the basic ingredients, such as bread or rice.

Include preparation time as part of the process. Guide the young people as they chop or combine the ingredients to be used.

As the meal is shared, talk about ways in which the contributions and cooperation of many people could help individuals and groups affected by HIV/AIDS. Emphasize cooperation in neighborhoods as a way of dealing with HIV/AIDS.

Dance

PURPOSE   To improvise Biblical themes that illustrate ways of responding to persons infected and affected by HIV/AIDS.

PREPARATION   *Materials*

- Bibles
- Paper and pencils or pens

PROCEDURE   Christians are called to respond to the AIDS crisis in many ways. Besides making responsible decisions about their own behavior, people of faith are challenged to minister to the needs of persons infected and affected by the deadly virus, HIV. Scripture suggests attitudes and actions to help people show Christ's compassion and concern for individuals and groups in various situations. Involve the participants in gestural improvisations to illustrate some of these important Bible verses.

Arrange the learners in small groups. Distribute paper, pens or pencils, and Bibles to each team. Ask the students to write the words "love," "justice," "healing," and "forgiveness" on the paper. Assign each group to locate verses that refer to the given words. Ask them to write down ways that Jesus showed healing, love, justice, and forgiveness. Suggest other feeling words as well, such as "mercy" and "compassion." Give the students enough time to brainstorm words and to find scripture references for them. Encourage the participants to share their passages with the group.

Once the students have completed this part of the activity, invite them to improvise several of the passages located in the Bible. Improvisation is an activity performed with little or no preparation. Encourage the young people to think about their drama in light of the AIDS epidemic. How would Jesus show compassion to a person living with AIDS. What does the Gospel tell us about living justice in the face of discrimination? How can hope be given to a world living with a disease for which there is no cure?

Invite the participants to stand and to form a circle. Lead the students in using their bodies to sculpt the feeling words. Hands, arms, and facial expressions are very important in this activity. Tell the group that a biblical theme will be stated and each person or persons in turn are to take a pose to illustrate it. For example, if the leader says "Sculpt compassion," the students may feel the need to embrace one another. To illustrate healing, pupils may reach out or touch the head or hand of a neighbor. Directing the group to "sculpt joy" may result in a simple dance movement.

Remind the learners that body language is more than a gestural activity. What people "say" with their bodies is just as important as what they say with their words. When visiting a person living with AIDS, the language of the body must exhibit care and concern. It is important to remember that love, compassion, and healing can be shown to another without the use of words.

Drama/Clown/Mime

PURPOSE To teach children problem-solving methods and to use drama to act out possible solutions.

PREPARATION *Materials*

- Newsprint or chalkboard
- Marker or chalk
- Paper and pencils

PROCEDURE Teach the children a step-by-step method for solving interpersonal problems. Focus on the theme of "AIDS in the Neighborhood" for this activity. Use drama to act out the alternatives and options for resolving conflict situations.

Present the key words of the problem-solving plan to the students. List them on newsprint or on a chalkboard. Discuss each of them as it is listed. The steps are:

1. Stop. Think. Remain calm.
2. Identify the problem. What is causing the problem? What does the other person need and want?
3. Brainstorm. Generate a list of all the possible ways to solve the problem.
4. Select three acceptable solutions and one unacceptable solution. Star the solutions that are acceptable to everyone.
5. Evaluate. What will happen with each of the ideas? What are the consequences? How practical will they be to implement? Why will they be effective?
6. Decide. Make a group decision on which solution will meet the needs of the most people in the most acceptable way.
7. Plan the best way to carry out the idea.
8. Re-evaluate the decision within a certain time.

Have the children suggest problems common in a neighborhood, especially as they relate to HIV/AIDS issues. These could include peer pressure to take drugs, temptation to share needles for ear piercing, tattooing and blood pacts, and enticement to engage in sexual activities. Other neighborhood problems might involve a child with AIDS, a single person who is infected and needs help with yard work, and a youth service agency that requires funds to continue. Brainstorm all of the possible solutions and give individuals and small groups an opportunity to act them out. This will aid the learners in understanding why some possibilities will work better than others.

Pass out paper and pencils and encourage the children to write down and remember the problem-solving steps and to suggest them to other people when conflict situations arise.

Games

PURPOSE To use a game to teach ways in which the AIDS virus is passed from one person to another.

PREPARATION *Materials*

- Shoebox
- Construction paper
- Scissors

- Glue
- Newspapers and magazines
- Index cards and pens or pencils
- Resource materials about HIV/AIDS

Advance Preparation

- Cover the shoebox with construction paper
- Prepare index cards with true and false statements about HIV/AIDS. Use the list provided for ideas. Write one statement on each card.

PROCEDURE It is very important to make clear what is true and what is false in talking about HIV and AIDS. Misinformation is one of the major causes for the fear and panic often associated with the disease. Neighborhoods are places where correct and incorrect information abounds. Invite the group to cite some situations in which this is true. For example, a student is not

Fact Cards

- HIV is the AIDS virus.
- AIDS is a disease that attacks the body's immune system leaving it unable to fight certain kinds of diseases.
- Homosexual is a person showing sexual preference for another person of the same sex.
- The AIDS virus can be transmitted by sexual intercourse.
- The AIDS virus can be passed from female to male.
- The AIDS virus can be passed on from male to male.
- The AIDS virus can be passed on from male to female.
- The AIDS virus can be passed on from female to female.
- Children can get AIDS.
- A woman infected with HIV can pass the virus on to her baby during pregnancy.
- HIV is transmitted through the sharing of dirty needles.
- There is no present cure for AIDS.
- AIDS does not discriminate.
- HIV can be transmitted through the use of shared needles for tattooing or ear piercing.
- T-cell is the cell that HIV attacks when it enters the body.

False Cards

- It is possible to become infected with HIV by donating blood.
- Only homosexuals get AIDS.
- HIV can be transmitted from a mosquito or other insect.
- Only a few countries of the world are affected by AIDS.
- Drinking fountains are a potential source of acquiring AIDS.
- Sneezes spread the virus that causes AIDS.
- People get AIDS from kissing.
- Once infected with the HIV virus a person will die.
- You will always get AIDS if you have a blood transfusion.
- HIV can live outside a person's body.
- HIV can be transmitted from a toilet seat.
- People with AIDS should not be touched.
- Children can get AIDS from attending class with an infected child.
- AIDS is as easy to catch as the common cold.
- There is a test to determine if a person has AIDS.

allowed to attend the neighborhood school because he or she has AIDS, a person is not invited to swim at the neighborhood pool because he or she has HIV infection, or a family is shunned at the local congregation because one of their children has AIDS.

Use a game involving true and false statements to help the participants separate some of the myths and the realities related to HIV/AIDS. In advance cover a shoebox with construction paper. Invite the group to decorate the box with headlines related to HIV/AIDS. Provide newspapers, magazines, and brochures, as well as scissors and glue. While the group is working, note that people often have a hard time separating myth from reality when it comes to AIDS. Invite the learners to play a game to help them identify correct information about HIV/AIDS. Place the playing cards, the true and false statements that were written on index cards in advance, in the decorated shoebox. Gather the group in a circle and invite each person, in turn, to draw a card from the box. Tell the individual to read the statement and to indicate whether it is true or false. Encourage cooperation rather than competition, and urge the group members to help one another come up with the right answer. Share correct information for each of the false statements. Display the true and the false statements on separate posters.

Another way to play the game is to have each participant draw a card from the box. Instruct the players to read their sentences silently. Tell the people who think that they have true statements to go to one side of the room and those who feel that they have false information to go to the other side of the room. Take turns having each side read their statements. Determine whether the information is actually true or false and adjust the sides accordingly.

Regardless of the way in which the game is played, help the students to know what is true and what is not true with regard to HIV/AIDS. Remind the group that one way to fight fear is with facts.

Music

PURPOSE To write verses for the song "This Little Light of Mine" on a theme related to AIDS and the neighborhood.

PREPARATION *Materials*

- Music, "This Little Light of Mine"
- Accompaniment (optional)

PROCEDURE There are many ways in which people can let their "lights" shine in their neighborhood to show their concern for AIDS-related topics. They might turn on a porch light during a food collection drive, place a candle in a window as a sign of support, or hold a light while participating in a neighborhood vigil. People can also sing songs about being "lights." Ask the group to think of a song on this theme. Although there might be several songs that would work well, "This Little Light of Mine" is a good one to use for this activity. Make up new words about ways in which people can address HIV/AIDS in their own specific community. Challenge the group to try the following approach.

Sing the chorus of the song "This Little Light of Mine." It goes:

"This little light of mine,
I'm gonna let it shine.
This little light of mine,
I'm gonna let it shine,
Let it shine, let it shine, let it shine."

As the first verse, use the following words:

"Let it shine in the neighborhood,
I'm gonna let it shine.
Let it shine in the neighborhood,
I'm gonna let it shine,
Let it shine, let it shine, let it shine."

Ask the children to name ways they can let their lights shine to do something about AIDS. Possibilities include visiting a child who has AIDS, doing errands for a neighbor with AIDS, and participating in a food collection drive. Put these ideas into verses, such as:

Collect food for AIDS ministries,
I'm gonna let it shine.
Bring some flowers to Pat and Phil,
I'm gonna let it shine.
Let it shine, let it shine, let it shine.

Continue creating and singing verses as long as the children are enjoying the activity. Remind them to let their lights shine in all situations in their neighborhoods.

Photography

PURPOSE   To hold a video-a-thon to view HIV/AIDS information and to raise funds for HIV/AIDS causes.

PREPARATION   *Materials*

- Videotapes, videocassette player, and TV monitors
- Notebooks and pencils
- Snacks and meals
- Sponsor sheets
- Information about HIV/AIDS organizations

PROCEDURE   *Advance Preparation*

- Prepare and distribute sponsor sheets to each participant
- Designate the organization to receive the collected funds
- Collect pledges for segments of time videos are viewed
- Obtain videotapes and videocassette equipment
- Enlist personnel to run the equipment and to chaperon the event

Learning about HIV/AIDS can be done through many formats. Interesting, informative, instructional videotapes are available from a variety of sources. Films are produced for people of all ages, with subjects ranging from transmission to testing. Hold a video-a-thon as a way to educate people about HIV/AIDS. Designate a time and place where videos will be shown continuously. Begin on a Friday evening and run nonstop through Saturday night, or hold the event for an entire day.

Preparation for the event must begin in several ways. If part of the purpose of the video-a-thon is to raise funds for an AIDS ministry or service organization, prepare sponsor sheets and distribute them to the participants. Challenge the group to find people who will pledge money for each minute, half hour, or hour that they view videos. Also, gather videotapes from various sources. Secure the required equipment and find people to run it. Distribute the equipment throughout the building, designating rooms for different age levels. Participants may be asked to bring a notebook and pen or pencil to record information about the videos. They should also be told to bring pillows, sleeping bags, and snacks.

At the beginning of the video-a-thon, gather the group and explain the policies and procedures. Each person must keep track in their notebooks of the videos they've viewed and the amount of time they watched. Encourage everyone to keep watching videos until the time runs out, stopping only for snacks, meals, stretching, and bathroom breaks. If varying age groups are involved, assign people to chaperon designated rooms.

At the conclusion of the event, instruct the participants to collect pledges and to return them to a designated person by a specific date.

At another time, hold a read-a-thon to share HIV/AIDS information through books, magazines, journals, and cartoons.

Puppetry

PURPOSE To learn about "The Kids on the Block" and specific ways in which puppets are being used to educate about AIDS.

PREPARATION *Materials*

- Information on "The Kids on the Block" and the organization's AIDS program

Advance Preparation

- Obtain information on "The Kids on the Block," 9385-C Gerwig Lane, Columbia, Md. 21046 (telephone: 410-290-9095; 410-290-9358, FAX)

PROCEDURE "The Kids on the Block," created in 1977, features life-size puppets designed to teach children and adults to understand, accept, and appreciate children who are different. Children learn about disabilities and differences through a one-to-one dialogue with puppets and, as a result, become more sensitive and appreciative of all kinds of people. The puppets dress and act like real children. Like real children, each has definite likes and dislikes, hopes and fears, talents and limitations. And, like real children, some have differences such as mental, physical, or emotional disabilities and some have lives touched by abuse, drugs, or AIDS.

"Kids on the Block" offers a program on AIDS, featuring puppets Natalie Gregg and Joanne Spinoza. Natalie Gregg is a twenty-five-year-old married woman who recently has learned that she has AIDS. When her friend, Joanne Spinoza, questions Natalie about her health, Natalie tells Joanne about her disease. Through Joanne, Natalie explains about AIDS in practical terms and how you get AIDS and how you don't.

In the script "Birdhouse," which is intended for fifth grade through adult audiences, Joanne relates that she's heard rumors that Natalie has AIDS. When Natalie tells her the truth, Joanne is shocked and frightened. Natalie tells her story calmly and with great consideration for her friend. They discuss myths and misconceptions about how the disease is spread as well as facts about AIDS.

"Talking about Death" is a script intended for third grade through adult audiences. As Natalie teaches Joanne how to play chess, Joanne talks to her friend about the progression of her condition. They talk about AIDS and Natalie's plans now that she knows that she has a disease for which there is no cure. Joanne learns to accept a person with AIDS as a person first and to attach an individual personality to what has become a public source of fear and panic.

Make the students aware of "The Kids on the Block" programs and the ways in which these unusual puppets are used to educate people about AIDS. Show pictures and share literature that has been obtained from "The Kids on the Block" national office. Investigate the location of puppet groups that present "Birdhouse" and "Talking about Death" and arrange for a performance. If there is no existing "Kids on the Block" troupe in the immediate vicinity, challenge the students to organize support from neighborhood businesses, service groups, hospitals, and school districts to begin a company in the community. Many students have organized troupes and perform at local elementary and middle schools.

Storytelling

PURPOSE To create flannelgraph stories to address ways the AIDS virus cannot be transmitted.

PREPARATION *Materials*

- Pellon (available at fabric stores)
- Scissors
- Markers
- Patterns (optional)
- Cardboard or thin plywood

- Background material such as felt, flannel, or indoor/outdoor carpeting
- Stapler and staples

Advance Preparation

- Prepare the flannelgraph background

PROCEDURE

Untrue stories concerning ways in which the AIDS virus is transmitted are prevalent. Unfortunately, children have heard, and often believe, rumors and myths that are not accurate. Actually, AIDS is very difficult to get since it requires the transfer of blood, semen, or vaginal secretions from an infected person. This does not occur in a child's normal everyday activities. Help the youth name ways in which the virus cannot be transmitted. Use a storytelling method involving flannelgraph pieces to show things that children can do without fear of contracting AIDS.

Brainstorm ways that the HIV virus cannot be transmitted from one person to another. Suggestions might include:

Sharing a picnic
Playing basketball
Kicking a ball
Swimming
Taking a walk

Give each student the opportunity to form a flannelgraph piece depicting one way in which the AIDS virus cannot be transmitted. Create an object to represent each theme. A picnic basket would illustrate sharing a picnic, a basketball would symbolize playing basketball, and a foot could suggest taking a walk. Prepare figure patterns, if desired, by cutting pictures from coloring books or by providing stencil sheets. Pellon, a stiffening material used in sewing, will be used for the figures. Supply pellon, markers, and scissors, and instruct each person to trace or draw an object or picture onto the fabric. Color and highlight the pieces and cut them out. As an alternative, children's drawings or other paper figures may be used. Back them with sandpaper or felt to make them adhere to the background material.

Construct the background by covering a piece of cardboard or plywood with felt, flannel, or indoor-outdoor carpeting. A large bulletin board may also be readied in this way. Staple the material in place.

Invite the students to take turns sharing stories using the pictures and the background board. For example, using cut-outs of a picnic basket, a ball, a swimming suit, and a soda can, the story might be: "I went on a picnic with a group of friends, we played kick ball, went swimming, and drank a lot of soda pop. We had so much fun." During the storytelling, emphasize ways in which the AIDS virus is not transmitted from one person to another.

1. Doris Janzen Longacre, *More with Less Cookbook* (Scottdale, Penn.: Herald Press, 1977), pp. 50–51.

CHAPTER 7
School

The arts-related activities in this "School" section suggest ways in which students can make their educational environment a place in which facts are learned, fears are addressed, and compassion is emphasized.

Architecture

PURPOSE To illustrate the important role a living environment plays for persons with AIDS.

PREPARATION *Materials*

- Chalk board and chalk or newsprint and marker
- Markers
- Heavy-weight drawing paper, construction paper, wallpaper samples
- Shoeboxes
- Glue
- Scissors
- Old magazines

PROCEDURE "Raising the Roof, Opening Doors" was a national architectural competition sponsored by the Boston Public Facilities Department and the Boston Society of Architects. Its intent was to heighten awareness of HIV/AIDS and the types of living environments needed by persons living with the infection. Blueprints, models, and scale drawings were submitted by architects throughout the United States. As part of a school AIDS-awareness emphasis, involve students in a similar experience. Through this project they will discover some of the special needs of persons with AIDS and identify ways to meet them through appropriate living environments.

Brainstorm the kind of living environments that would be important for a person living with AIDS. Record the suggestions on a chalkboard or a piece of newsprint. Talk about the type of living space that would make life easier and more comfortable for the person with HIV/AIDS. In the brainstorming be sure to mention factors such as: lighting, temperature, levels, stairs, handicapped access, color, noise, decorations, plants, maintenance, and so forth.

Invite the participants to create a living space incorporating the suggested ideas. Arrange the young people into teams of four or five persons. Ask each team to select a different environmental consideration from the list. Tell the groups to discuss the needs of a person with HIV/AIDS as they relate to that particular living factor. For example, explain that extremes in temperature cannot be tolerated by a person with AIDS who has pneumonia, and excessive light is difficult for a person with AIDS-related vision problems. Provide time for the participants to discuss each factor. Take turns sharing the ideas with the entire group.

Distribute a shoebox to each group. Place additional materials within sharing distance of the participants on each team. Challenge each group to create a composite house reflecting a comfortable living environment for a person with HIV/AIDS. Use the magazines, markers, drawing paper, glue, and scissors to encourage students to build a model home or room to illustrate the type of living environment that would help meet the needs of a person living with HIV/AIDS. Heavy-weight paper, construction paper, and wallpaper samples may be used to create walls. Magazine photos of plants, comfortable furniture, pictures, and so forth will enhance the space. Answer questions and provide additional information about HIV/AIDS as the participants complete the project.

Display the models for others to view as part of an AIDS-awareness week at school.

Art

PURPOSE	To use posters to explore themes of transmission and prevention of AIDS.
PREPARATION	***Materials***

- Posters related to AIDS themes
- Poster contest guidelines
- Awards

Advance Preparation

- Obtain AIDS-related posters from organizations such as the American Red Cross
- Form a poster contest committee
- Duplicate guidelines
- Secure judges

PROCEDURE Health education for youth is one of the most effective weapons against the spread of AIDS. Education is critical in preventing the transmission of HIV. When young people know the facts about HIV infection and AIDS, they can take steps to protect themselves and others. Schools play an important role in communities and in the lives of people who will eventually be affected directly or indirectly by HIV/AIDS. It is important to know the facts about HIV infection and AIDS. Young people and school personnel must understand how to avoid becoming infected with the AIDS virus as well as how to respond to people who are infected. Posters that convey information related to HIV/AIDS are effective tools to use to educate young people about transmission and prevention themes.

On a popular poster, a young child is standing with arms outstretched, amidst a garden of flowers. The caption on the poster reads "I have AIDS. Please hug me. I can't make you sick." This poster, available from the Center for Attitudinal Healing (19 Main Street, Tiburon, Calif. 94920; telephone 415-435-5022), plus others distributed through organizations such as the American Red Cross, help to make students aware of AIDS information in affective and effective ways. Display a variety of posters such as:

American Red Cross

AIDS: See and Believe
Don't Listen to Rumors about AIDS. Get the Facts!
Red Cross Is Helping
Respect Yourself. Protect Yourself.
You Can't Get AIDS

U.S. Public Health Service

AIDS Is Scary, But a Zit Is Real, Right?
Do You Talk about AIDS on the First Date?
I Didn't Know I Had AIDS . . . Not Until My Baby Was Born with It
If You're Dabbling in Drugs . . . You Could Be Dabbling with Your Life
No Matter What Shape You're in, Anyone Can Get the AIDS Virus

Review the themes and topics presented in the posters. Discuss ways in which AIDS is spread and ways in which it can be stopped. Provide accurate information about transmission and prevention.

Challenge the students to create posters on AIDS-related themes. Hold a poster contest for the entire school, church school, or community. Print and distribute guidelines containing the following information:

Sponsors: List the name(s) of the sponsoring group(s).

Theme: Pick an open-ended theme around which entries can be based; for example: "You can't get AIDS by . . ."; :You can get AIDS by . . . "; "AIDS can be prevented."

Age Categories: List grades or ages which may enter.

Format: Name the styles of artwork that are eligible: paintings, drawings, collage, and so forth. State how entries are to be submitted, for example, on one side of an 8-1/2" x 11" paper. Note that name, grade, school or congregation, and phone are to be printed on the back of the page.

Deadline: Include day, date, and time.

Submit to: Provide the name of the person or place and the address where the entries may be delivered or mailed.

Judging: Indicate the criteria upon which the entries will be judged, such as imagination, style, content, neatness, and so forth. Name categories of judges such as teachers, librarians, artists. Give specific names, if possible.

Awards: Give a prize, perhaps a button or certificate, to everyone who enters. List first, second, and third prizes. These could be money, t-shirts, or books. Note any other type of recognition, such as displaying the entries at a public function or awarding something special to the school or congregation submitting the most entries.

Other Information: Note whether the entries will become the property of the sponsoring group(s) or be returned to the artist. Indicate that the decision of the judges is final.

Contact Persons: List the names and phone numbers of people who may be called for questions or information.

After the Contest: Mount the entries and display them in public locations. Compile an anthology of some of the pieces. Thank all those who organized the event.

Banners/Textiles

PURPOSE To use HIV/AIDS-related acronyms in a banner-making project.

PREPARATION *Materials*

- Wide ribbon (various colors and lengths)
- Dowel rods
- Scissors
- Permanent markers
- Tacky glue
- Glossary

PROCEDURE HIV. AIDS. ARC. STD. PWA. Learning the letter combinations of phrases related to HIV/AIDS is almost like learning a new language. Although there are many familiar acronyms associated with HIV/AIDS, it cannot be assumed that people understand their meaning. Help the students research some of the acronyms that are associated with the AIDS crisis and use them in a ribbon-banner-making activity.

Be sure that the participants understand the meaning of the word "acronym." An acronym is a word formed from the first letters of other words. An acronym is often pronounced as a word and is sometimes written in capital letters. For example, AIDS is an acronym made up of the first letters of the words "Acquired Immune Deficiency Syndrome." This acronym names a disease that attacks the body's immune system, making it unable to fight off illnesses.Invite the learners to name other acronyms associated with AIDS, such as:

ARC—Aids Related Complex. A chronic disease people may develop if they are infected with HIV.

HIV—Human Immunodeficiency Virus. The virus that causes AIDS.

STD—Sexually Transmitted Disease. Infectious disease spread by sexual contact with an infected person.

AZT—Azidothymidine. An antiviral drug used to treat HIV infection.

CDC—Centers for Disease Control. An agency of the United States Public Health Service responsible for monitoring and controlling various diseases.

PWA—Person with AIDS. Individual diagnosed as having HIV infection and the symptoms associated with AIDS.

Additional acronyms may be found in the Glossary at the end of this book.

Use a banner-making activity to help the students understand the acronyms and their meanings. This can be done as a class project, with each person contributing a piece to the banner. Help each student select a different acronym to use for the project.

Distribute a piece of ribbon and a permanent marker to each participant. Direct the learners to print one acronym and its meaning vertically down the length of the ribbon.

Invite the pupils to create new words for the letters of their acronyms. The new words should describe another aspect of HIV/AIDS, relate to attitudes and actions, or highlight methods of care and concern. For example:

AIDS—Anger Incorrectly Directed at Self
HIV—Hug Individuals with the Virus
PWA—Positive Winning Attitude

Invite the students to turn their ribbons over and to write the acronyms and their new meanings on the blank side of the pieces.

When the young people have completed their ribbons, construct the banner. Glue each ribbon to the dowel rod. Additional ribbon or string may be added to each end of the banner to serve as a hanger for the piece. When the project is completed, display it in a location where many people will see both sides of the ribbons.

ANGER	**H**UG	**P**OSITIVE
INCORRECTLY	**I**NDIVIDUALS WITH THE	**W**INNING
DIRECTED AT	**V**IRUS	**A**TTITUDE
SELF		

Cartoons

PURPOSE To read comic books to learn facts about AIDS.

PREPARATION *Materials*

- Comic books on AIDS such as:

    "AIDS News," edited by P. Catlin Fullwood. Seattle: People of Color Against AIDS Network (POCAAN), 1988

    "Andrea and Lisa." Baltimore: HERO, 1987

    "Anyone Can Get AIDS." South Deerfield, Mass.: Channing L. Bete, 1991

    "A Christian Response to AIDS." South Deerfield, Mass.: Channing L. Bete, 1990

    "Corey's Story." Minneapolis: Minnesota AIDS Project, 1987

    "Dying to Get High—AIDS and Shooting Drugs." South Deerfield, Mass.: Channing L. Bete, 1991

    "Get the Facts," by Ellen G. Feiler, Jennie Hefelfinger, Diane S. Scalise, and Charles Thompson. Fort Lauderdale, Fla.: Broward County Public Health Unit, 1991

    "Jeffrey Wants to Know," by Betsy Randall-David and Amit Pieter. Gainesville: Florida Association of Pediatric Tumor Programs, 1987

    "Let's Talk about AIDS." South Deerfield, Mass.: Channing L. Bete, 1992

    "Making Responsible Choices about Sex." South Deerfield, Mass.: Channing L. Bete, 1987

    "Rappin': Teens, Sex, and AIDS," by Sala Udin and Brian Clarke. San Francisco: Multicultural Training Resource Center, n.d.

    "Risky Business," by Sterling A. Winterhalter, III. San Francisco: San Francisco AIDS Foundation, 1988

    "Risky Stuff," by Carlos Morton. Washington, D.C.: American Red Cross, 1990

    "Rubber Bros. Comics," by Paul Mozeleski and Peter Mozeleski. Wilbraham, Mass.: Rubber Bros. Reading Club, 1990

    "Sex and STDs—How to Stay Safe." South Deerfield, Mass.: Channing L. Bete, 1992

    "Sex Is Safer with a Condom." South Deerfield, Mass.: Channing L. Bete, 1991

    "Space Age Smarts," by Betsy Randall-David and Amit Pieter. Gainesville: Florida Association of Pediatric Tumor Programs, 1987

    "What Everyone Should Know about AIDS." South Deerfield, Mass.: Channing L. Bete, 1983

    "What Young People Should Know about AIDS." South Deerfield, Mass.: Channing L. Bete, 1987

    "Worried about AIDS? Have an HIV Test." South Deerfield, Mass.: Channing L. Bete, 1992

    "Young People Get AIDS." South Deerfield, Mass.: Channing L. Bete, 1991

Advance Preparation

- Obtain comic books

PROCEDURE Comic books are an engaging and effective way to acquaint youth with issues involving AIDS. Since young people are so attracted to this type of reading material, comic books are an important educational tool. There are several inexpensive cartoon-style books appropriate for various age groups (especially young teens) that explore various aspects of the subject. Themes of transmission, prevention, responsible decision making, and self-esteem are emphasized in all of them.

Choose one comic book and provide a copy of it for each participant. Have them read the material and do the activities individually or as a group. Collect a variety of titles and distribute a different comic book to each student or small group. Allow time to review the information. Invite each group, in turn, to share what they have read and learned from the comic book they reviewed. Remind the young people that education is one of the weapons they can use to fight the disease.

Since the comic books were designed to provide information about AIDS, encourage each student to take one to show to their friends and family.

Creative Writing

PURPOSE To guide children in creative writing opportunities that can be used in every section of the school or community newspaper.

PREPARATION *Materials*

- Newspapers
- Paper and pens
- Envelopes and stamps

PROCEDURE Show the children copies of daily and weekly newspapers that are published in the community. Also display a copy of the school newspaper if one is published. Invite the group to participate in a creative writing project, or several of them, that will encourage the inclusion of information about HIV/AIDS in various sections of the papers. Try some of these ideas:

Editorial Page

Write a "Letter to the Editor" or a "Point of View" article on ways in which communities can provide services for persons with AIDS.

National News

Encourage the inclusion of news of treatment options.

Metro Section

Submit news releases on drug prevention programs taking place in the area.

Religion Page

Request a feature on AIDS-related projects and programs of local congregations.

Culinary/Food Section

Suggest an issue devoted to nutrition requirements for HIV-infected persons and ways in which individuals can become involved in food collection, preparation, and distribution.

Entertainment Section

Highlight performances related to AIDS themes or that serve as fund raisers for AIDS organizations.

Travel Page

Research interesting places throughout the world and cite statistics on AIDS transmission and prevention in these locations.

Women's Page

Create opportunities for interviews with local women who are infected or who are working to promote awareness of AIDS issues related to women.

Youth Page

Ask the paper to print children's poems or essays on AIDS topics.

Sports Page

Supply a story on athletes infected and affected by HIV/AIDS.

Book Reviews

List and critique books on AIDS themes.

Invite individuals and groups to choose a section of the newspaper and to write an AIDS-related article to submit to a local publication. Provide resource materials, paper, pens, envelopes, and stamps. Encourage the writers as they compose their stories. Remember to submit information and articles to church and school newsletters and newspapers as well.

Also use the newspaper as a resource. Have the youth clip articles that can be used to compile a scrapbook of stories about HIV/AIDS themes or to form a news bulletin board.

Culinary Arts

PURPOSE   To share a potluck of "Stone Soup" as a means of learning the ingredients of a school AIDS education program.

PREPARATION   *Materials*

- *Stone Soup*[1]
- Large pots
- Stones
- Markers (permanent)
- Cans of vegetable soup and can opener
- Stove
- Bowls and spoons
- Napkins
- Beverage and cups
- School AIDS education policies

Advance Preparation

- Invite students to bring cans of vegetable soup

PROCEDURE   Cooperation is a theme found in the German folktale "Stone Soup." When soldiers come into a village proclaiming that they are hungry, the townspeople respond that they have no food to share. As the soldiers begin to make "stone soup" from water and a few rocks, the fascinated folk bring contributions, such as potatoes, carrots, and meat, which greatly improve the quality and quantity of the product. All share a delicious dinner as well as a new-found friendship. Tell this interesting and important story to the students.

Compare this cooperative endeavor to ways in which a community and a school can collaborate in addressing AIDS education issues. The scope and content of AIDS education for students should be locally determined and consistent with parental and community values. Broad community participation will ensure that school AIDS education policies and programs reflect local values.

- Education about AIDS for students in early elementary grades should be designed to reduce unnecessary fear of the epidemic and fear of becoming infected.
- Education about AIDS for students in late elementary/middle-school grades should provide students with basic facts about the nature of viruses and the ways the AIDS virus (HIV) is transmitted.
- Education about AIDS for students in junior/senior high school should provide basic facts about the AIDS virus and HIV infection/AIDS transmission and prevention.

Discuss AIDS education in the school. What is or is not being done? Using a "stone soup" method, ask the students to name the ingredients, or components, of a school AIDS education policy. Place a large pan or soup pot in the middle of the group. Pass out a stone and a permanent marker to each person. Challenge the participants to write one ingredient of a school AIDS education policy on each rock, such as:

- Classroom time
- Parents
- Teachers

- School board members
- State board of education
- Students
- Textbooks
- Community representatives
- Volunteers
- AIDS educators from community organizations
- Counselors
- Nurses
- Comprehensive school health education program
- Health classes
- Age-appropriate information
- Prevention emphasis
- Training programs
- Educational materials
- Evaluation

Take turns placing the rocks in the pot, discussing each contribution as it is made. Remind the students that developing, implementing, and assessing AIDS education policies and programs is an ongoing task, and one in which they are a key ingredient.

Emphasize the theme of cooperation and the necessity of combining many ingredients to obtain the finished product by holding a "Stone Soup" potluck. Invite each person to open the can of vegetable soup he or she brought and to pour it into a large cooking pot. While the soup is heating, ask the participants to prepare the other ingredients of the meal such as setting the table and pouring beverages. Share the meal together.

At the end of the activity, distribute a small stone to each person with the reminder that each student is an ingredient in determining AIDS education policies and programs in the school.

Dance

PURPOSE To use folk dances from various cultures to help participants learn to appreciate differences between people.

PREPARATION *Materials*

- Folk dance instructions and music
- Record, cassette, or CD player
- Photographs of folk dancers
- Videotapes on folk dance
- Videocassette player and monitor
- Items such as Lifesavers candy, toothpaste, toilet paper, shoe, magazine, soda pop can

Advance Preparation

- Select folk dances
- Obtain folk dance music
- Practice the folk dance steps
- Invite folk dance groups and leaders to visit the class

PROCEDURE People are different in many ways. One way to illustrate this point is through the use of folk dance. Folk dances throughout the world vary from culture to culture. This uniqueness is something to be celebrated.

Before introducing the theme of folk dance, focus attention on the fact that all people are different. Invite the participants to stand in the center of the room. Tell the group that a list of statements will be read and that each phrase has something to do with common differences among people. Instructions will be provided for ways in which the group may respond to each item. For example: Show the roll of Lifesavers. Ask all those who lick Lifesavers to walk to the right side of the room and all those who chew them to move to the left. Continue the activity by showing commonly used items and naming different ways that they are used. Suggestions include:

With a tube of toothpaste: People who squeeze, go right. People who roll, go left.
With toilet paper: Those who hang it so the paper unrolls on the outside, move right. Those who hang it so the paper unrolls on the inside, move left.
With shoes: Those who put on the left one first, move right. Those who put on the right one first, move left.
With a magazine: Those who read from the back, move right. Those who read from the front, move left.
With an empty soda pop can: Those who dent it, go to the right side. Those who leave it alone, go to the left side.

Continue the activity with additional statements. Once this portion of the exercise is concluded, ask the group to share their reactions and responses. What point did these simple statements make? Emphasize that all people are different, even in their everyday activities.

Folk dance is an interesting, involving way to celebrate the differences among cultures. Folk dancing is thought of as traditional ritualistic and recreational dance forms, anonymous in origin, and handed down from generation to generation in specific areas of the world. Many of the movements are symbolic and represent the actions of or reactions to nature, people, birds, and animals. Tell the students that they will be learning a variety of folk dances from other countries.

Begin by showing photographs of folk dancers or viewing a videotape of people dancing different steps. If a folk dance group or instructor has been invited to share with the students, introduce them to the group and ask the guests to perform. Invite the group to learn folk dances from different cultures, such as:

Scotland—Highland fling
Ireland—Jig
Philippines—Liki
Moravia—Handkerchief dance
Mexico—La Cucaracha
Poland—Polka
Caribbean Islands—Calypso
Greece—Trata
Israel—Hora
Spain—Paso Doble

Provide instructions and guide the group as they listen to the music and learn the steps.

After the dancing, remind the participants to respect all people, regardless of their differences. Tie the activity into the theme of HIV/AIDS by reminding the group that there are many people living with HIV and dying from AIDS. These individuals are sometimes considered "different" by society. They, too, are "folk" who need to be celebrated.

Drama/Clown/Mime

PURPOSE   To use the game of Charades to teach that AIDS can happen to anyone.

PREPARATION   *Materials*

- Index cards and pens or pencils
- Shoebox

Many people think that they are not at risk of being infected with HIV, the virus that causes AIDS. These people need to think again. Many people who are infected with HIV didn't think they were at risk either. Many didn't know how to keep from getting infected with

HIV. Many people pretend that HIV/AIDS isn't a problem—at least not their problem.

Charades is a dramatic game that involves pretending. During charades the words or situations to be guessed are pantomimed without spoken words. Play a game of charades to address the theme that HIV/AIDS can infect anyone.

Pass out index cards and pens or pencils. Ask the students to write one HIV/AIDS-related behavior or situation on each card. Explain that the cards will be used as clues for a game of charades. Point out that many people think that HIV/AIDS cannot happen to them. Just like people who play a game of charades, they are pretending. When preparing the cards, be sure that each of them conveys a different theme. Situations could include:

Person injecting drugs
Teens on a first date
Prostitute soliciting for sex
Woman receiving a blood transfusion
First grader who sits next to a child with AIDS

After the cards are prepared, place them in a shoebox. Explain the procedure for playing a game of charades. Tell the students to take turns drawing a card from the box and acting out the situation written on it. Direct the rest of the group to guess the behavior related to AIDS. Once the situation is named, discuss how it is connected to HIV/AIDS. Ask how people in this situation might pretend that HIV/AIDS isn't involved or that it doesn't affect them. The person who guesses correctly gets the next chance to act out a topic. Continue in this manner until many behaviors are illustrated.

Charades may also be used to help talk about other AIDS-related problems such as:
People will die from AIDS
There is no cure for AIDS
There are no vaccines for AIDS
Tests for HIV are not 100% accurate
Some people kill themselves once infected with HIV
Not all students are learning about AIDS
Some people with AIDS are subjects of discrimination

Allow an opportunity for the students to discuss the theme that people cannot pretend that they are not at risk of HIV/AIDS. HIV/AIDS affects everyone and can infect men, women, and children of all ages. Suggest that people need to become "AIDS Smart." Although this can be done through education, counseling is also an important factor involved in dealing with the pretending. Counseling involves the exchange of ideas between two people. Although one of the parties may be a friend, a professional counselor is often involved in helping people deal with issues related to HIV/AIDS. Inform the participants that it is appropriate to talk to others about feeling and fears associated with the AIDS epidemic. Addressing HIV/AIDS issues in concrete ways is much better than pretending that it isn't a problem.

Games

PURPOSE   To learn the mime technique of isolation and to relate this term to the ways some persons infected and affected with AIDS are treated.

PREPARATION   *Materials*

- 5" x 7" cards and markers
- Props that facilitate recognition of AIDS symptoms

Advance Preparation

- Prepare one card for each participant. On half the cards write "AIDS" and one of its symptoms. On the other stack of cards write "AIDE" and one of the symptoms used in the first pile on each card. Refer to pages 17–18 for a list of symptoms.

PROCEDURE "Isolation" is the mime technique of moving each segment of the body independently. In an isolation exercise a person stands straight and motionless.

The next step is to move one element of the body without moving any other part. In other words, the individual isolates one part from the rest of the body. This may sound simple and easy. It is simple, but not easy. The body is not used to staying still. When one part moves, the parts that surround it naturally wish to move. It is relatively easy to move most segments of the body; it is more difficult not to move.[2]
Invite the group to try the mime technique of isolation.

Ask the students to stand up straight and to become motionless. Tell everyone to hold one hand in front of them. Now, suggest that they try to bend the thumb at the knuckle. They are to bend only the thumb without moving any other parts of the hand or arm. Next, try bending only the first finger, then the second, the third, and finally the little finger. Sometimes the isolation is easy to achieve; other times, it is hard. Continue practicing until the isolation exercises become more comfortable. Switch to the other hand and repeat the exercise. The activity may be continued with the wrist, arm, head, neck, and so forth.

Isolation is a mime technique; it is also an activity and an attitude found in everyday life. Ask someone to give another definition of the word "isolation." It means to set apart from others or to place alone. Many times people infected with HIV and those with AIDS are isolated physically, emotionally, and spiritually. Think specifically about ways that isolation may occur at school. Children with the virus may be left out of games on the playground, set apart during social functions, or ignored in the course of classroom discussions.

Engage the children in an activity to help them experience how it might feel to be someone with AIDS who is isolated. This exercise will also encourage them to think about ways to assist people who have AIDS. Invite each person to draw one of the cards that was prepared in advance. Tell those with the "AIDS" cards to go to one area of the room and to prepare to identify themselves as a person having the symptom listed on the card. They may use any props or materials available. Those with the "AIDES" cards should cluster together. Tell them that when the activity begins they are to ignore the students with "AIDS." Later in the project, they will offer assistance. The "AIDES" students should begin to brainstorm ways in which they can help the students who have "AIDS." Each person should think of ways to aid the student who has the corresponding symptom on his or her card. Remind the "AIDES" group not to talk to the persons with "AIDS" when they return. Explain that this is often how persons with AIDS are treated in real life. In other words, they are isolated.

The "AIDS" students return, displaying their symptoms, and are treated poorly by the players with "AIDES" cards. After a short time, stop the process and engage in discussion about how each group feels. Resume the activity, only this time have each "AIDES" card holder find the "AIDS" individual with the corresponding symptom on his or her game piece. "AIDES" should help "AIDS" in ways appropriate to the symptoms they are displaying. All "AIDES" can assist in general ways by being friendly to the "AIDS" players.

Gather the participants together to summarize the activity. Point out that it is easy to isolate people in real life. Once a person learns to isolate someone else, it can be hard to unlearn the behavior. It often takes a lot of work, just like isolating various body parts in the art of mime. Encourage the group to include rather than exclude persons infected and affected by AIDS in school activities and in other situations and circumstances.[3]

Music

PURPOSE To use a familiar song to help young people learn methods of assertive communication.

PREPARATION *Materials*

- Newsprint and markers
- Masking tape
- Music, "If You're Happy and You Know It"
- Accompaniment (optional)

Advance Preparation

- Prepare a poster on a sheet of newsprint that lists "Tips for Assertive Communication." Include ideas such as:

  Speak distinctly and firmly
  Remain calm
  Stand erect
  Look directly at the other person
  Use "I" messages
  Avoid accusatory remarks that include the word "you"

- Tape the poster to a wall

PROCEDURE Some of the decisions young people face involve choices about drug and alcohol use and sex. Because HIV is spread through sexual intercourse or sharing drug needles and syringes, youth need to learn how to make decisions that keep themselves and others from being infected with the virus. Besides making the decisions, young people need to know how to communicate effectively their thoughts and feelings to others. Emphasize the use of the word "No" and the importance of stating "I" rather than "You" messages. Ideas generated by the participants will be reported by writing new words to a familiar tune.

Organize the participants into two groups. Group One will consider situations involving sexual relations; Group Two will consider situations involving drug use. Tell Group One to imagine themselves as a person being pressured to have sexual intercourse, especially without the use of a condom. Explain that Group Two should pretend to be someone who is being persuaded to use drugs or to share needles or syringes. In both cases the individuals in these predicaments want to say "No." Tell the two groups that their task is to determine ways to say "No" to these risky activities. Distribute sheets of newsprint and markers and suggest that each team generate a list of ideas and answers.

Before the groups begin the activity, call attention to the poster listing "Tips for Assertive Communication." Review each of the statements on the list. Instruct the group to incorporate these suggestions into their responses.

Provide time for the groups to develop ideas and phrases to respond to their imaginary, yet very realistic, situations. These could include:

Sexual Relations

- "I am just not ready for sex yet."
- "I know it feels right for you and I care about you. But I'm not going to do it until I'm sure it's the right thing for me to do."
- "I feel good about not having sex until I'm married. I've made my decision and I feel comfortable with it."

Drugs

- "I want to go to college. I can't risk getting hooked on drugs."
- "Drugs are illegal. I won't break the law."
- "I love my life. Drugs can kill me."

Share the responses of the two groups. Next, challenge each team to put their words to music. Sing the familiar song "If You're Happy and You Know It" with the young people. Tell each group to change the words of the song to a message related to HIV/AIDS, especially as it correlates with transmission and prevention through drug use and sexual activity. For example new words could be:

If you're drug free and you know it, just say "No."
If you're drug free and you know it, just say "No."
If you're drug free and you know it, just saying "No" will show it.
If you're drug free and you know it, just say "No."

Other ideas include:

If you're AIDS smart and you know it, just say "No."
If you respect yourself and others, just say "No."
If you can say "No" and mean it, do it now.
Let me tell you how I feel by using "I."

After the new words are written, invite each group to share their songs as a way of emphasizing the importance of assertive communication, especially as it relates to HIV/AIDS themes.

Photography

PURPOSE To make and use calendars that illustrate ways in which the AIDS virus is not transmitted.

PREPARATION *Materials*

- Paper, 11" x 17" (seven sheets per calendar)
- Stapler and staples
- Scissors
- Glue
- Markers
- Photographs and pictures from many sources
- Calendar pages for each month; blank

PROCEDURE Calendars are a rich resource for exploring many themes related to numerous subjects. Calendar pictures are wonderful tools for curriculum enrichment and classroom activities. When a calendar is displayed in a classroom, hallway, or lunch room, awareness of its theme is promoted each time a person glances at it, checks a date, or writes something in a space. To help the children learn more about ways in which the AIDS virus is not transmitted, use this topic as the basis of calendar illustrations. Make a calendar for the classroom or have each participant construct a calendar to use at home.

Explain the calendar project to the group. Tell them that different pictures will be used each month to illustrate ways that the AIDS virus is not transmitted from one person to another. Invite the group's help in naming twelve ways, one for each month of the year and related to specific school activities. For example:

January—Building a snow person together
February—Shaking hands or giving a hug
March—Drinking from a water fountain
April—Sharing a book
May—Playing in the playground
June—Having fun at a picnic
July—Going to camp together
August—Swimming in a pool
September—Riding on a school bus
October—Playing football or another game
November—Eating lunch together
December—Receiving a Christmas gift from someone

If one calendar is to be made, assign twelve individuals or small groups to illustrate one month. If individual calendars are to be made, all themes will be used by each person. For individual calendars, distribute seven pieces of paper. The paper can be any size, although a large size, such as 11" x 17", allows the students room to create interesting, inviting pictures. Tell the participants to fold the seven pages in half and to staple the sheets in the middle, on the crease line. Challenge the group to create each month's illustration from photographs and pictures. Twelve suggestions include using pictures from:

Magazines
Cards

Snapshots
School newspapers
Local and national newspapers
Postcards
Brochures
Newspaper inserts
Stickers
Other calendars
Catalogs
Posters

Show the students a variety of materials, as well as basic tools such as markers, scissors, and glue. Instruct them to use the twelve top sections of their calendar to create various illustrations of ways the AIDS virus cannot be transmitted from one person to another. To make the pages for each month, dates may be copied off of another calendar or calendar pages may be duplicated and glued to the bottom of the corresponding sheet. Tell each person to design a cover and to write additional information about HIV/AIDS transmission and prevention on the remaining blank pages. Invite each person to write his or her name somewhere on the calendar.

Gather the participants, with their calendars, in a circle on the floor, on chairs, or around tables. Instruct everyone to pass his or her calendar around the circle and to look carefully at the ways the various themes have been depicted by other people. Continue passing calendars until each person ends up with his or her own again.

Puppetry

PURPOSE To make and use glove puppets to learn proper procedures for handing contact with body fluids and blood.

PREPARATION *Materials*

- Rubber gloves
- Scissors
- Felt and Velcro pieces
- Glue
- Paper and pencils
- Information on Universal Precautions
- Poster board
- Markers

Advance Preparation

- Obtain information on Universal Precautions for handling body fluids
- Prepare a poster listing the Universal Precautions steps

PROCEDURE Since HIV, the virus that causes AIDS, is transmitted from one person to another through the transfer of body fluids and blood, it is extremely important to teach students "Universal Precautions." Universal Precautions are the proper procedures for handling contact with blood and body fluids. Explain that although the virus is transmitted primarily during sexual contact or through the sharing of intravenous drug needles and syringes, it is also possible to spread the virus in other ways. If body fluids from an infected person are spilled and not cleaned up properly, the virus may enter an uninfected person's body through a cut or open sore. Discuss situations in the school setting in which body fluids or blood may be exposed to others. These instances include times when a child has a bloody nose or when a person is injured during an activity.

Show the students a chart containing the Universal Precautions. Discuss each step of the procedure.

Universal Precautions

Procedures for handling contact with blood and body fluids

1. Put on disposable or utility gloves.
2. Use paper towels to absorb spill, then place used towels in a red plastic leak-proof bag.
3. Flood spill area with a freshly prepared bleach solution or with a hospital-grade disinfectant. The bleach solution must contain one part bleach to ten parts water and should be less than 24 hours old.
4. Clean area with paper towels, broom, or vacuum.
5. Place used paper toweling in red plastic bag.
6. Remove soiled gloves by turning inside out, placing one within the other; if wearing utility gloves, remove and then disinfect appropriately; proceed to step 8.
7. Place red bag in appropriate infectious waste container.
8. Immediately wash hands with soap in running water.

After the participants understand each step of the procedure, invite them to write short puppet scripts and to make glove puppets to use to impart this important information to other people. Pass out pencils and paper and instruct the children, individually or in small groups, to write a puppet show about the Universal Precautions. The story needs to have a beginning, a middle, and an end. These can also be called Acts I, II, and III. Begin by selecting the theme of the show. Decide the action that takes place in each scene and the characters that are needed. Write short, simple dialogue for the characters.

Characters, such as health-care workers, children, or adults, may be added to each finger of the glove, or felt pieces representing the objects named in the Universal Precautions, such as gloves, bleach, and soap, may be made and attached to the fingers. Provide a glove for each child, as well as felt pieces, scissors, Velcro, and glue. Instruct the group to construct the figures that will help them tell their stories. Glue Velcro pieces to the fingertips of the glove and to the back of each felt figure. Place the glove on the hand. Attach the characters to the glove at the appropriate time in the puppet show. Practice the story and present the puppet show to help people of all ages understand the proper way to handle body fluids and blood. This is an important way to help prevent the spread of HIV infection.

Storytelling

PURPOSE To use a cooperative method of storytelling as a pretest and post-test for teaching information about HIV/AIDS.

PREPARATION *Materials*

- Resource materials on HIV/AIDS

PROCEDURE "Round Robin" is a cooperative method of telling a story. Each participant adds a certain number of words or a sentence or a statement. Invite the children to tell a round-robin story addressing different topics related to HIV/AIDS. Use this method as a pre- and post-test when teaching information on this subject. It is an interesting and involving way to determine what the children already know and what they have learned.

Gather the participants and ask them to sit in a circle on the floor or on chairs. Explain that the group will be telling stories related to different issues of HIV/AIDS. Each person will have an opportunity, in turn, to add five words to it. If the group is large, change the number of words to three; if it is small, increase the number of words to more than five. Tell the participants that the collaborative account will help everyone learn new facts about this disease. It will also aid them in separating fact from fiction.

Begin the narrative for the group with five words, such as "HIV is a virus that . . ." Go around the circle and provide an opportunity as well as cues and encouragement for each child to contribute to the story. Continue the process by introducing new themes. Include categories and examples such as:

Countries of the world: "Haiti is a country where . . ."
States: "New York state has the . . ."
Professions: "Paramedics are important people who . . ."
Categories of people: "Women can become infected by . . ."
Vocabulary: "HIV stands for the words . . ."
Prevention methods: "Abstinence is one of the . . ."
Transmission: "Injecting drug users who share . . ."
Places: "School is a place where . . ."
Involvement: "Bringing food to a family . . ."
Groups: "The American Red Cross produces . . ."

Continue until each story seems to be concluded or until the children run out of ideas. Following the stories, discuss the information that was presented. Correct misinformation and teach facts related to the various topics.

Although there are no supplies required for this activity, it may be helpful to have pictures, key words on cards, or resource materials to use to prompt the children during the round-robin review.

1. Marcia Brown, *Stone Soup* (New York: Macmillan, 1947).
2. Claude Kipnis, *The Mime Book* (Colorado Springs, Colo.: Meriwether Publishing, 1974), p. 7.
3. Ideas for the "AIDES" and "AIDS" activity were contributed by Tanya Harmon and used by permission.

CHAPTER 8
Congregation

The activities included in the theme "Congregation" center on enabling young people to understand and to put into practice God's teachings on care, compassion, and justice. The exercises suggest possibilities and projects through which people in a congregation may become involved in HIV/AIDS awareness and action.

Architecture

PURPOSE To overcome obstacles and to promote congregational awareness of HIV/AIDS.

PREPARATION *Materials*

- Obstacles: furniture, tires, logs, etc.
- Blindfolds
- Newsprint and markers
- Materials for selected activities

Advance Preparation

- Prepare the obstacle course

PROCEDURE An "obstacle" is defined as anything that stands in the way, an obstruction, something that hinders or blocks. Sometimes persons infected and affected by HIV/AIDS face many obstacles to full participation in the life of a congregation. Use this architecture-related activity to explore some of the barriers, both physical and emotional, that face persons with HIV/AIDS and their families and friends and to discover ways to heighten AIDS awareness in the community of faith.

As the students arrive, or after the entire group has gathered, tell the participants that they will be walking through an obstacle course. Be sure that everyone understands the meaning of the word "obstacle." Divide the players into walkers and guides. There should be at least one guide for each walker. While the contestants are maneuvering through the obstacle course, it is the guide's role to protect them from harm. After the instructions are given, blindfold each walker. The game begins with the blindfolded contestants leaving the starting point. The contestants must travel the full length of the obstacle course without touching one another or talking. When the last contestant has finished, the game is over. Ask the participants to remove their blindfolds and to gather in a circle on the floor, on chairs, or around tables.

Ask the group for their reactions to walking the obstacle course. Explain that this game was set up to help them understand that sometimes there are obstacles in the way of persons infected and affected with HIV/AIDS who want to fully participate in the life of a congregation. Ask the group to think together about what some of these barriers might be. Record the answers on newsprint. Answers could include:

Handicapped access: Some people with AIDS use a wheelchair or are unable to climb steps.

Sound systems: Persons with AIDS who experience hearing loss may not be able to understand the words being spoken.

Vision problems: Because of deteriorating eyesight, a person with AIDS may be unable to read the bulletin, the hymnbook, and the Bible.

Even if there are ramps, elevators, large-print worship aids, and hearing systems, attitudes can also shut people out of a community of faith. People who pass judgment on lifestyle or background, those who do not extend a warm welcome, and individuals who do not allow their children to participate in classes with young people or leaders who are infected with HIV also present obstacles to full participation in the life of the body of Christ. Physical appearance because of hair and weight loss, lack of transportation, and similar factors also pose barriers that might prevent the person with HIV/AIDS from attending worship, education, nurture, and outreach activities of a congregation.

After some of the obstacles have been identified, invite the participants to suggest ways in which they may be overcome. One suggestion is to hold an HIV/AIDS awareness Sunday. Involve the young people and other members of the congregation in planning and presenting this type of event. A special Sunday focused on HIV/AIDS is intended to increase the members' awareness of and interest in local, nation, and international projects and programs. Its aim is also to encourage and challenge people to expand the mission of the church beyond their own walls. This activity is a way to involve all of the church-school classes as well as other church groups in planning a one-day festive event that is meaningful and fun.

Materials required will vary with the selected activities. Advance preparation includes:

- Request permission to hold the event.
- Set the date.
- Organize a planning committee, involving the youth group, women's groups, church school, Christian education department, worship committee, social concerns committee, outreach committee, mission committee, and other groups.
- Publicize the event with posters, banners, bulletin announcements, and newsletters.

Some of the components of the day could include:

Displays: Create HIV/AIDS awareness displays.
Bulletin boards: Use materials available through denominations or AIDS service organizations to create bulletin boards.
Table of materials: Free materials are available through many agencies and organizations. Provide them for people for further reading and reference.
Bulletin Inserts: Obtain and use pertinent bulletin inserts about HIV/AIDS.
Music: Learn and sing songs with HIV/AIDS-related themes during the worship service. The church-school youth can provide special music.
Prayer: Remember persons infected and affected with HIV/AIDS during individual and corporate prayer times.
Communion: If the Lord's Supper is part of the worship service for this event, use different types of bread as a reminder that God's love is for all peoples of the world.
Church school classes: Invite persons living with HIV/AIDS and/or representatives of AIDS ministry organizations to speak to church school classes.
Benefit sale: Hold a sale, related to a special project, and donate the money to further ways in which God's love can be shared with other people.

After the special Sunday, continue to focus on HIV/AIDS themes in some of these ways:

Keep the theme as an integral part of worship.
Share updated information in church newsletters and displays.
Participate in projects that further the cause of HIV/AIDS understanding.
Study HIV/AIDS related themes in church school sessions.

Remind the participants that by holding an HIV/AIDS awareness Sunday, they are doing nothing more or less than challenging the church to be the church. Read to the group the words spoken by the angel in Luke 2:10,11. When a congregation can proclaim the glad tidings of great joy to all people, then it will be the church it is called to be.

Art

PURPOSE To view the icon and read the prayer for "Mother of God Light in All Darkness."

PREPARATION *Materials*

- Icon poster or card of "Mother of God Light in All Darkness"
- Candles and matches

Advance Preparation

- Obtain icon poster or card(s) from: National Catholic AIDS Network, P.O. Box 422984, San Francisco, Calif. 94142

PROCEDURE "Icon," from the Greek word *eikon*, means image or figure. Used primarily in the Eastern Orthodox Church, icons are sacred images or pictures of Jesus, Mary, and saints. The National Catholic AIDS Network commissioned an icon, "Mother of God Light in All Darkness," for all of us living with HIV and AIDS. It is based on the Russian icon "The Pimen Mother of God" and was painted, technically "written," by Fr. William Hart McNichols, who worked in AIDS ministry at St. Vincent's Hospice and throughout New York from 1983 to 1990. In the autumn of 1990, Fr. McNichols moved to Albuquerque, New Mexico, to study the theology, history, and craft of icon painting with the Russian-American master Robert Lentz.

Explain the meaning of an icon to the participants and show them a poster or card of "Mother of God Light in All Darkness." Continue the story by telling the group that the artist says of the icon,

> I wanted to create a contemplative image of absolute unconditional love, and of hope amidst the varied experiences of darkness people with HIV and AIDS, and all of us encounter in this life. The Mother of God holds the Christ Emmanuel who guards and is the living flame of love, warmth, promise and joy. She gently repeats his gesture of shielding the Light.

Allow time for the group to view the painting and to share their responses to it.

Tell those gathered that there is a prayer associated with this icon and invite them to offer the words to God together. Explain that the leader will say a line and the group will repeat it in unison. This process will continue for the entire prayer. If possible, distribute a candle to each person to hold during the prayer to symbolize the light of Christ represented in the icon. Provide safety instructions and light the candles. If lighted candles are not a good option for the group, substitute a battery-operated type. Offer the words of the prayer for all of us living with HIV and AIDS.

> *Mother of God*
> *Light In All Darkness,*
> *shelter Him*
> *our flame of hope*
> *with your*
> *tender hands.*
> *And in our times*
> *of dread and nightmares,*
> *let Him be our*
> *dream of comfort.*
> *And in our times*
> *of physical pain*
> *and suffering,*
> *let Him be*
> *our healer.*
> *And in our times*

of separation
from God and one another,
let Him be
our communion.
Amen.[1]

If possible, distribute an icon card to each person to keep. Encourage the group to pray daily for persons infected and affected by HIV/AIDS.

Banners/Textiles

PURPOSE   To make and send greeting cards to persons with AIDS.

PREPARATION   *Materials*

- Materials will vary with selected method
- Envelopes and stamps
- Names and addresses of persons with AIDS

Advance Preparation

- Obtain the names and addresses of persons with AIDS

PROCEDURE   Make "mini-banners" in the form of cards and use them to express care and concern to persons living with AIDS. Cards communicate greetings when personal visits are not possible, convey thoughts that are difficult to speak, and cheer homebound and hospitalized patients. Organize a congregational card-making event. Obtain the names and addresses of church members who are HIV infected as well as information about persons with AIDS who are family members and friends of persons connected with the congregation. In addition, gather the names and addresses of persons living in various care facilities in the community or in homes and hospitals sponsored by the denomination.

Add interest to the project by making the cards in unusual ways. Set up learning centers around a large room or in several smaller rooms, each containing supplies and suggestions for making cards by various techniques. For special and unique greetings, make the cards or notes using several of these methods:

Block prints: Print designs by using linoleum or eraser cut-outs as printers.
Bulletin covers: Write a message on the inside of a blank bulletin cover.
Cake, cupcakes: Decorate a cake or cupcakes with a special greeting.
Calligraphy: Inscribe a message in a calligraphy style.
Re-cycled cards: Use pictures from used cards and write the message on the back.
Collage: Arrange a variety of pictures to form a collage.
Coloring book: Trace a picture from a coloring book or color a page and use it as a card.
Computer: Use a computer program, such as "Print Shop," to make a card.
Construction paper: Fold a piece of construction paper in half and decorate it with stickers and seals.
Doily: Pick a colored or patterned doily to use as a card.
Felt scraps: Organize felt scraps to create a design.
Magazines: Choose letters from a magazine to form words such as "love," "joy," "peace," or "hope."
Newspaper: Write or glue words on a piece of newspaper and include a message.
Paper strips: Loop strips of paper and staple them together to form a chain. Write one word of the message on each piece.
Pompons: Glue pompons together to create a design.
Ribbon: Write the message on a piece of ribbon or the streamer of a bow.
Rubber stamps: Press a rubber stamp on paper to make a picture.
Shapes: Combine shapes to form a design.
Silk screen: Screen print a meaningful message.

Spatter paint: Spatter paint a card using a piece of window screen and a toothbrush.

Stencil: Stencil a pattern on fabric or paper.

Tissue paper: Piece tissue paper scraps together to create a stained-glass effect.

Torn paper: Tear a design out of paper and glue it to a note.

Watercolors: Paint a picture and add a scripture passage as the message.

Wrapping paper: Pick colorful wrapping paper, cut a piece, fold it in half, and write a message inside.

As the card makers arrive, allow them to choose the names of several people for whom they will make greetings. Invite the "artists" to explore various learning centers and to experiment with several card-making techniques. After the event, mail or deliver the cards to the recipients.

Cartoons

PURPOSE   To discover ways in which individual members and entire congregations are ministering to persons infected and affected by HIV/AIDS.

PREPARATION   *Materials*

- "I'm Involved" Game
- Paper and pens or pencils
- Duplicating or photocopying equipment
- Camera and film (optional)
- Self-adhesive labels
- Scissors
- Photographs of AIDS ministry projects and programs
- Tape or tacks
- Bulletin board, wall, or poster board
- Chalkboard and chalk or newsprint and marker
- Markers or colored pencils

Advance Preparation

- Duplicate "I'm Involved" games
- Locate photographs of AIDS ministry projects and programs

PROCEDURE   "What can I do?" is a question individuals often ask when the topic of AIDS arises. "What can we do?" is the query of many congregations. The answer to both is, "A lot!" In this activity the participants will explore ways in which individuals and entire congregations are already involved in many aspects of AIDS ministry. They will also explore new possibilities for service.

Use the "I'm Involved" game as a way for the children to explore ways in which individuals are involved in AIDS ministry opportunities. Distribute a copy of the game and pen or pencil to each person. Instruct the group to move around the room or to take the paper to other groups or classes in the church to find people who fit the descriptions on the sheet. Once a person who can answer "Yes" to a category is found, that person is to write his or her name in the blank on the sheet. Different names must appear in each blank. Allow time for this part of the activity.

Regather the group and read each statement on the sheet. Talk about the answers. Were people found for each category? What did the children discover in the process? Were they surprised at the number of people involved in AIDS-related projects and programs?

On a chalkboard or a sheet of newsprint, compile a list of ways in which people are addressing AIDS issues. Focus the group's attention on what the congregation is doing to address AIDS-related themes in worship, education, outreach, and nurture ministries. Begin another list to record projects and programs that individuals and groups could do. These listings could include:

- Welcome people with HIV/AIDS, their caregivers, family members, and friends to church services and programs.
- Remember infected and affected persons during the congregational prayer.
- Hold AIDS education classes, lectures, and workshops.
- Visit people in hospitals, hospices, or homes.
- Investigate foster parenting programs for children with HIV and AIDS.
- Offer opportunities for caregivers to have a rest.
- Provide transportation to doctor's appointments.
- Go grocery shopping.
- Do laundry.
- Clean the house.
- Send cards.
- Prepare meals.
- Touch someone by offering a handshake or a hug.
- Share a meal.
- Let someone cry.
- Listen to a life story.
- Sit quietly with someone and watch TV or a movie.
- Participate in Adopt-a-Family programs.
- Rent or purchase medical supplies and equipment.
- Hold memorial services.
- Start support groups.
- Organize a fund-raising event.
- Write letters to support the rights of people with HIV and AIDS.
- Provide a holiday meal.

I'm Involved Game

INSTRUCTIONS: Get the signatures of different people who have done or are doing each of the following things related to HIV/AIDS.

_____ read a newspaper article about HIV/AIDS.

_____ prayed for a person with AIDS.

_____ viewed the NAMES Project AIDS Memorial Quilt.

_____ volunteers for an AIDS ministry organization.

_____ watched a TV program about HIV/AIDS.

_____ sent a card to an infected person.

_____ visited the family of a person with AIDS.

_____ read a book about AIDS.

_____ picked up a brochure to learn more about AIDS.

_____ knows the AIDS Hotline number.

_____ attended a lecture about AIDS.

_____ drove someone with AIDS to a doctor's appointment.

_____ donated money to an AIDS organization.

_____ wrote a letter to a congressperson regarding AIDS.

_____ has seen a poster or billboard about AIDS.

- Learn more about becoming a "Covenant to Care" congregation, a ministry of the United Methodist Church. Members make this promise: "As members of The United Methodist Church we covenant together to assure ministries and other services to person with AIDS . . . We ask for God's guidance that we might respond in ways that bear witness always to Jesus' own compassionate ministry of healing and reconciliation; and that to this end we might love one another and care for one another with the same unmeasured and unconditional love that Jesus embodied."
- Provide office space for AIDS ministry organizations.

Continue exploring the theme of AIDS ministry opportunities by drawing, finding, or taking pictures of projects and programs offered by one or several congregations. Tell the children that they will be creating a cartoon strip on a bulletin board, wall, or large piece of paper to illustrate this subject. If pictures are to be drawn, provide paper and markers or colored pencils and instruct each person to depict a different way individual members and entire congregations can share Christ's care and compassion in AIDS-related situations. If photographs are found or taken, distribute one or several to each person in the group. Supply self-adhesive labels, scissors, and pens and tell the students to draw conversation balloons to add to the pictures. Each "balloon" should contain words, real or imaginary, that the people in the picture might be saying. Tell the participants to cut out the balloons, peel off the backing, and stick the words to the proper picture. Tape or tack the completed pictures to the background material. Encourage the group to look at the pictures. Challenge the group to respond to the question "What can I do?" by getting involved in AIDS ministry projects and programs.

Creative Writing

PURPOSE To enable participants to write petitions for a prayer calendar with HIV/AIDS-related themes.

PREPARATION *Materials*

- Paper and pens
- Duplicating or photocopying equipment
- Newsprint
- Tape
- Markers
- Bulletins and posters from AIDS prayer services

PROCEDURE Prepare a prayer calendar with specific petitions related to HIV/AIDS themes that can be used by members of the congregation every day for a month. Begin the activity by showing the participants materials, such as bulletins or posters, from prayer services and events connected with the AIDS epidemic. For example, during the October, 1992, display of the NAMES Project AIDS Memorial Quilt in Washington, D.C., an interfaith prayer service was held at the National Cathedral; ecumenical services are generally scheduled on World AIDS Day; individual congregations may arrange prayer vigils for infected and affected family members and friends associated with the faith community; memorial services are offered by groups in remembrance of the lives of their members. Discuss specific ways in which prayer is used by entire congregations and communities to express their care and concern for people infected and affected by HIV/AIDS. Obtain materials on the "Harlem Week of Prayer for the Healing of AIDS," which was started in 1989. During this week in the fall, the religious communities of Harlem, New York, unite in prayer and education by holding worship services, seminars, and concerts related to HIV/AIDS themes.

Challenge the participants to think of prayer needs and requests related to HIV/AIDS. Ideas could include causes for praise, specific people who work in the field, situations in which conflicts have arisen or been resolved, countries where needs are great, organizations that provide education and assistance, and local opportunities for involvement. Invite the group to prepare petitions for a month-long prayer calendar that will be duplicated and distributed to members of the congregation. Begin the project by brainstorming and recording on newsprint as many prayer petitions as there are days for the month the calendar will be used. Provide information on specific events that will take place during the month, such as a meeting of the AIDS ministry committee, World AIDS Day, a food drive, or a local display of the NAMES Project AIDS Memorial Quilt. Incorporate prayer petitions related to these activities on the proper days. Examples of prayer petitions for a thirty-one day month include:

- Pray for people who will be tested for HIV infection today.
- Remember medical workers who provide care for persons with AIDS.
- Say a prayer that persons addicted to drugs may find ways to address this problem.
- Pray for the meeting of the AIDS ministry committee that will be held today.
- Pray for persons who will view the exhibit of the NAMES Project AIDS Memorial Quilt today.
- Pray for care partners.
- Pray for persons who share long-kept secrets related to their sexual orientation.
- Pray for parents who are grieving the loss of a child.
- Pray for teachers who educate children about AIDS-related themes.
- Pray for denominational executives who make AIDS-related statements.
- Pray for school board members who make AIDS-related policy decisions.
- Pray for persons who live with guilt for transmitting the virus to someone else.
- Pray for persons who counsel people with HIV/AIDS.
- Pray for children who must decide whether or not to play with someone with HIV/AIDS.
- Pray for scientists who seek to find a cure for the virus.
- Pray for children who have lost parents to AIDS.
- Pray for people who have become infected through blood transfusions.
- Pray for medical supplies for countries in need.
- Pray for volunteers for AIDS ministry organizations.
- Pray for funding for AIDS-related projects and programs.
- Pray for the president of the United States who makes AIDS-related decisions.
- Pray for legislators to pass laws that are fair to all people.
- Pray for the interfaith worship service for the healing of AIDS that will be held today.
- Pray that people who need medical treatment will find access to complete and compassionate care.
- Pray that people will view sexuality as a gift from God.
- Pray that persons with AIDS will find comfort from the Scriptures and from caring individuals and congregations.
- Pray for volunteers to meet the numerous needs related to HIV/AIDS.
- Pray for persons who are facing the loss of control of their bodies and their lives because of weakness and dementia.
- Pray for conflict resolution in families facing AIDS-related illness.
- Pray for husbands and wives who have been infected by a spouse.
- Pray for those who face the loss of their lives at an early age.

Compile the requests into a calendar that can be duplicated and distributed, not only to each participant, but also to the entire congregation. Challenge the participants to pray for an AIDS-related concern every day.

Culinary Arts

PURPOSE To prepare a congregational cookbook listing AIDS-related symptoms and side effects and hints on food preparation to help meet nutritional needs of persons with AIDS.

PREPARATION *Materials*

- Resources on nutrition and AIDS

Mouth Pain or Sores:

Mouth pain or sores can make it hard to eat because of discomfort and difficulty in swallowing.

HINTS

- Cool, smooth, and mildly flavored foods make eating more enjoyable.
- Eat foods served at moderate temperatures rather than extremes in temperature, hot or cold, which may be irritating.
- Choose mild food and drinks like apple juice rather than acidic food such as oranges, grapefruit, or pineapple, which may cause a burning feeling in the mouth.
- Limit spices such as chili powder or red pepper and salted foods.
- Dunk toast, cookies, and crackers in liquids such as milk, soup, or tea to make them softer.
- Eat foods like puddings, eggs, canned fruits, baked fish, soft cheeses, noodle dishes, and ice cream.
- Popsicles can be a tasty way to numb the pain.
- Add a nutritionally balanced drink to the regular diet to help boost calories when it is difficult to eat.

- Index cards and pens
- Recipe box or duplicating equipment and paper

Advance Preparation

- Obtain copies of the pamphlet *Nutrition and AIDS: Taking Charge of Your Diet* from: Task Force on Nutrition Support in AIDS, Wang Associates, Inc., 19 West 21st Street, New York, N.Y. 10010.

PROCEDURE New member breakfasts, leadership luncheons, potluck suppers, sub sandwich sales, pizza parties, church cookbooks, parent and child banquets, cookouts and picnics, meals-on-wheels—all of these congregational projects and programs, and many more, involve food. Food is almost synonymous with the worship, education, outreach, and nurture ministries of many churches, synagogues, and religious bodies. Food ministries to persons with AIDS, however, require special planning, precautions, and preparation. Create a church cookbook that will assist people in the congregation as they facilitate food-related ministries to persons living with HIV and AIDS.

When the immune system is weakened, as it is with AIDS, it is particularly important to maintain good nutritional habits. Eating both the right amounts and the right types of food will provide strength and improve the ability to fight infection. Various types of foods are needed by persons with AIDS as they experience the various symptoms and side effects associated with the disease. To educate the congregation about these special needs make recipe cards and produce a unique church cookbook. On one side of the card, write an AIDS-related symptom; on the other side, list one or more hints to help with the situation.

Additional symptoms or side effects to include are:

- Difficulty swallowing

- Dulled taste sensation
- Diarrhea
- Anorexia
- Nausea/vomiting
- Precautions

Assign a different symptom or side effect to each individual or small group. Provide resource materials, index cards, and pens. Instruct the participants to locate information related to the symptoms and to prepare cards containing the categories and the helpful hints. Once the groups have completed the cards, share the information. Place the cards in a recipe box to leave in the church kitchen or duplicate the cards and distribute them to members of the congregation.

Dance

PURPOSE   To show how Jesus used his hands to touch people who were ill and hurting and to use a dance activity as a way of reaching out to others in prayer and hope.

PREPARATION   *Materials*

- Cassette tape of "Healing Hands," by Elton John, and cassette player
- Bibles
- Index cards, pens, and envelopes
- Camera and slide film or source of theme-related slides
- Slide projector and screen

Advance Preparation

- Take or find slides of people using their hands to help other people.
- Practice projecting and coordinating the slides and the background music.
- Write one word of each of the following Bible verses on an index card. Place the cards for each verse in a separate envelope.

  Matthew 8:3—Healing the leper
  Mark 5:41—Healing Jarius' daughter
  Mark 10:16—Jesus blesses the children
  John 9:6—Healing the man born blind
  Matthew 8:15—Healing Peter's mother-in-law

PROCEDURE   In the New Testament there are many stories of ways in which Jesus used his hands to touch people both to heal them and to show them his care and concern. Invite the participants to review Scripture passages that illustrate Jesus' attitude and action on this theme. Explain that the words of the verses have been written on separate index cards and that they must be put in order before they can be read. Determine whether the students will work alone or in small groups for this portion of the activity. Distribute an envelope to each person or team. Tell the learners that the envelopes contain the words to a New Testament verse related to touching and healing. One word of the verse is written on each card in the envelope. Their challenge is to put the words together in the proper order to form the verse. Once they think the words are in order, the learners may use a Bible to check their work. Provide time for the children to complete this portion of the activity. Once completed, allow the children to share what they found. Talk about how Jesus was always reaching out and touching people. At one point in the discussion, ask the students to shake hands with the people around them as a way to reach out and touch.

Talk with the students about people today who need a loving touch. Since Jesus is no longer on the earth, ask the group who can provide this important physical contact. Mention the families and individuals who are affected by AIDS. Let the children share their thoughts and feelings related to reaching out and touching these people. Often people with AIDS are viewed as untouchable and unlovable. They are seen as ugly and dirty. Because of this, people are afraid to reach out and touch them. But they, like everyone, need a healing hand to touch both their hearts and their bodies.

Play the song "Healing Hands" by Elton John and show the slides of people using their hands to help other people. If there are no slides, play the song and ask the children to listen to the words. Play the song again and invite the participants to add gestures to the music, reaching their hands out to one another at the appropriate times. Play the song over if the children request it. Encourage the participants to talk about what it felt like to reach out and to take hold of another person's hand. Discuss ways in which this can be done on a daily basis, especially in relation to HIV/AIDS.

Conclude the activity by reciting one of the following two prayers written by the National Episcopal AIDS Coalition:[2]

> Lord Jesus, you reached out in eager compassion to touch and heal people whom others shunned. Help us who bear your Name eagerly to follow your example by reaching out to all who suffer from AIDS or HIV infection, that through us they may feel your love and know the power of your healing. Amen.

> Merciful God, we remember before you all who are sick this day, and especially all persons with AIDS or HIV infection. Give them courage to live with their disease. Help them to face and overcome their fears. Be with them when they are alone or rejected. Comfort them when they are discouraged. And touch them with your healing Spirit that they may find and possess eternal life, now and forever. Amen.

Drama/Clown/Mime

PURPOSE To debate the question "Is AIDS a judgment from God?"

PREPARATION *Materials*

- Bibles
- Paper and pens

PROCEDURE Is AIDS God's judgment? This difficult question challenges denominations, congregations, and individual Christians to make hard choices. Should the faith community respond by showing God's love and compassion or do they view the disease as a sign of God's punishment and avoid involvement? It's not hard to understand why many Christians have associated AIDS with God's punishment. The first known persons to acquired AIDS were primarily sexually active homosexuals and intravenous drug users. But the disease is not limited to people in those groups. Sufferers today include people who received contaminated blood transfusions, babies born to mothers with AIDS, and heterosexual spouses of AIDS carriers. Discuss this controversial topic through the format of a debate.

Divide the participants into two teams. Designate one team as those who view AIDS as God's judgment, and the other group as those who do not view AIDS as God's punishment. Let each team confer for five minutes to come up with arguments on the question "Is AIDS a judgment/punishment from God?" One side should come up with reasons to support this position; the other side should offer reasons to contradict it. Let every participant pair off with a member of the opposite team for a ten-minute debate. This activity could be staged as a panel debate, using two team members from each side, with a moderator. At the conclusion of the debate, reconvene the whole group. Discuss which arguments on both sides made the most sense. Which statements challenged the group's own attitudes and actions?

Tell the group that people in Jesus' time had similar questions. Then, as now, many assumed that suffering was a direct result of sin. But Jesus himself challenged that assumption. Read the participants the Scripture story, John 9:1-41, of the man born blind. Jesus declined to connect the blind man's suffering with sin. He instead spoke of it as an opportunity to display God's glory by restoring the man's sight. Jesus chose to focus on the alleviation of human pain rather than on discerning God's intention. Jesus did not reflect on why the man was blind; Jesus healed his blindness. Rather than retribution, suffering becomes an occasion for God's love to be demonstrated. Christians need to stop asking why certain people get AIDS and begin asking what God is calling the church to do to help. Actually, Jesus' words in the New Testament provide that answer, too. Like Jesus with the leper, people of faith are called to eat with people with AIDS and share their home with them (Matthew 26:6); touch people with AIDS and give them their intimacy (Matthew 8:2-4); and to heal people with AIDS (Luke 17:11-19).

Conclude the activity by offering the students the opportunity to summarize the information and insights they have gained by writing a diamonte (diamond-shaped) poem. In the five-line diamonte, the subject at the top of the poem is in opposition to the subject at the bottom. The formula is as follows:

Line One—One word that is an opposite of line five.
Line Two—Two words that describe line one.
Line Three—Three words that resolve the conflict.
Line Four—Two words that describe line five.
Line Five—One word that is an opposite of line one.

Write a diamonte together using the word "Judging" as the first line and the word "Forgiving" as the fifth line. Invite the group to contribute ideas for words and phrases that will resolve these two opposing views. For example:

Judging.

Behavior. Beliefs.

Compassion. Care. Concern.

Attitudes. Actions.

Forgiving.

Provide paper and pens and invite each person to write his or her own diamonte poem on the topic. Encourage willing individuals to share their responses with the entire group.

Games

PURPOSE   To emphasize the importance of education about HIV/AIDS in all areas of congregational life.

PREPARATION   *Materials*

- Construction paper
- Paper cutter or scissors
- Markers
- Stapler and staples

Advance Preparation

- Cut sheets of construction paper into 1" strips.
- Write one of the AIDS-related acronyms, the capital letters, on each strip of paper. Write a definition on each strip of paper. Suggestions to use include:

    KS: A type of cancer, frequently seen in people with AIDS, that causes purple blotches on the skin.

AIDS: An infection that attacks the body's immune system, leaving it unable to fight certain kinds of disease.

HTLV-III: The name first given to the AIDS virus by American scientists.

T-Cell: The cell that HIV attacks when it enters the body.

ELISA: The name of the blood test initially done to detect the presence of antibodies to HIV in the body.

AZT: An antiviral drug used to treat HIV infection.

IV: Injection from a needle inserted directly into a person's bloodstream.

STDS: Infectious diseases spread by sexual contact with an infected person.

CDC: An agency of the U.S. Public Health Service, responsible for monitoring and controlling various diseases.

LAS: Disease, often seen in people with HIV, that causes chronic enlargement of the lymph nodes.

LAV: The name originally given to the AIDS virus by French scientists.

HIV: Human immunodeficiency virus, the virus that causes AIDS.

ARC: A chronic disease people may develop if infected with HIV.

PCP: A type of pneumonia caused by a parasitic infection of the lungs, which some people with HIV contract.

HIV-2: A second type of AIDS virus, discovered in West Africa in the 1980s.

PROCEDURE Use a game to join the people in a congregation together to emphasize the importance of individual and collective education about various aspects of HIV/AIDS. Tell the group that each person will receive a strip of construction paper. Half of the papers have letters that are abbreviations or acronyms associated with HIV/AIDS. The other half have phrases or sentences that are definitions related to HIV/AIDS. Their task is to match the letters and definitions. When a match is made, the two players are to staple their strips to form links and join them together. Pass out the construction paper pieces that were prepared in advance. Instruct the players to move around the room, ask questions of one another, and locate the correct letters or phrase. When everyone has made a match, go around the group asking one person to read the letters and the other to give the definition. Supply additional information about the meaning of the terms, as needed. As each set of players completes a turn, have them add their links to the chain, using blank strips to make the connections.

Play the game again, only this time pass around construction paper strips and have each participant choose a piece. Distribute markers. Instruct each person to write his or her name on the strip. Also ask each individual to write one way he or she will learn more about HIV/AIDS and one place that AIDS education should occur in the congregation. Both sides of the strip may be used. For example:

Ways to learn more about AIDS

Read a book
Watch a video
Talk to a medical worker
Visit an infected person
Write to an organization

Education opportunities in the congregation

Sunday school classes
Youth group
Adult education courses
Intergenerational events
Service projects

Go around the group and have each person share the information that has been written on the strip. When the first person finishes, have him or her staple the strip to form a link. As others report, have them add their links to the chain. Continue the process until everyone has had a turn. Discuss the importance of working as individuals and as a congregation to promote AIDS education in all areas of church life.

Music

PURPOSE   To explain the significance of the shofar and to demonstrate it as a way to call people to action against AIDS.

PREPARATION   *Materials*

- Shofar (or picture of one)
- Paper plates (two per person)
- Hole punch
- Yarn, string, lacing cord, or shoelaces
- Scissors
- Markers
- Shofar patterns
- Tape recording of shofar sounds and tape player

Advance Preparation

- Invite a guest, such as a rabbi or a member of a Jewish congregation, to share the symbolism and sound of the shofar.
- Make shofar patterns using the illustration provided.

PROCEDURE   Sound the shofar as a way to call people to action against AIDS. Show the children an example or a picture of a shofar. Explain its symbolism and significance. The shofar is an instrument made of a ram's horn that is primarily used by the Jewish people during their high holidays. The ram's horn serves as a reminder of the Hebrew scripture story, recorded in Genesis 21, in which Abraham substitutes a ram as a sacrifice in place of his son Isaac. Originally, the shofar was used as a way to send messages from one hillside to another. It signaled the need for immediate action, such as in the case of fire or attack. The shofar was also used as a trumpet in battle.

Sounding the shofar consists of making a set of sounds repeated three times, followed by a longer sound. Demonstrate the sounds for the group. Hebrew words are spoken to describe the sounds. In order to perform the duty of the shofar, both the Bal Tekiah, the one who sounds the shofar, and the listeners must intend to sound and to listen. Today, the shofar is sounded at the time of the highest Jewish holidays, Rosh Hashanah and Yom Kipper, to herald a need for action. Sound the shofar again to signal a call to action against AIDS.

Since the sounds of the shofar, like the sounds of a trumpet, call people to action, ask the participants to suggest ways in which congregations are being called to action regarding HIV/AIDS. Responses might include:

- Working to break down prejudice regarding people with AIDS
- Educating about ways people can and cannot get AIDS
- Delivering meals to homebound persons with HIV infection
- Donating resources to AIDS ministries
- Volunteering time to work on HIV/AIDS-related causes

Invite the group to make simple shofars from paper plates to serve as symbols that they have been called to become personally involved in actions to fight AIDS. Place the supplies within sharing distance of the participants. Instruct the learners to cut a shofar shape from a paper plate. They may use the patterns provided or create the design freehand. Tell them to turn the shape over and to trace it on another paper place. Cut it out. Place the two shapes together to form a shofar. Using a paper punch, make evenly spaced holes along the two sides of the ram's horn shape. With yarn, string, shoelaces, or lacing cord, sew the two pieces together. Challenge each person to use a marker to write at least one way in which he or she will respond to the sound of the shofar and take action to help people infected and affected by HIV/AIDS.

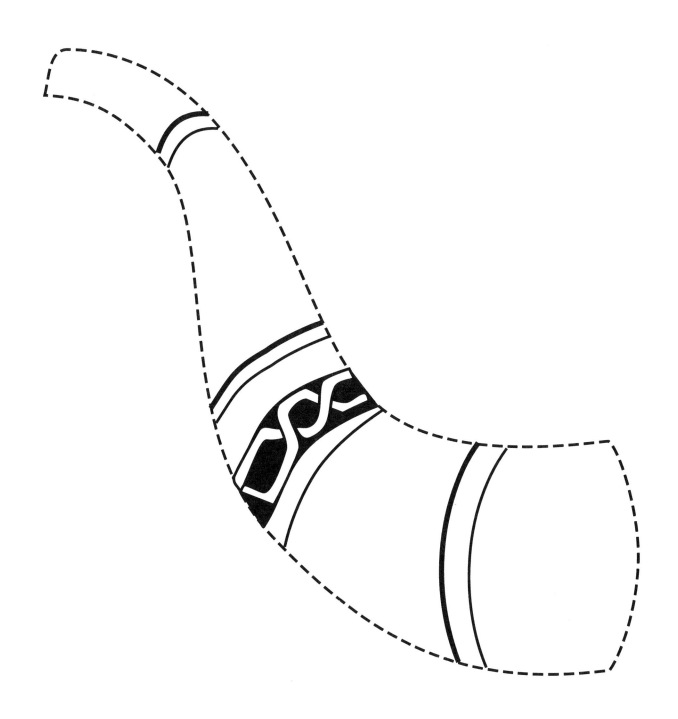

Photography

PURPOSE To illustrate Psalm 23, and other Scripture passages, with overhead projections depicting the theme.

PREPARATION *Materials*

- Overhead projector and screen
- Acetate transparencies
- Permanent markers
- Bibles

PROCEDURE Inspiration. Insight. Instruction. The psalms offer these gifts, and more, to their readers. Popular speaker and writer Tony Campolo shares a sensitive and sincere story in his book *20 Hot Potatoes Christians Are Afraid to Touch*.[3] Campolo relates an incident in the life of his friend, a pastor in Brooklyn, who was called by the local undertaker to conduct a funeral for a man who had died of AIDS. Throughout the service at the funeral home and the committal at the cemetery, the twenty-five men who had gathered remained completely motionless. Finally, the pastor looked at the crowd and asked if there was anything more he could do for them. One of the men replied, "I was looking forward to somebody reading the Twenty-third Psalm." One by one, the men made special requests for the pastor to read their favorite passages of Scripture. Their inspiration, insight, and instruction came from the words of the Bible.

Although many litanies have been used in connection with AIDS healing and worship services, an especially meaningful and memorable one is a version of Psalm 23 from the Interfaith Conference of Metropolitan Washington, D.C.'s prayer service on AIDS entitled "Cry Pain, Cry Hope." Read the litany together, assigning parts as desired.

Litany from Psalm 23[4]
(Adapted from the Revised Standard Bible)

Leader
God is faithful and full of compassion,
God knows our needs before we ask.
Tell of the tender love of God.

All
The Lord is my shepherd:
I shall not want.

Leader
With God alone there is security and peace,
The ways to salvation and rest are with God.
Tell of the guiding love of God.

All
He maketh me to lie down in green pastures;
He leadeth me beside the still waters.

Leader
When sin and despair lead us from God's will,
God seeks us and finds us and makes our life anew.
Tell of the redeeming love of God.

All
He restoreth my soul;
He leadeth me in the paths of righteousness
for his Name's sake.

Leader

In the midst of darkness the light of God will not be dimmed.
In the face of death God's promise of life remains sure.
Tell of the abiding love of God.

All

Yea, though I walk through the valley of the shadow of death,
I will fear no evil, for thou art with me;
Thy rod and thy staff they comfort me.

Leader

Blessing and honor await those who love God,
Their trust will be crowned with joy.
Tell of the promises of God.

All

Thou preparest a table before me in the presence of mine enemies;
Thou anointest my head with oil;
My cup runneth over.

Leader

If God is for us, who can be against us?
The corners of the earth and all that is in them
are in the hands of God.

All

Surely goodness and mercy shall follow me all the days of my life
and I will dwell in the house of the Lord forever.

Talk about the images that come to mind from this reading, especially as they relate to HIV/AIDS. Invite the participants to illustrate some of these thoughts and themes on acetate transparencies which can be shown on an overhead projector. Invite each person to choose a different line or phrase to depict. Distribute a piece of acetate to each person and place permanent markers within sharing distance of the artists. Allow time for the learners to complete their pictures.

Explain the procedure for placing the pictures on the overhead projector during the litany. Retell, recite, or read the litany based on Psalm 23, placing the pictures on the overhead projector at the appropriate points in the passage.

Additional Scripture passages to use with this process include Psalm 142; Psalm 27; Psalm 46; Job 14:1-10; Romans 8:31-35, 37-39; Isaiah 41:8-10; I John 4:16b-21; James 5:13-15; II Kings 20:1-5; and Mark 8:1-11. Invite the group to compose phrases and to create pictures based on one or more of these portions of Scripture. Share the results and offer them for use during a special congregational or community worship service on HIV/AIDS.

Puppetry

PURPOSE To make and use rod puppets to explore Gospel themes related to AIDS issues.

PREPARATION *Materials*

- Styrofoam balls
- Plastic tubs
- Polyfoam carpet pad
- Dowel rods or chopsticks
- Pantyhose
- Felt, fabric, yarn, trims
- Glue
- Scissors
- Sharp art knife

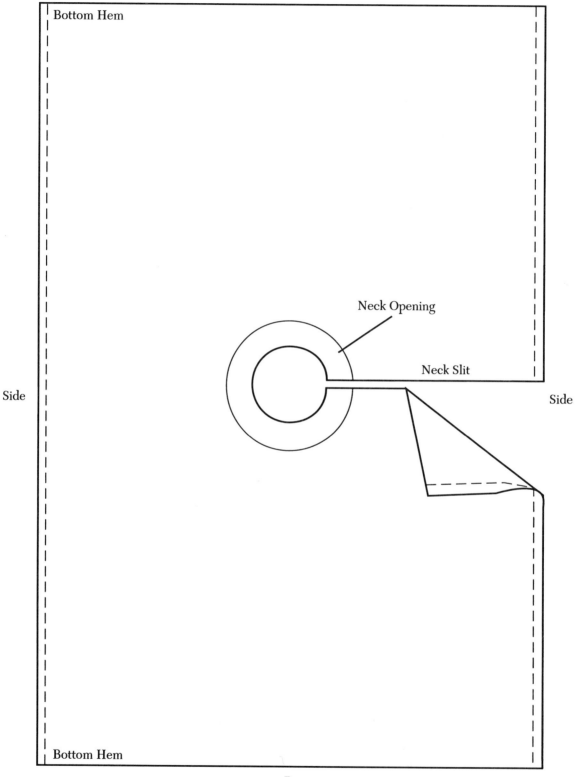

Top

Bottom Hem

Neck Opening

Neck Slit

Side

Side

Bottom Hem

Bottom

Place over puppet, bring bottom hems together, then stitch neck slit and underarm seams.

- Needles and thread
- Bibles

PROCEDURE   Although the Bible does not address AIDS directly, it does address related issues: healing, caring for others, relationships between spiritual brokenness and sickness, and forgiveness. Examine these passages in the current context of AIDS. Make rod puppets from recyclable materials and use them to illustrate these Scripture stories.

Working as individuals or in small groups, distribute Bibles and ask the participants to look up several scripture passages. Include verses such as:

Matthew 7:1-5: Luke 6:37-42: Judging others
Matthew 8:1-4: Healing a person with leprosy
Matthew 12:1-13: Healing and gathering food on the Sabbath
Luke 10:25-37: Parable of the Good Samaritan
Luke 15:11-31: Parable of the Prodigal Son
John 5:1-14: Healing the man by the pool
John 8:1-11: Woman caught in adultery
John 9:1-3: Illness and spiritual brokenness

Invite each person or group to read the passage and to share a summary of their story. Discuss ways in which these passages relate to issues involved in the AIDS epidemic. For example, what does the story of the woman caught in adultery have to say about the way people should respond to persons who contracted AIDS through high-risk behavior? How does the parable of the prodigal son illustrate ways in which congregations should respond to persons with HIV infection? Based on the account of the Good Samaritan, what are some of the risks involved with helping a person with AIDS?

Invite the entire group to choose a Scripture story, or have each small group choose a passage, and construct puppets to use in retelling these Gospel accounts. Decide which characters are needed for each narrative.

Demonstrate the process for making the rod puppets. The parts of this puppet are made from several recyclable objects. A styrofoam ball forms the head, pantyhose becomes the skin, and a plastic tub (from margarine or frozen whipped cream) serves as the shoulders. Strips of carpet pad turn into two arms and the dowels or chopsticks become the rods used to work the puppet. Follow the simple directions to put the pieces together.

Insert a dowel into the bottom of the styrofoam ball. After the hole is made, remove the dowel. Spread glue in the hole and on the dowel, and re-insert the dowel. Allow the glue to dry.

Cut a hole for the dowel in the bottom of the plastic tub. Then make a small slit on each opposing side; the arms will be attached at these points. Cut arms from polyfoam carpet pad and fit one into each side slit.

Cut a 6" length of pantyhose. Tie off one of the loose ends, pull the hose over the head, and secure it to the dowel with a strip of yarn. Choose yarn to make hair. Wrap it around your hand or a piece of cardboard several times. Snip open the ends or leave them looped. Glue or sew the hair to the top of the head.

Using felt scraps, cut out eyes, nose, and mouth. Glue them to the head.

Turn the plastic container upside down. Insert the dowel through the hole in the bottom and push the container up until it touches the head. Pull the pantyhose through the hole and tape it to the dowel. Place a large piece of tape under the plastic carton to hold the container in place.

Choose fabric for the costume. Cut a rectangle the width of the puppet's shoulders and long enough that, when doubled, it will make a tunic of sufficient size for the finished puppet. Cut a hole in the center of the fabric for the dowel, and cut a slit from the hole to a side edge. Place the costume over the puppet's shoulders and stitch the slit closed. Fold the front and back hem together, pull the arms through, and stitch the side seams from under the arms to the hem. Add trims to complete the costume.

Attach the other dowel rod to the end of one of the puppet's arms with thread or a rubber band. To operate the puppet, hold the dowel under the costume in one hand and work the dowel on the arm with the other hand.

Provide the necessary supplies and allow time for the participants to make their puppets. Guide and encourage the process. After the characters are completed, ask each person or group to improvise the story for which they made puppets. Take turns sharing these Gospel accounts of Jesus' teachings on ways in which people should relate to one another.

As an added dimension to this project, ask members of the congregation to provide the puppet supplies. Advertise the list of required items in the bulletin or newsletter. In the process of collecting the materials, tell the contributors what will be done with the objects they donate. After the puppets are completed, invite the congregation to a puppet show. Explain ways in which this project relates to the theme of HIV/AIDS.

Storytelling

PURPOSE   To write a story describing the events of a biblical narrative or principle in a contemporary setting.

PREPARATION   *Materials*

- Bibles
- Paper and pens or pencils

PROCEDURE   Stories from Scripture, such as the parable of the Good Samaritan in Luke 10:30-37, illustrate that Jesus wants his followers to express love even to those considered "unlovable." Parables were Jesus' method of helping people understand difficult truths and themes. These passages can be made even more memorable and meaningful for today's young people by rewriting them in contemporary settings with modern-day characters.

Read the story of the Good Samaritan to the group from one or more versions of the Bible. Invite the group to rewrite the message of these verses in a modern-day setting with modern-day people playing the parts. Provide an example, such as:

Once there was a girl named Tanya who was heavy into drugs. Tanya had been kicked out of her home by her parents. She had also been expelled from school. Unknown to both her parents and her principal, Tanya had recently been tested and discovered that she was HIV positive. Besides doing drugs, she had been sharing needles with other users. Unsure what to do, and not willing to face her problems, late one night Tanya decided to run away from home. She waited at the entrance to the toll road until a car driven by a teenage girl picked her up. Going down the highway, far over the speed limit, the car crashed into a bridge abutment. Tanya was thrown from the car and seriously injured. The driver, who only had minor injuries, sped off, leaving Tanya in serious shape on the side of the road. Tanya saw the first car whiz by her and then the second. Her feeble cries for help and her fragile waving motions went unattended. Finally a woman stopped and ran to help Tanya. From her car phone, the woman called an ambulance. Soon the emergency workers were on the scene, giving Tanya the medical attention she required. As Tanya was rushed to the hospital, the woman followed in her car. At the treatment center, the woman even called Tanya's parents, told them what had happened, and asked them to come to be with their daughter. She also called her own pastor, who came to visit Tanya and her family. When Tanya was released from the hospital she went back home, and she and her family are addressing their problems in various ways. The woman, as well as the pastor, continue to call on them from time to time, offering care and concern with each visit.

Discuss ways in which the story of the Good Samaritan relates to issues connected with HIV/AIDS. Many people who are infected and affected require the basic necessities of life such as food, shelter, and companionship. Challenge the learners to reflect these themes in their contemporary parables. Organize the participants into teams of three and instruct them to write a brief contemporary story, five to eight lines, based on Luke 10:30-37. Remind the group that the concept they are illustrating is Jesus' philosophy of loving the unlovable. They are to parallel the biblical account and to bring the biblical principles into a fresh focus. Distribute paper and pens or pencils and encourage the groups as they write.

Invite the teams to read their contemporary stories to one another and to discuss the comparisons and contrasts with the biblical passage. Conclude the activity by offering a prayer thanking God for the "Good Samaritans" in the world.

1. National Catholic AIDS Network, *An Icon of Darkness and Light* (San Francisco, Calif.: National Catholic AIDS Network, n.d.).
2. National Episcopal AIDS Coalition, *AIDS Spoken Here* (Washington, D.C.: National Episcopal AIDS Coalition, n.d.).
3. Tony Campolo, *20 Hot Potatoes Christians Are Afraid to Touch* (Dallas: Word, 1988).
4. Interfaith Conference of Metropolitan Washington, *Cry Pain, Cry Hope: An Interfaith Prayer Service on AIDS* (Washington, D.C.: Interfaith Conference of Metropolitan Washington, n.d.). Reprinted by permission.

CHAPTER 9
Family

Activities encompassing a broad range of creative methods and dealing with numerous concepts and concerns are provided to promote the skills and strengths needs to address the issues of AIDS and the "Family."

Architecture

PURPOSE To illustrate the importance of building bridges as a way of including rather than excluding people.

PREPARATION *Materials*

- Pictures of bridges
- Blocks, Legos, or Tinker Toys
- Paper and markers
- Duplicating or photocopying equipment

Advance Preparation

- Duplicate copies of the "Bridges" dot-to-dot game

PROCEDURE A bridge may be a huge architectural structure that spans a major body of water or a modest board placed over a small stream. Regardless of its size, its function is to connect two areas and to enable people to get from one place to another.

Show the students pictures of bridges or build one out of blocks, Legos, or Tinker Toys. Talk about the ways in which bridges are needed in families affected by AIDS. Unfortunately, there is often great distance between a person infected with HIV and his or her family members, extended family, and friends. Sometimes parents, children, and siblings have not seen or talked to one another in years. Strained relations among people may exist over lifestyle, including drug use and sexual preference. Often people living with the AIDS virus return home once they become too sick to live alone and care for themselves. One of the best places for a person with AIDS to receive care is at home, surrounded by those who can provide love and care. Most people with AIDS can lead an active life for long periods of time. In fact, most of the time a person with AIDS does not need to be in a hospital. A person with AIDS often recovers from AIDS-related illnesses more quickly and comfortably at home with the support of family, friends, and loved ones. Also, home care can help reduce the stress and cost of hospitalization. Having a person with AIDS living in a household may also cause distance between family members and other individuals and groups, such as neighbors and acquaintances who do not understand the disease. Bridges are needed in many places. Help the children think of some of the bridges that are needed in these situations. Brainstorm words such as "communication," "honesty," "imagination," "knowledge," and "support."

Distribute the "Bridges" dot-to-dot game sheets and markers. Use this activity to illustrate building bridges of friendship and understanding by having the students take turns connecting the dots. Invite the children to work in groups. Once the bridges are connected, ask the participants to draw people on both sides of the structures. Tell the group to list words or to draw pictures between the spans that describe ways in which people build bridges associated with AIDS issues, especially as they relate to families.

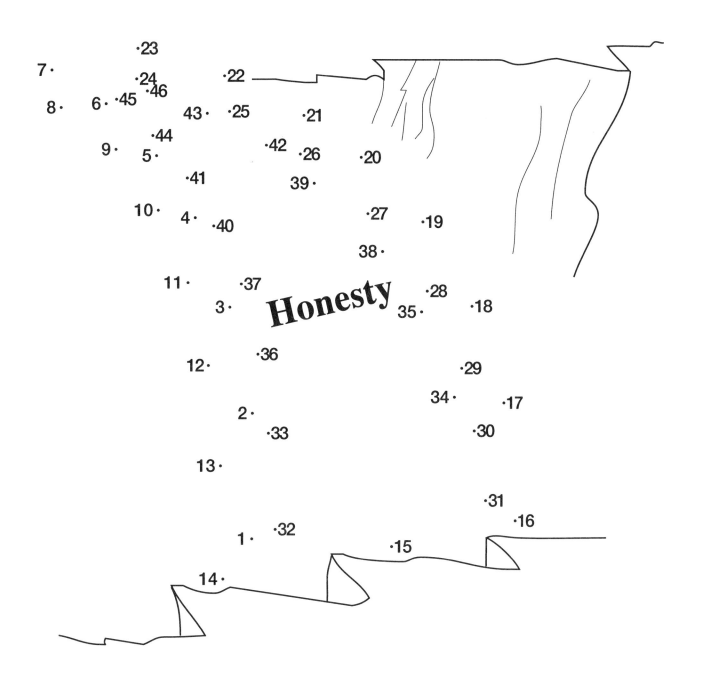

Honesty

Art

PURPOSE   To offer unique expressions of affirmation in the form of printed pillowcases to persons with AIDS.

PREPARATION   *Materials*

- Pillowcases (white or light colors)
- Paper and pencils
- Crayons
- Newspaper
- Paper towels
- Iron and ironing board
- Bibles
- Names and addresses of persons with AIDS or institutions and organizations that care for infected persons.
- Packaging materials

Advance Preparation

- Obtain the names and addresses of persons who will receive the completed pillowcases

PROCEDURE   Everyone needs messages of affirmation and acceptance, especially persons with AIDS. Because the HIV virus weakens a person's immune system, individuals with HIV/AIDS often spend a lot of time resting. Create perky pillowcases with meaningful messages and give them as special gifts to men, women, or children suffering from the disease. Choose people to receive the gifts or determine an organization or institution that would welcome the presents.

Tell the participants about the pillowcase project and ask them to think of messages of affirmation, in words and pictures, that could be drawn and written on the fabric. Suggestions include:

- You are special
- Have a good day
- God loves you
- We care about you
- An appropriate Bible verse

Demonstrate the process for making the pillowcase designs. Sketch the rough design on paper and color it. Place several layers of newspaper inside the pillowcase. Copy the design onto the pillowcase and color it; be sure to press hard when using the crayons. Place one layer of paper toweling over the illustration and iron over it until all the wax melts onto the paper towel. Remove the paper towel. Show the group the results. Tell the learners that the picture is now permanently printed on the pillowcase.

Distribute paper and crayons and guide each person as he or she creates a message. As the students complete this part of the project, iron their designs onto the fabric. This should be done by an adult unless the participants are older youth. Place the completed pillowcases on a table and invite everyone to look at the results.

Package the unique greetings and send or deliver them to the appropriate people and places. Enjoy the good feelings that come from expressing care and concern for others.

Banners/Textiles

PURPOSE   To learn about ABC Quilts and to make quilts to give to HIV infected persons.

PREPARATION   *Materials*

- Fabric

- Scissors
- Permanent markers or liquid embroidery pens
- Sewing equipment
- Backing material (optional)
- *Kids Making Quilts for Kids*[1]

Advance Preparation

- Obtain additional information about ABC Quilts by sending a stamped, self-addressed business-size envelope to ABC Quilts, P.O. Box 107, Weatherford, Okla. 73096.
- Cut a 4" x 4" or larger fabric square per person; a total of 26 squares if the "ABC" theme is used for the project.

PROCEDURE   ABC Quilts, which stands for "At Risk" Babies Crib Quilts, is a volunteer, nonprofit organization founded in 1988 by Ellen Ahlgren to give love and comfort in the form of a quilt to each small child under age six who tests positive for the HIV/AIDS virus, is born with problems related to alcohol or other drug addiction, or who is abandoned. Since its inception, ABC Quilts has expanded to a national and worldwide network of volunteer individuals, groups, and organizations. So far, over 100,000 quilts have been given to babies and children through ABC Quilts. *Kids Making Quilts for Kids: A Young Person's Guide for Having Fun While Helping Others and Learning about AIDS and Substance Abuse* is a book written by the people of ABC Quilts to tell their story and to challenge people to become involved in this project. Show the book to the participants and tell them about this important venture.

Besides sharing the story of ABC Quilts, *Kids Making Quilts for Kids* contains complete instructions for constructing four different types of quilts or quilt faces. These include printed panel quilts, traditional patchwork quilts, block-and-lattice quilts, and creative designs. Patterns for and photographs of a variety of quilts are provided in the book.

Challenge the group to make a quilt to donate to ABC Quilts or to give to a person with AIDS who is known by the participants. Combine the thoughts and talents of the students or of an entire organization or congregation as they work together to make a patchwork quilt. This project involves the cooperation and invites the contributions of many individuals. The finished product serves as a reminder of what can be accomplished when people work together.

Discuss a theme for the quilt that relates to the topic of family. Challenge the group to create a block for every letter of the alphabet, each suggesting a way in which families can get involved in AIDS-related concerns. Each square could contain a letter of the alphabet, a word or phrase related to HIV/AIDS that begins with the letter, and a drawing to illustrate the theme. Some examples include:

A — Activities: Encourage children to participate in healthful activities.
B — Bake: Bake and bring the results to another family.
C — Call: Call to communicate.
D — Drive: Drive persons with AIDS to appointments and activities.
E — Example: Set an example by not using drugs and alcohol.
F — Facts: Share facts about HIV/AIDS transmission and prevention.
G — Give: Give money to AIDS organizations.
H — Help: Help with a fund-raising project for HIV/AIDS causes.
I — Interest: Show interest in children's activities.
J — Join: Join AIDS ministry organizations.
K — Kindness: Show kindness in many ways.
L — Love: Demonstrate love with words and actions.
M — Mothers' Voices: Mother's Voices, P.O. Box 708, Merrick, N.Y. 11566-9913 (telephone: 212-366-9217), is a group seeking to mobilize the hearts and voices of mothers, together with their families and friends, in a campaign to end the AIDS crisis. Contact the organization for additional information.
N — Needs: Develop empathy for the needs of others.
O — Opinions: Offer opinions in congregational and community meetings.

P— Peer pressure: Teach children ways to resist peer pressure.

Q— Question: Question unusual behavior of family members and offer care and concern.

R— Respect: Respect family members and other people.

S— Self-esteem: Encourage positive self-esteem.

T— Talk: Talk to family members.

U— Use: Use time and talents to help others.

V— Volunteer: Volunteer as a "buddy" to a child or adult with AIDS.

W— Work: Work for an end to AIDS.

X— Xtra: Go the eXtra mile to help an infected person.

Y— Yes: Say "yes" to advocating for the needs of persons with AIDS.

Z— Zillions: Find zillions of other ways to become involved.

Once the themes have been identified, invite different people to choose one or more of the letters to illustrate. Regardless of the subject selected, the process for completing the project is the same. Distribute the patches and the supplies needed to decorate them. Encourage the use of drawings, symbols, and words. Talk with the learners as they work on the project.

Sew the squares together. This portion of the project should be done on a sewing machine by an adult or older youth. Back the piece, if desired. Display the completed project in a prominent place to remind people of the many ways in which families can respond to the AIDS crisis.

Cartoons

PURPOSE   To identify ways in which young people obtain information about HIV/AIDS and to review data appropriate for various age groups.

PREPARATION   *Materials*

- Chalkboard or newsprint
- Chalk or marker
- Paper and pencils or pens
- Markers
- Masking tape
- Resource materials

PROCEDURE   Where do young people learn about HIV/AIDS? Ask the participants to generate a list of responses to this question and record their answers on a chalkboard or a sheet of newsprint. Youth learn about HIV/AIDS at home from parents, caregivers, and siblings; at school from teachers, staff members, and other students; and in the community from medical workers, clergy persons, and social service employees. Young men and women, as well as boys and girls, also obtain information related to the infection from television, radio, books, pamphlets, mailings, magazines, advertisements, billboards, graffiti, and street talk. To help prevent the spread of HIV infection among youth of all ages, adults and children need to talk with one another about HIV/AIDS facts. HIV/AIDS prevention is most effective when young people hear these messages early. Accurate information at an early age will lay an important foundation for good self-esteem and health in the future.

Many experts, from AIDS researchers to the surgeon general of the United States, have called upon parents to talk to their children about AIDS, to make sure young people understand how the disease is spread and how to avoid it. Different information is appropriate at various ages.

Preschool

- Teach children the correct names for body parts. Using coy terms for the sex organs creates confusion and embarrassment.

- Encourage good hygiene habits to prevent the spread of disease.
- Emphasize saying "No" to experiences that make the child feel uncomfortable.
- Answer questions accurately and sensitively.
- Stress that AIDS is hard to get.
- Promote positive self-image.

Ages 5–8

- Discuss infections and viruses.
- Promote a sense of open communication.
- Correct misperceptions.
- Explain sexuality in understandable terms or with the aid of children's books.
- Emphasize healthful behaviors.

Ages 9–12

- Present basic information about HIV transmission and prevention.
- Emphasize values.
- Find out what young people think they know about HIV/AIDS. Correct misinformation.
- Reassure youth that although AIDS is dangerous, they can avoid it and stay safe.
- Emphasize respect for self and for others.
- Be sure that children understand that sexual behaviors can be ways to share pleasurable, loving feelings within an intimate relationship but that emotional maturity is needed to handle the responsibilities that go along with sexual behavior.
- Stress the dangers of drug abuse.

Teenagers

- Stress that a person can avoid getting HIV/AIDS by making good decisions, using good judgment, and refraining from high-risk behavior.
- Talk with teens about safe and unsafe sex.
- Suggest ways to express feelings without having sex.
- Use explicit language to discuss ways in which HIV is spread.
- Emphasize the dangers of drugs, especially of injecting drugs with needles.

Tell the participants that they will be making cartoons which have two parts. The first part, or top half, will be a drawing of a way or ways in which young people obtain accurate information about HIV/AIDS. The second part, or bottom half, will focus on information appropriate for specific ages. Organize the learners into four small groups. Assign a different age level to each of them: preschool, ages 5–8, ages 9–12, and teenagers. Tell the students that their assignment is to gather data on age appropriate information for the category to which they have been assigned. Direct attention to reference materials that are available for their use or distribute pamphlets and resources to each team. Pass out paper, pencils, and markers. One cartoon may be made per group or each person in the group may illustrate his or her idea individually. Remind the pupils to use the top half of the sheet to draw the way youth obtain data about HIV/AIDS and the bottom half to highlight information appropriate for the assigned age group. Circulate through the room as the learners work on the projects. Answer questions and supply accurate information.

When the cartoons are completed, hang them around the room and encourage the students to walk around to look at them.

Creative Writing

PURPOSE	To send a recorded letter to affirm and show care for a family living with AIDS.
PREPARATION	*Materials*

- Paper and pencils
- Blank cassette tapes and cassette recorder

- Mailing envelopes and postage stamps
- Tape of instrumental music

Advance Preparation

- Obtain the names and addresses of families that have lost a loved one to AIDS or who are taking care of a family member or friend with AIDS.

PROCEDURE Many times the emotional and physical stress that comes with caring for the terminally ill can be lightened or lifted by words of care and concern. Invite the children to extend a message of compassion to individuals and families living with AIDS. Rather than the usual format of writing a letter or sending a card, the participants will prepare recorded messages and mail or deliver them to persons in need. Note some of the reasons that recorded, rather than written, messages will be used for this project. Depending on the stage of AIDS a person is experiencing, blindness is a frequent occurrence, making it impossible to read mail or letters. Voiced greetings can help to cheer a person struggling with AIDS.

Distribute paper and pens and help the students prepare information for their recordings. Guide the participants in writing cheerful notes using poetry, stories, and happy thoughts. Encourage creativity in producing the voice mail greetings. Remind the group that introductions are important. They should tell their names, ages, and fun trivia about themselves and their own families. Let the children express their concern and prayers as a sign of love and kindness to a family struggling with AIDS.

Once the messages are prepared, help the children record their thoughts. Soft music and other cheerful sounds could be used as background to the messages.

Package and send the tapes to the selected families. Invite the receiving family to record a message and send the tape back for future greetings.

Culinary Arts

PURPOSE To raise money for a local AIDS organization and to increase AIDS awareness through a "Kool-Aid" bake sale.

PREPARATION *Materials*

- Index cards and pens
- Kool-Aid
- Recipes and ingredients
- Utensils and equipment
- Chalkboard and chalk or newsprint and markers

Advance Preparation

- Write the word "_____-Aid" on a chalkboard or newsprint.

PROCEDURE Band-Aid. Kool-Aid. Farm-Aid. The word "Aid" is connected with many forms of help and assistance. A Band-Aid is used to bind or cover an injury. Kool-Aid is a popular drink that quenches thirst. Farm-Aid was a musical event that raised money to assist persons involved in the farm crisis. Many forms of "Aid" are needed to address the AIDS epidemic. Enlist the help of the participants and their families in organizing a Kool-Aid bake sale to raise funds for a local AIDS organization and to increase awareness of various aspects of the disease.

As the participants arrive or at the beginning of the activity, call attention to the word "_____-Aid" on the chalkboard or newsprint. Invite the participants to fill in the blank by suggesting a variety of words associated with the word "Aid." Write the responses in a web format around the word "Aid." Ask the group to suggest ways to aid local AIDS organizations or persons with AIDS. One way is to hold a Kool-Aid and baked goods sale and to donate the proceeds of the project to these persons and places.

Locate a central site in the neighborhood for the sale. Select a date and time. Invite adults to help with the baking as well as with the sale of the items. Prepare advertising for the event.

Brainstorm clever names for the foods to be sold. Names attached to the products can bring added awareness of the AIDS issue and show care and concern for those living with the disease. For example:

Caregiver Cup Cakes
Drugfree Donuts
Compassionate Chocolate Chip Cookies
Meditation Muffins
Prayerful Peach Pie
Wishful Wheat Bread
Safer Sex Sugar Cookies
Living Longer Lemon Squares

Encourage the students to add their own ideas to the suggestions. Prepare index cards that can be displayed with the items on the day of the Kool-Aid bake sale. For example:

Caregiver Cup Cakes: A caregiver is an important partner in the life of a person with AIDS. Caregivers provide ongoing support, comfort, and care for the infected person. Often caregivers are family members, friends, or strangers who become good friends.

Living Longer Lemon Squares: Many people who are HIV positive are living longer and healthier lives because of a "take charge" attitude. Many persons with AIDS diet, exercise, find a spiritual life, choose healthful behavior, and therefore live longer with the virus.

Invite the children to a baking day before the Kool-Aid sale. Encourage families to bake at home and to donate items to this sale. On the day of the sale, prepare Kool-Aid to sell with the other goodies.

Dance

PURPOSE   To explore and experience a variety of ways to pray with and for persons infected and affected by HIV/AIDS.

PREPARATION   *Materials*

- Varies with selected method

PROCEDURE   Prayer is an important part of the Christian life. Prayer is a vital source of strengthening and supporting the bond among members of a family. It is also an essential element of help and hope for persons infected and affected by HIV/AIDS. Make a commitment to spend time in prayer each day, centering on the various aspects of the AIDS epidemic. Pray for people living with the virus as well as for those dealing with the disease in other ways, but also pray with persons and families affected by the infection. Begin by using dance and movement as prayer and continue by choosing a unique model of prayer and using it each day for a month. Prayer suggestions include:

- Use gestures and motions as expressions of prayer.
- Learn a prayer in sign language and teach it to others.
- Pick a Scripture passage and use it as a prayer.
- Use watercolors and paint a prayer.
- Pray the words of a meditation as it is read.
- Weave a prayer with yarns and fabric.
- Use guided imagery as the focus of prayer.
- Use clay and sculpt a prayer.
- Write a poem and read it as a prayer.
- Read a favorite piece of poetry and let it become prayer.
- Find a story and allow it to speak as prayer.
- Pray for each person in the family.

- Record daily activities and offer them to God as prayer.
- Allow a walk in nature to become prayerful.
- Express a prayer of thanks for a special gift.
- Play a prayer on a musical instrument.
- Reflect on each year of a person's life and offer a prayer of thanks.
- Sit in silence and listen to God.
- Say the Lord's Prayer and reflect on each line.
- Listen to a favorite hymn as a prayer.
- Name something for every letter of the alphabet and give thanks for it.
- Remember care partners in a special way.
- Pray for people in the north, south, east, and west of the world.
- Find and use prayers from various faith traditions.
- Pray for the leaders of the countries of the world.
- Reflect on the words of Psalm 23.
- Invite people to contribute words or phrases to a prayer.
- Create a collage as the basis of a prayer.
- Call someone and offer a prayer over the phone.
- Praise God from whom all blessings flow.

Drama/Clown/Mime

PURPOSE To explore the theme of care partnership by creating skits using objects related to attending to someone with AIDS.

PREPARATION *Materials*

- Large paper or plastic bags
- Assorted items related to caring for a person with AIDS

Advance Preparation

- For each group of three to six persons, fill a paper or plastic bag with five items associated with caring for a person with AIDS. Items could include pillow, blanket, bleach bottle, thermometer, books, brochures from various AIDS service organizations, telephone, telephone book, dishes, etc.

PROCEDURE AIDS is a challenging disease that stresses both the person who is sick and those who provide care. Although hospitals and health-care facilities supply medical attention, being at home helps a person with AIDS maintain independence and a normal way of living. Remaining at home reduces stress and medical costs as well. Someone who attends to a person with AIDS is generally called a caregiver, however, the term "care partner" is also commonly used and in most cases preferred. Explore various aspects of care partnership through the use of dramatic skits.

Invite the students to participate in short skits on the theme of care partnership. Arrange the players into groups of three to six. Explain that one person in each group will play the role of the person in need of care and one person will portray the caregiver. Remaining students may play the parts of additional caregivers, such as family members or friends, medical workers, or AIDS-organization personnel. Distribute a bag to each team. Inform the groups that they will go to separate areas of the room and prepare a skit using the five objects in the bag they received. Tell the students that the objects may or may not be used for their normal functions; however, each object must be used and each player must participate. Note that the skits are to run approximately three minutes and that they may be presented verbally or nonverbally. Allow preparation time. After the skits are planned and rehearsed, tell the groups to return and to take turns presenting them.

At the conclusion of the skits, invite each small group to consider another question related to care partnership. Tell each person to assume the role of the person providing care. If no objects or items were available, what could they still offer to the person for whom they were caring. Give each group a few minutes to brainstorm answers. Invite each team to report their ideas by miming, or silently communicating, words and actions. Themes and thoughts could include a listening ear, a loving heart, and a sensitive spirit. Emphasize the importance of care being a partnership. Those involved must face difficult decisions regarding treatment and care together. Stress that it is important for people with AIDS to do all that they can for themselves for as long as they are able. Allowing the person with AIDS to make decisions regarding needs, schedules, activities, exercise, and diet provide a sense of control and independence.

Continue by suggesting ways in which the caregiver may become equipped for his or her task. Note that the Red Cross, Visiting Nurses, and AIDS service organizations offer home-care courses, and many groups provide support systems. Suggest that the caregiver must also know how to protect him or herself from infection with the virus that causes AIDS.

If appropriate, conclude by inviting care partners to speak to or visit with the students. By having a person living with AIDS and the individual(s) providing care interact with the participants, the learners will have the opportunity to explore many aspects of care partnership.

Games

PURPOSE   To use the game format "Go Fish" to teach ways in which people can help persons living with AIDS.

PREPARATION   *Materials*

- Index cards and pens
- Chalkboard and chalk or newsprint and markers

Advance Preparation

- Write the family "Need" statements listed below on a chalkboard or newsprint

PROCEDURE   People living in various family situations have needs that can be met by other family members. Direct the group's attention to the statements written on a chalkboard or newsprint. Ask the students to suggest solutions to these needs.

Need: I need a ride to choir rehearsal.
Response: I will take you in my car.

Need: I have to work overtime tonight and need someone to start the supper.
Response: I will be home in time to start it.

Need: I'd sure like to talk to someone about my day.
Response: Let's have a cup of coffee together.

After the students have suggested responses to a variety of situations, tell them that individuals with HIV/AIDS have many needs that can and must be met by other people. Play a modified version of the children's game Go Fish to help the participants explore the needs of persons with HIV/AIDS and ways in which people can respond to them.

Guide the students in making a deck of Go Fish playing cards. Provide index cards and pens for this purpose. Instruct each person to think of a need and than a remedy for the need and to write them on separate index cards.

Need: I need a ride to the doctor's office.
Response: I have a car.

Need: I need groceries, but I have no money.
Response: I work as a volunteer in our community food pantry.

Need: I'd like some books to read.
Response: I'm going to the library.

Create at least five sets of cards per player. To make the game more interesting and informative for the students, come up with many different needs and remedies. Stress ways in which people are interdependent. When the cards are finished, use them to play a game of Go Fish. Shuffle the cards and distribute five cards to each player. Place the remaining cards face down in a pile in the center of the table. One person starts by stating a need from one of the cards dealt to him or her and asks a specific person for a remedy. If the person has it, he or she must hand the card to the asker. If not, he or she says, "Go Fish," and the player takes a card from the pile of remaining cards. For example:

John: Mary, I need a place to sleep tonight. Do you have a remedy?
Mary: Yes, John, I work at a shelter for the homeless.

Mary turns her card over to John. John sets both cards on the table in front of him. Since John made a match with the person he asked, he may take another turn. If he did not make a match, he would pick a card from the pile. If it matches, he takes another turn. If it does not match, someone else takes a turn.

Continue playing until all of the cards are used. Emphasize that everyone wins when people help each other.

Music

PURPOSE   To listen to songs compiled on a recording to benefit the Pediatric AIDS Foundation.

PREPARATION   *Materials*

- *For Our Children* tape (Burbank, Calif.: Disney Press, 1991)
- Tape player

PROCEDURE   *For Our Children* is a very special musical endeavor, produced by Walt Disney Records, to benefit the Pediatric AIDS Foundation. It is designed to offer families songs to enjoy together, as sung by today's most talented superstars in music and film. These celebrities have joined together to present songs that have been loved by children of all time and others to treasure for years to come. The idea for the project began when recording artist James Taylor created a tape of songs for Ariel Glaser, daughter of Elizabeth Glaser and Paul Glaser (Starsky of the television show *Starsky and Hutch*). Ariel contracted the HIV virus from her mother, who in 1981 had received an emergency transfusion of blood that was unknowingly infected with HIV. The virus was passed to Ariel through breastfeeding and to her brother Jake *in utero*. While Ariel was sick she heard a song on television that made her laugh more than anything. It was called "Jellyman Kelly" and was sung by James Taylor. One day someone told James Taylor that Ariel was sick and that she loved his funny song. He recorded "Jellyman Kelly" and other happy songs on a tape and sent it to Ariel as a very special present. Whenever Ariel didn't feel well, she listened to the tape and it made her smile. After Ariel's death from an AIDS-related illness, her mother approached Walt Disney Records with the idea for a compilation album to benefit the Pediatric AIDS Foundation, an organization she co-founded to address problems unique to children with the HIV virus and AIDS. All profits from *For Our Children* are donated to the Pediatric AIDS Foundation to assist its efforts in funding critically needed pediatric AIDS research, education, and services.

Share the love and joy of this unique album with children, for it was made to provide a better future for all young people. Perhaps it will even inspire the listeners to compile an recording of their own to share with children with AIDS.

Songs and recording artists are: *Side One*: "Give A Little Love," Ziggy Marley and the Melody Makers; "This Old Man," Bob Dylan; "Cushie Butterfield," Sting; "Mary Had a Little Lamb," Paul McCartney; "The Ballad of Davy Crockett," Stephen Bishop; "Itsy Bitsy Spider," Little Richard; "Chicken Lips and Lizard Hips," Bruce Springsteen; "Country Feelin's," Brian Wilson; "Blueberry Pie," Bette Midler; "The Pacifier," Elton John. *Side Two*: "Getting to Know You," James Taylor; "Autumn to May," Ann and Nancy Wilson; "Child of Mine," Carole King; "Tell Me Why," Pat Benatar; "A Medley of Rhymes," Debbie Gibson; "Blanket for a Sail," Harry Nilsson; "Good Night, My Love

(Pleasant Dreams)," Paula Abdul; "Gartan Mother's Lullaby," Meryl Streep; "Golden Slumbers," Jackson Browne and Jennifer Warnes; "A Child Is Born," Barbra Streisand.

Supplement the activity by sharing the book *For Our Children* (Burbank, Calif.: Disney Press, 1991) and by showing the video of the same title.

Photography

PURPOSE   To teach the importance of sharing and celebrating the lives of people living with AIDS and to create memories for families who have lost a loved one to AIDS.

PREPARATION   *Materials*

- Camera and film
- Addresses of AIDS families
- Scrapbook and photo album
- Diary or journal
- Memorabilia box (a box with pictures, newspaper clippings, and other mementos)
- Cardboard box
- *Wilfred Gordon McDonald Partridge*[2]

Advance Preparation

- Obtain the names and addresses of families where a member is living with AIDS
- Place "memory" objects in a large cardboard box

PROCEDURE   One way to become better acquainted with another person is by sharing photographs. Photos, in the form of snapshots, formal portraits, movies, slides, videos, and clippings, record significant events and stories in the life of individuals and families. Memories of special times are important to persons living with AIDS as well as to their family members and friends. Use this project to help the participants become better acquainted with a person with AIDS and to help the person accumulate and acquire photo memories that will celebrate his or her life story.

Begin by showing the children the large carton filled with memory-related articles. Distribute one item at a time to a different person in the group. Take turns having each recipient name and describe the piece. After all of the objects have been shared, ask what the items have in common. They are all ways to record memories and to remember special events.

Read the group a wonderful book about memories, *Wilfred Gordon McDonald Partridge*. This is a story about a young boy who lives next door to an old people's home. Wilfred Gordon McDonald Partridge knows all of the people who reside there, but his favorite person is Miss Nancy Allison Delacourt Cooper, because she, too, has four names. One day Wilfred overhears his parents talking about Miss Nancy. When they say that she has lost her memory, Wilfred seeks to find it for her again. As Wilfred asks the people in the retirement community what a memory is, they all supply part of the answer. They tell him that it is something that is from long ago, that makes one feel warm, that may make a person cry, that causes a person to laugh, and that is precious as gold. Wilfred sets out to find items that fit each of these categories and brings them to Miss Nancy. As she explores each object, she remembers significant situations and stories. Miss Nancy regains her memory through the help of a young child.

State that persons living with AIDS have special stories that need to be recalled, recorded, and remembered. Explain that there are several ways in which this can be done and that one way is to become a "buddy" with someone, to get to know the person and to help him or her share memories. Present the details of the project. If possible, provide each participant with the name of a person living with AIDS and arrange opportunities for the two people to get together. Suggest that a good way to get acquainted is by looking through photographs. Invite the person with AIDS to share his or her life story by talking about the pictures. Help the person collect pictures of favorite things such as foods, restaurants, vacations, beaches, parks, plays, movies, music, and more, and organize them into a scrapbook, photo album, or memory box. Create a legacy to celebrate the person's life and to leave to family members and friends.

Offer the children additional options, especially those involving photography, for staying in touch with their "buddies." Sending photos of family members, pets, and favorite places would be a good way to issue greetings and good wishes. Send the person living with AIDS prayers written on the back of nature photos as a way to convey comfort and compassion. Books filled with personal photos and messages are a wonderful way to share love and life with another person.

Regardless of the project that is chosen or the way in which it is carried out, encourage the children to use creativity and originality in celebrating the lives of persons with AIDS.

Puppetry

PURPOSE   To make and use paper-bag and paper-plate animal puppets to learn safe pet guidelines.

PREPARATION   *Materials*

- Paper lunch bags and paper plates
- Markers or crayons
- Construction paper
- Scissors
- Glue
- Trims
- Paint stirrers
- Duct tape
- Fabric, plastic bags, or tissue paper
- *Safe Pet Guidelines*

Advance Preparation

- Obtain *Safe Pet Guidelines* from: Pets Are Wonderful Support Education Department, P.O. Box 460489, San Francisco, Calif. 94146-0489 (telephone: 415-824-4040)

PROCEDURE   In many households, pets are important members of the family. Ask the participants if any of them have or have ever had a pet. Take time for volunteers to share stories of their pets. Tell the children that pets are often very important companions for persons with HIV and AIDS. Pets offer unconditional love and acceptance which is often missing in human relationships. This is especially important to infected persons when their human contacts diminish through isolation because of the disease. Besides the benefits of companionship, there are also many risks for HIV-infected persons with pets. When a person's immune system is suppressed through disease or medical treatments, they become more vulnerable to infections. When this happens they may become fearful of contact with other living creatures, including pets. While there are a number of diseases people can catch from animals, very few of them pose a threat to life. The Centers for Disease Control state that there is no evidence that dogs, cats, or other nonprimate animals can contract the human immunodeficiency virus or transmit it to human beings. "Zoonoses" refers to those diseases that can be contracted by humans from other animals. People with suppressed immune systems are more susceptible to all kinds of disease, including the zoonoses. People need to know about the risks of catching diseases from their pets. Tell the group that they will learn more about safe pet guidelines through involvement in an animal-puppet-making project.

Pets Are Wonderful Support, PAWS, is a volunteer, nonprofit group that helps improve the quality of life for persons with HIV disease by offering them emotional and practical support in keeping the love and companionship of their pets and by providing information on the benefits and risks of animal companionship. The organization publishes a brochure *Safe Pet Guidelines*. If possible, distribute a copy to each participant. Review some of the guidelines, such as washing hands after touching pets, keeping animals clean and well groomed, and maintaining the pet's living and feeding areas. Fleas must be eliminated, contact with a pet's bodily fluids should be avoided, and visits to the veterinarian need to be made regularly. Animal bites must be tended immediately to help avoid infection, pet diets must be regulated to prevent the animal from acquiring diseases that can be passed on to humans, and new pets need to be examined and tested for diseases and parasites. Pets to avoid include stray animals, animals with diarrhea, exotic animals, sick animals, wild animals, and monkeys.

Tell the class that they will be working in small groups to research and report on safe pet guidelines for specific types of animals such as dogs, cats, fish, and birds. Arrange the participants into groups and assign each team a specific type of pet to study. Explain that they are to use the information in *Safe Pet Guidelines* as well as additional information that has been provided. Distribute paper and pens or pencils for recording the findings. As a unique way to report the data, each person is to construct an animal puppet from a paper bag or a paper plate. Review the procedure for making the puppets.

For a paper-bag puppet, the bottom flap of the bag becomes the head. Fold the flap flat against one side of the bag. Use markers or crayons to draw the facial features on the flap or cut the pieces out of construction paper and glue them in place. Decorate the body of the bag with paper pieces or marker drawings. Add trims such as feathers for a bird or fake fur for a cat. To operate the puppet, insert one hand into the bag. Place four fingers inside the flap and the thumb in the bag. Move the fingers to make the puppet talk.

Try a paper-plate animal puppet, too. Use marker paper or construction paper scraps to form a face on one side of the plate. Add hair made from these and other materials. Glue the pieces in place. Tape or glue a paint stirrer, craft stick, or dowel rod to the back of the plate to use as the handle by which the puppet is operated. Fabric pieces, plastic bags, or tissue paper can be added to the rod to create a costume.

Allow time for the groups to gather information and to make puppets. Take turns having each group or individual make a report on safe pet guidelines for the type of animal researched.

When the stories and summaries are completed, emphasize that in most cases the benefits of animal companionship outweigh the risks for persons with HIV and AIDS. Challenge the group to use their animal puppets to make other people aware of safe pet guidelines.

Storytelling

PURPOSE   To use pictures as story starters to encourage young people to discuss ways in which HIV/AIDS is transmitted and prevented.

PREPARATION   *Materials*

- Magazine pictures
- Scissors
- Paper and pens
- Glue

PROCEDURE   Discussion about the transmission and prevention of HIV can be facilitated in many ways. One way is by using pictures of people as story starters. Participants are to find pictures of people and suggest ways in which their lives might be touched by HIV/AIDS.

Provide a variety of magazines, catalogs, and newspapers containing pictures of people. Direct each participant to find one or more of the following pictures:

Baby
Preschool child
Elementary-school child
Middle-school child
Teenager
Woman

Man
Man and woman
Two men
Two women
Mother and baby

Gather the group in a circle on the floor, on chairs, or around tables. Ask each student, in turn, to choose a picture depicting a different person and to tell a story about one way HIV/AIDS might touch the subject's life. For example, if someone shows a picture of a mother and a baby, the story could be: The woman in this picture used to be a drug user. She shared dirty needles with other people when shooting up drugs. The woman became infected with the HIV virus; and when she became pregnant, she passed the virus to her baby. When showing the photo of the elementary-school child, the story could be about hemophilia. The picture of the adults might be accompanied by an account on sexual transmission. Encourage children to add information and insight to one another's stories. Continue this process by showing and sharing a number of pictures.

During the course of the activity, supplement the information the children are stating by supplying specific facts about HIV/AIDS transmission and prevention. Keep in mind that AIDS is caused by a virus, HIV, that is transmitted when body fluids such as blood, vaginal secretions, and semen are transferred from an infected person to someone else. Transmission generally occurs by having sex with someone who has the virus, by sharing needles and syringes with infected persons, from a pregnant women who passes the infection to her unborn or newborn child, and, less frequently, through blood transfusions. High-risk ways of acting are important factors to keep in mind when talking with the students. These include having sex with strangers, having sex with many different people or with people, such as prostitutes, who have sex with many other people, having anal sex, having sex with someone who shoots drugs, sharing drug needles and syringes, and having sex without using condoms. Prevention methods include abstinence, safer sex, and condoms and avoiding drugs, the sharing of needles, or the cleaning of needles with bleach if they are reused.

An alternate or additional way to use this activity is to invite each person to choose a picture, to glue it to a piece of paper, and to write a short story about the way in which the subject of the photo might be affected or infected by HIV/AIDS. Once the stories are completed, arrange the participants into small groups, have them exchange pictures, and read and learn from one another's work.

1. ABC Quilts, *Kids Making Quilts for Kids* (Gualala, Calif.: Quilt Digest Press, 1992).
2. Mem Fox and Julie Vivas, illustrator, *Wilfred Gordon McDonald Partridge* (New York: Kane Miller, 1985).

CHAPTER 10
Self

Activities in this chapter are intended to encourage a positive sense of self-worth in the participants so that they may address the many issues of HIV/AIDS that affect them and the people around them.

Architecture

PURPOSE   To help participants explore "doors" that are open or closed to persons in various AIDS-related situations.

PREPARATION   *Materials*

- Door
- Roll of paper such as paper tablecloth, newsprint, or butcher paper
- Tape
- Scissors
- Markers or crayons
- Dictionary
- Magazines or catalogs (optional)
- Paper and pencils
- Maze
- Duplicating or photocopying equipment

Advance Preparation

- Cover a door with paper. Depending on the size of the group, one or both sides of the door may be used
- Write the word "WELCOME" vertically down the center of the paper
- Duplicate the maze game

PROCEDURE   As the participants arrive, invite them to gather around the door to the room. Greet each person individually and encourage the children to also welcome one another. After everyone has assembled, use the dictionary to look up the exact meaning of the word "welcome." Talk about times and places where the participants have felt welcome and about situations when they did not feel welcome. Next, look up the meaning of the word "door." One definition is "a means of access." Explain that a door is often associated with the word "welcome." A door can be opened or closed. A door can help make a person feel welcome or unwelcome. Now, use the door to list things people can do to make another person feel welcome. This can be done in a number of ways:

- The words or phrases can begin with or include the letters of the word "welcome"
- Children can write their own words and phrases directly on the door
- Young children can draw pictures of their ideas or they can suggest words and themes and a leader can write them on the door for them

Before beginning the project, brainstorm a few words or phrases to use such as wave, call, and eat lunch together. Provide markers or crayons. Pictures may be cut from magazines and added to the door. Review the results of the project together.

Gather the group. Ask the children if all doors are open for people living with the AIDS

virus. Unfortunately, the answer is "no." Distribute a maze sheet and pencil to each person and invite the group to complete the game. Discuss places people can go to get help and to have their questions answered. Some ideas should include the buildings pictured on the maze: hospital, community health clinic, school, home, and church. Tell the group that it is "a-mazing" how many doors are actually closed to persons with AIDS. Name some of the sites and situations where doors might be closed to persons with HIV/AIDS. Include the themes of housing, employment, medical treatment, and insurance, among others. Tell the group that each person has the responsibility to help to open doors to persons with HIV/AIDS-related needs. Continue the activity by inviting the learners to construct a maze together on the paper on the door. Involve the children in the process of discussing and drawing doors that should be open to persons with HIV infection and ways in which they can work to be sure that persons with AIDS have access to them.

Art

PURPOSE   To learn that it is safe to give and to receive blood in the United States.

PREPARATION   *Materials*

- Adhesive-backed name tags
- Red ink pads
- Paper towels
- Fine-tip markers

PROCEDURE   As the participants arrive, ask each person to place his or her finger on a red ink pad and to make a fingerprint impression on a plain adhesive-backed name tag. Set the stickers aside. Talk about the uniqueness of fingerprints. Make sure the students realize that before they were born, God made a special design on their fingers. Their design is different from everyone else's in the world.

Something else that is unique to each person is the decision to give and to receive blood and blood products. There are many differing and conflicting stories in newspapers and magazines and on television about AIDS. These stories often confuse people about how safe it is to give and to receive blood. Some people are so confused about HIV and AIDS that they no longer give blood or plasma. Others believe that receiving blood is so dangerous that they would even refuse a necessary transfusion. Having the facts can help people make these important and often life-saving decisions.

Ask if anyone in the group has ever had his or her finger pricked for a blood test, possibly for cholesterol screening or for blood typing. Inquire if anyone has ever donated blood or if they know people who have given blood. Encourage answers to the question "What does blood have to do with HIV and AIDS?" Explain that the HIV virus must enter the blood in order to live and to do its damage. Once in the blood, the virus attacks the white blood cells, and the body's immune system is impaired and ultimately destroyed. HIV enters the blood in ways such as:

Hemophilia

To control bleeding, people with hemophilia need clotting factor concentrates made from the blood of many donors. New methods used to produce these concentrates have been shown to greatly reduce the risk of HIV transmission; however, before identification of the AIDS virus and proper testing procedures, many hemophiliacs contracted the infection.

Blood Transfusion

In this medical procedure a person, usually in a life-threatening situation, receives someone else's blood. Since testing for the AIDS virus was devised in 1984 and 1985, blood transfusions are nearly 100 percent safe. Before then, people who received blood transfusions were at risk of infection.

Drugs

When an infected person injects drugs, blood can be trapped in the needle, then injected into the bloodstream of the next person who uses the needle. Even the smallest amount of blood left in a used needle or syringe can contain HIV.

Tell the group that it is safe to donate blood in the United States. This is because every piece of equipment, such as needles, tubing, and containers, used to draw blood is sterile. No piece of equipment has ever been used before, and all needles are discarded properly after the blood is drawn. Receiving blood is safer than ever before, too. The chances of becoming infected from receiving blood are very small. All donors are interviewed for risks of HIV infection. People who want to donate blood are asked specific questions to determine if they have done anything that may have exposed them to HIV or other viruses. If their answers suggest that they may be at risk, they are not allowed to donate. In addition, when someone gives blood or plasma, it is tested for signs of HIV, hepatitis, syphilis, and certain other diseases. If these tests reveal infection, the donated blood or plasma is destroyed. Although the current tests are nearly 100 percent accurate, testing is being improved to make blood and plasma products even safer.

Refer to the fingerprints the students made as they entered the room. State that just as each fingerprint is unique to its maker, the decision to give and to receive blood is unique to each person as well. To stress the safety of these processes, invite the group to turn their fingerprint impressions into stickers that encourage people to donate blood and assure them that blood donations and blood transfusions are safe. Make fine-tip markers available and suggest that the students draw around their print and turn it into an illustration of a person or a drop of blood. Words such as "It's safe to donate blood" or "Give Blood. Give Life" may be added. Ask each person to find the fingerprint he or she made earlier. Challenge the students to find their fingerprints without referring to the name on the back of the name tag! Even though they are unique, it is hard to tell one from the other by casual observation. As the students create their stickers, circulate through the group and answer any questions people may have about giving and receiving blood. Once the projects are completed, invite the group to wear the stickers or to give them to someone else.

Remind the group that giving and receiving blood saves lives. The gift of blood helps others; someday it could save the donor's own life or the life of a loved one.

Banners/Textiles

PURPOSE   To make computer banners as symbols of commitment to personal involvement in the fight against AIDS.

PREPARATION   *Materials*

- Computer, printer, "Print Shop" or similar software, and computer paper
- Pencils
- Poster paints, brushes, and containers for paint
- Newspapers
- Cleaning supplies
- Masking tape

Advance Preparation

- Arrange for computer equipment and personnel to make computer banners
- Prepare the painting area by covering the work surface with newspapers and providing cleaning supplies

PROCEDURE   Whether a person becomes involved in the fight against HIV/AIDS is an individual choice. Each man, woman, teenager, boy, and girl must make a personal decision for him or herself. Once a commitment to get involved is made, this pledge can be evidenced in numerous ways. In this activity participants will explore methods to educate others about AIDS and ways to directly help persons and families living with AIDS. Computer banners will be created and displayed as signs of the commitment made by each person.

Tell the group that they will be making computer banners. For the messages on the banners, each person will choose one or more ways in which he or she will commit to doing something about AIDS. Ask the group to name slogans that would educate others about HIV/AIDS. Ideas include:

- Fight AIDS, not people with AIDS
- Hate is not a family value
- AIDS can't be spread through friendship
- Have you hugged a person with AIDS today
- AIDS is everyone's disease
- Be AIDS smart
- Just say NO!

If the banner will be used to remember someone who has died of AIDS, phrases such as these could be used:

- Remember their names
- In the presence of absence
- Mr., Ms., Mrs. _____, we loved you

On a more personal level, think together about special and specific commitments each person could make to directly assist, advocate for, and affirm persons and families living with AIDS. Suggestions, based on ideas in the book by Shireen Perry with Gregg Lewis, *In Sickness and in Health: A Story of Love in the Shadow of AIDS* (Downers Grove, Ill.: InterVarsity Press, 1989), include:

Practical Help
- Prepare and deliver meals for the patient and/or family.
- Do grocery shopping.
- Drive the patient to medical and other appointments.
- Pick up prescriptions.
- Do laundry.
- Help with housecleaning.
- Tackle a fix-it job that is going undone around the house.
- Deliver and pick up mail.
- Find or offer housing for out-of-town family and visitors.
- Pay some of the bills.

Personal Help
- Read a good book onto a tape and leave it for the person to listen to at his or her convenience.
- Play games such as checkers.
- Bring a special treat such as gourmet ice cream.
- Give a hand or foot massage.
- Make regular phone calls to encourage the person.
- Spend time together.
- Take the person for a ride.
- Go to a special event, such as a play or concert, together.
- Make physical contact by offering handshakes and hugs.
- Send notes and cards.

Spiritual Help
- Read Bible passages, especially the psalms, aloud.
- Sing together.
- Bring recorded music.

- Pray with the person.
- Share the love of Christ through words and actions.
- Hold a prayer service for the person.
- Have members of a congregation coordinate support services.
- Check with the patient's caregiver and offer support to this person.
- Hold a Bible study class at the person's home.

Ask each person to think about one or more ways in which he or she will become involved in the AIDS issue. Distribute paper and pens or pencils and tell the group to write their personal commitments in simple sentences or phrases on the paper. Use these statements as the basis of computer banners. Using a computer software package, such as "Print Shop," help each person create a banner displaying a personal commitment to fight AIDS. Once the banners are printed, allow the group to decorate them with paints, markers, or crayons.

If computers are not available, facilitate the project in an alternate way. Tell the group that they will be painting their phrases on pieces of computer paper. Distribute long pieces of computer paper. Place containers of poster paint and brushes around the work area. Have pencils ready for those who choose to draw first before painting. Allow time for the participants to paint their banner strips.

Once the children have painted their banners, hang them for viewing. Tell the participants to take time to read the phrases and to learn from one another's work. Instruct the students to take their banners with them and to display them in places where they will be reminded of their personal commitments to get involved in the fight against AIDS.

Cartoons

PURPOSE   To discuss transmission of the AIDS virus through sexual activity and to suggest condom use as a method of prevention of the infection.

PREPARATION   *Materials*

- Condom sample
- "The Rubbers Bros. Comics"

Advance Preparation

- Obtain samples of "The Rubber Bros. Comics" from: The Rubbers Bros. Reading Club, P.O. Box 431, Wilbraham, Mass. 01095-0431 (telephone: 413-734-1057 or 800-745-1057)

PROCEDURE   Sex is a special gift from God. Sexuality affects who people are and how they interact with one another. Sexual activities include romantic talking, holding hands, kissing, petting, and very intimate acts involving genital contact. Most religions teach that sexual intercourse is an expression of love that should be saved until a person is in a faithful, monogamous marriage.

One of the main ways that people are exposed to the AIDS virus is through the high-risk behavior of unprotected sexual contact. Sexual contact may be defined as any contact between a person's sexual organs, sometimes called genitals, and another person's genitals, mouth, or anus. The AIDS virus may be spread through sexual activities such as vaginal sex, oral sex, or anal sex. During any of these activities there is the possibility for the AIDS virus to be spread through the exchange of body fluids, such as blood, semen, and vaginal secretions, to the moist linings of the openings to the body. Every time someone has unprotected sexual intercourse with another person, male or female, the person is subject to illnesses to which that partner and his or her previous sexual partners have been exposed.

Abstinence from sexual intercourse is the only sure way to avoid exposure to the AIDS virus. Another way is to limit sex to one partner who also limits his or her sex in the same way. Persons who do have sexual intercourse should protect both themselves and their partner by using a condom. A condom, sometimes called a rubber or a prophylactic, is an expansive cover for the penis that catches semen when the man ejaculates. A condom acts as a barrier to keep blood, semen, or vaginal fluids from passing from one person to the other during sexual intercourse. Condoms are not 100 percent safe but, if used properly, will reduce the risk of sexually transmitted diseases, including AIDS.

Discuss the sexual transmission of the AIDS virus, and especially its prevention, through the use of a special series of comic books and cartoons called "The Rubbers Bros. Comics." Almost every era in the twentieth century has had a comic book hero to right the wrongs of the world, and the Rubbers Brothers are no exception. Fred and Gene, two tough dancing condoms, will stop at nothing to defeat A-Man, the evil AIDS virus. Creators of the Rubbers Bros. Dance Team, Paul Mozeleski and his father Peter, say the comic book series promotes AIDS prevention awareness and safer sex through the use of condoms.

Show the students samples of the comic books. Discuss the sexual transmission of the AIDS virus and also the use of condoms. Display a condom sample, if desired. Explain that the effective use of condoms is one of the best forms of protection against HIV for persons engaging in sexual activity. Condoms must be used each time a person has sex, from the beginning to the end of the sexual act, as it only takes one sexual encounter without a condom to become infected with HIV. Latex condoms are most effective since natural condoms made of animal skin have pores that allow HIV to pass through. Packages should indicate that the condoms are to prevent disease and that the product is treated with a spermicide called nonoxynol-9, a chemical used to kill sperm and also the AIDS virus during intercourse. Only water-based lubricants should be used with a condom; oil-based lubricants can weaken and break the condom. A condom should be used once and then properly discarded. Proper use of a condom may also be taught or demonstrated.

Creative Writing

PURPOSE
To use journal writing as a way of helping children express their feelings on a variety of themes related to AIDS.

PREPARATION
Materials

- Three-ring notebooks with pockets and notebook paper
- Permanent markers and pens or pencils

PROCEDURE
Start the children on a journal-writing project as a way of helping them explore several themes associated with AIDS. A journal is a daily record of events and the emotions associated with them. Explain the project and inspire the group to use their personal pages as a way to communicate thoughts and feelings and to explore problems and possible solutions. Make the children aware that although writing is a good way to do this, art is also encouraged.

Distribute three-ring notebooks with pockets and permanent markers. If the group is notified in advance, it may be possible to have each person bring his or her own supplies. Provide time for the boys and girls to decorate the covers with words and symbols representing themselves. This could include drawings and designs about their hobbies, family, school, pet, favorite places, special foods, and so forth. Tell each person to write his or her name on the cover.

Pass out notebook paper and pens or pencils. Ask each participant to reflect on a variety of topics associated with HIV/AIDS. For example, tell the students to pretend that they have contracted AIDS from a blood transfusion they received before doctors started screening blood for the virus. Encourage them to try to capture their feelings, emotions, and experiences. How might their families and friends react to this news? How do they think or feel about having AIDS? What changes in their lifestyles will they make? What becomes most important now that they only have a short time to live? Encourage the children to write about the same topic every day for a week or to reflect on a new theme every day for a week. Other journal suggestions include:

- A parent has AIDS
- A brother or sister has AIDS

- A best friend has AIDS
- The doctor or dentist has AIDS
- A child with AIDS has just started attending school
- The neighbors have a baby with HIV infection

After engaging in the journal experience, provide an opportunity for the group to share thoughts and feelings with one another if they desire.

Culinary Arts

PURPOSE To use food packaging to illustrate that people should not be judged only by outward appearance.

PREPARATION *Materials*

- Labels and wrappers from food products
- Paper and pencils or pens
- Two boxes
- Snacks, one appetizing and one unappetizing

Advance Preparation

- Create a display of food-packaging materials
- Place the appetizing snack in an unappealing container, and the unappetizing snack in an appealing container

PROCEDURE Unfortunately, people are often judged by the way they look on the outside rather than by who they are on the inside. Illustrate this point by using packaging materials from a variety of food products. Wrappers and advertising may make food seem very appealing, but actually the products might not taste as good as they appear. Emphasize this point by offering the children a snack. Show the group two boxes and tell them that they must agree on the one from which they want their treat. One box should be extremely attractive, enticingly labeled and beautifully decorated. The other container should be extraordinarily unappealing in its outward appearance. Ask the group to choose one box, encouraging them to pick the most attractive one. Open the box and show the children a horrible snack. It could be a damaged or moldy product or a type of food they would not enjoy eating. Open the other box and show the group a treat they would all like. Set both boxes aside.

Invite the participants to look closely at the display of food-packaging materials. Challenge the group to think about a variety of questions. What do the labels tell? What don't they tell? Are they misleading in any way? Are some labels unattractive? Does unattractive mean what's inside isn't good? Do they recognize all the labels? Do people try the product if it doesn't look good? Might the product be good even if the packaging is unattractive? Provide paper and pens and encourage the students to record their responses. Ask if these questions also relate to people. Invite written and verbal discussion. How might people be different on the inside and the outside? Is it much like the labels of food?

Many people with AIDS are only seen from the outside. Too often people view them as unlovable or unclean. Because of the nature of AIDS, people with the disease lose weight, become blind, and develop cancerous blotches on the skin. Outwardly, their appearance is unattractive. Some people never look beyond what they see on the outside. People with HIV/AIDS become labeled, much like the food products. However, on the inside, there are beautiful qualities about these people. People with AIDS, regardless of external appearance, have needs for love and friendship.

Invite the children to compile a list of the "ingredients" that make them special. Emphasize that the list should include things that people can't tell just by looking at them. For example: artist, poet, cook, kind, loving, compassionate, lonely, afraid. Ask those who are willing to share some of their responses.

Once again, display the unappealing box containing the appealing snack. Ask the children if they would like to share the treat together, even though on the outside it doesn't look like something they would enjoy. Continue the discussion while eating together.

Dance

PURPOSE To add movement to Saint Francis' prayer and to use it as a catalyst for exploring individual responses to the AIDS epidemic.

PREPARATION *Materials*

- Paper and pencils
- "Lord, Make Me an Instrument" prayer

PROCEDURE " *Lord, make me an instrument of your peace . . .*" are the familiar words of Saint Francis of Assisi. They are often called a peace prayer. Read the lines to the children:

> *Lord, make me an instrument of your peace.*
> *Where there is hatred, let me so love,*
> *Where there is injury, pardon,*
> *Where there is darkness, light,*
> *Where there is sadness, joy,*
> *Where there is doubt, faith,*
> *And where there is despair, hope.*
> *O Divine Master,*
> *Grant that I may not so much seek*
> *To be consoled as to console,*
> *To be understood as to understand,*
> *To be loved as to love.*
> *For it is in giving that we receive,*
> *It is in pardoning that we are pardoned,*
> *And it is in dying that we are born to eternal life.*

Invite the class to add movements and gestures to express the meaning of the words. Assign each person or small group a phrase and take turns interpreting them.

Suggest that the children rewrite Saint Francis' thoughts as prayers using words connected with the AIDS epidemic. As a group, review each line of the prayer. For example, name situations where there is hatred and suggest ways that love can be shown or circumstances in which there is sadness and joy may be shared. Distribute paper and pencils or pens and ask each individual to focus on a way in which he or she can be an instrument of peace in some AIDS related situation. Share an example:

> *Lord, make me an instrument of your peace.*
> *Where there is name calling,*
> *Let me bring kind words.*
> *Where there is arguing,*
> *Let me bring problem solving.*

Allow time for the group to write their prayers. Encourage the children to interpret their new peace prayers through movement.

Drama/Clown/Mime

PURPOSE To help children describe emotions associated with HIV/AIDS.

PREPARATION *Materials*

- Index cards and markers
- Box

Feelings are as much a part of a child as fingers and toes, yet they are often much less obvious and need more clarification. When discussing and dealing with HIV/AIDS, feelings play an important role. A child with a sibling with AIDS may be angry that his or her brother or sister will die at a young age. A youth with an HIV-infected parent might feel scared at the thought of being left alone. A young person who experimented with drugs or sex only once could live in fear of contracting the virus. Part of the process of dealing with the many issues related to HIV/AIDS is learning to identify and express feelings. For children, this requires practice and participation.

Ask each child, in turn, to name a feeling. As the feeling, such as "happy," "sad," "angry," "confused," or "surprised," is named, write the word on an index card and place it in the box. Suggest various feelings if the children run out of ideas.

Gather the pupils in a circle. Ask one person at a time to pick a card from the box and to pantomime the feeling written on it through facial expressions and body gestures. There should be no talking. Invite the remaining learners to guess the feeling. Continue until everyone has had a turn.

Tell the children that people infected and affected by HIV/AIDS experience many feelings. Discuss a variety of situations and circumstances and ask the children to name, describe, or mime feelings that are specifically associated with them. Use several of these suggestions as guidelines for the activity:

- Jerry's test results indicate that he is HIV positive.
- Blake has AIDS and is dealing with the fact that there is no cure for it.
- Krista is told that she only has a few weeks to live.
- Karl has been caring for his son for many months without much time for himself.
- Hope's newborn daughter is HIV infected.
- Marla was at a party and injected drugs, only once, yet she wonders if she will become infected with HIV.
- Mark's younger brother has AIDS and the doctors say he will not live much longer.
- Michael, a person with AIDS, has been abandoned by his family and friends.
- Rick took steroids because he thought they would make him a better athlete and now he is HIV infected.
- Michelle, an extremely beautiful girl, is discovering that the infections associated with AIDS are causing her body to become drastically disfigured.
- Grant wonders how many other people he may have infected through sexual activity.
- Kaye is experiencing loss of control over all aspects of her life because of her weakened condition.

Help the children distinguish and discuss the many feelings associated with each of these scenarios. The participants may continue naming HIV/AIDS-related situations and stories and identifying the feelings associated with each of them.

Conclude the activity by reminding the children that everyone experiences feelings and that it is important to identify and express feelings in order to deal with them concretely and constructively.

Games

PURPOSE To use a game format to explore issues of loss and grief.

PREPARATION *Materials*

- Self-adhesive labels and markers

PROCEDURE Among the many aspects of dealing with the AIDS crisis is the challenge of responding in an appropriate way to the grief of those infected and affected by the disease. Use "The HIV Loss Exercise,"[1] developed by the AIDS Project of Contra Costa, California, as a way to explore this theme. This exercise is designed to awaken awareness of what people with HIV are experiencing in their lives—the uncontrollable, inexorable loss that leads to ultimate loss of life.

Have a small number of participants be the "HIV Virus." They will wait while the others do the following activities. Give each participant twelve to sixteen labels and one or more markers. Have them write several labels for each of the following categories: special people in their lives, favorite possessions, favorite activities, hoped-for dreams and goals. Have them stick the labels all over their chest and arms and then pair off. Each partner should have a few minutes to look at the other's list of things, and each should have a brief time to describe the meaning of the various labels.

The leader then explains that HIV entry into someone's life forces them to lose important parts of themselves. Ask each person voluntarily to take off one label. Give them a minute to think about the first loss and the feelings associated with the action. As HIV begins to destroy the immune system, more things are lost. Ask each person to remove one more label. At this point release the assigned "HIV people" to wander among the participants removing labels randomly. Give them time to circle the group. Expect emotional reactions from some people.

After ample time, tell the "HIV people" to gather in one corner of the room or space. Then start the discussion by asking the participants to respond to the experience. Use questions such as: What was taken? How did that feel? How did they feel about the one who did the taking? How did they feel about what happened to their partner? When there are no further comments, ask the "HIV people" to describe how they felt taking the labels. Did they look people in the eye? Did they crumple up the labels or treat them gently? Lead the discussion to the direct effect on people's lives of a slowly debilitating disease like HIV/AIDS that runs to an inevitable end. Discuss symptoms and stages of HIV/AIDS.

Tell the group that the stages of death and dying, as well as the stages of grief, have also been labeled. Create more labels and explain these phases. Elisabeth Kubler-Ross, in her acclaimed book *On Death and Dying*,[2] describes five stages of grief and loss:

- Denial
- Depression
- Anger
- Bargaining
- Acceptance

Everyone experiences these stages in different ways and for various amounts of time. Many people deny the reality of the HIV/AIDS virus, believing that it has no effect on them. Others bargain with their knowledge: not me, not my group, or I'm always careful. A large number are scared or angry. Too few have been reconciled to the fact that AIDS affects us all. Too few experience understanding, forgiveness, and gratitude for what life has to offer. It is important to emphasize that the experience is different for each infected and affected person. For most, reconciliation ultimately means a better understanding of the virus and a better plan about how to live with it and control its progression.

Provide information on ways to help people deal with loss and grief. Some options include individual or family professional counseling; support of family and friends; professionally led seminars and workshops; drop-in crisis grief counseling; fixed membership support groups with an agreed-upon time limit; open membership, ongoing support groups; funeral services; memorial services; anniversary observances; and gravesite visits.

Individuals in the group may be personally experiencing various stages of loss and grief. Stress that there are many factors involved in these phases and offer several options for support.

Music

PURPOSE	To use music to remind the participants that each person is created in the image of God.
PREPARATION	***Materials***

- Mirror
- Bible

- Music to "Beautiful"[3] and accompaniment (optional)
- Tape player

Advance Preparation

- Obtain a copy of the song "Beautiful" on the cassette tape *New Wine*. Contact: Jaime Rickert, Marydale, 945 Donaldson Highway, Erlanger, Ky. 41019 (telephone: 606-282-9080)

PROCEDURE Remind the participants that every person in the world is created in the image of God. Read Genesis 1:27 to the group: "So God created humankind in [God's] image . . . male and female [God] created them." Tell the students that because they are created in the image of God, they are unique and beautiful. Take a mirror and look into it. Pass the mirror around the circle and invite each person to look at him or herself. Remind each person, by name if possible, that he or she is created in God's image.

Ask the group to listen to the words of a special song titled "Beautiful." Read the words, sing the song, or play a recording of it.

It doesn't matter if I can't dance.
And it doesn't matter if I can't sing.
And it doesn't matter if I can't do most anything.
And it doesn't matter if I'm too short.
And it doesn't matter if I'm too tall.
And it doesn't matter if I'm too much of anything at all.
Because I'm beautiful because God made me,
Because God loves me just the way I am.
And I am beautiful like the stars that shine above.
And I'm not loved because I'm beautiful,
I'm beautiful 'cause I'm loved.
And it doesn't matter if I'm too shy.
And it doesn't matter if I'm too bold.
And it doesn't matter if I'm too young or too medium or too old.
And it doesn't matter if my eyes are too dark.
And it doesn't matter if my hair is to light.
And it doesn't matter if I'm too red, too yellow, too brown, too black or too white.
I'm beautiful because God made me.
Because God loves me just the way I am.
And I am beautiful like the stars that shine above.
I'm not loved because I'm beautiful,
I'm beautiful 'cause I'm loved.
And you are beautiful because God made you,
Because God loves you just the way you are.
And you are beautiful like the stars that shine above.
You're not loved because you're beautiful,
You're beautiful 'cause you're loved.
You're not loved because you're beautiful,
You're beautiful 'cause you're loved.
It doesn't matter if my eyes can't see.
And it doesn't matter if my ears can't hear,
And it doesn't matter if my lips can't talk, or my chair has wheels, or my thoughts
*   aren't clear.*
Because I'm beautiful because God made me.
Because God loves me just the way I am.
Because I'm beautiful like the stars that shine above.
I'm not loved because I'm beautiful,
I'm beautiful 'cause I'm loved.
I'm not loved because I'm beautiful.
I'm beautiful 'cause I'm loved.

Invite the participants to learn the words and to sing the song together.

Ask the students what this song has to do with people with HIV/AIDS. Sometimes persons with AIDS are not physically beautiful, especially during the last stages of the disease. Encourage discussion of the fact that each person, those infected and those not infected, are created in God's image; therefore, they are beautiful.

Photography

PURPOSE To use photography to teach that HIV/AIDS is not something to be viewed at a distance; it touches everyone.

PREPARATION *Materials*

- Camera and film
- Note books and pencils or pens
- Glue sticks

PROCEDURE For many people, and especially teenagers, AIDS seems a very distant problem—a problem they believe only afflicts homosexuals and drug users. Many people have a hard time imagining the AIDS epidemic becoming a real presence in their lives. Use photography to help the participants put themselves into the picture and to illustrate the point that objects, issues, and people look different up close from the way they do from a distance.

Invite the students to take two snapshots of a person or an object. Tell them that one picture is to be taken close-up and the other is to be taken from a distance. Both snapshots are to be of the same subject. Distribute cameras and film or have the pupils use their own equipment. Encourage each person to take a roll of twelve pictures, giving them six different people or objects to photograph. Provide time for this portion of the project.

Once the photographs are developed, direct the students to mount the photos in a notebook. Provide the necessary supplies. After the photos are mounted, ask the young people to compare and contrast each set of pictures. Observations are to be written in the note book. Guide the process by suggesting questions such as "What are the differences in the two snapshots?" "How are they alike?" "What can be seen in the close-up photo but not in the distant one?" "What can be told about the person or thing?" Encourage the group to write as many differences as possible.

Invite the children to discuss what they have discovered. Direct the subject to people who are living with AIDS or to AIDS in general. Ask how this compares with the activity. AIDS and people with AIDS are often looked at from a distance. AIDS is often seen as someone else's problem. The phrase "It can't happen to me" is frequently heard. HIV/AIDS is put at a distance. Individuals believe it touches others but not them.

Discuss with the students that AIDS means making choices. It means looking at people and situations up close. It means knowing the facts and letting others know the facts, too. It means getting to know other people up close. Explain that often persons with AIDS have few friends or no one to visit them. Taking a risk and getting to know a person with AIDS up close could make a big difference in that person's life.

Encourage the students not to remain in the distance but to be "close-up," a real part of the whole picture.

Puppetry

PURPOSE To make sock puppets to donate to children with HIV/AIDS.

PREPARATION *Materials*

- Socks
- Glue
- Scissors

- Felt
- Buttons and trims
- Yarn
- Needles and thread
- Plastic eyes (optional)
- Names and addresses of HIV-infected children
- Paper and pen

Advance Preparation

- Obtain the names and addresses of centers and treatment facilities that minister to children with HIV/AIDS

PROCEDURE Socks come in all shapes, sizes, and colors. Use them to remind the group of the variety of people, near and far, who are infected and affected by HIV/AIDS. Explain that some congregations, community organizations, and individuals offer day care as a special ministry to children infected by the AIDS virus. Hospitals and care facilities also minister to the needs of HIV-infected children. Name and describe specific places, if possible. Invite the class to make sock puppets to give as gifts to the children at some of these locations.

Show the children how to make a simple sock puppet. Select a sock to use for the demonstration. Tube socks work well. Cut two felt eyelashes and glue them to one side of the sock near the toe. Affix a plastic moveable eye to each eyelash. Depending on the ages of the children who will receive these puppets, an eye that will not fall off easily may be preferred. In this case, sew buttons to the sock to serve as eyes. Hair, formed from yarn, and other trims may be added to the puppet.

Put the puppet on one hand and arm. To form a mouth, use the other hand to press between the thumb and the four fingers of the hand inside of the sock. Move the thumb up and down to make the puppet talk.

Provide the supplies and guide the group as they construct their puppets. Encourage the children to continue this project at home by collecting lots of single socks and making puppets out of them.

When the puppet project is completed, deliver or send the gifts to one or several daycare centers or treatment facilities. Include a note asking the teachers or medical workers to use the puppets as tools for sharing love and comfort with the children in their care.

Storytelling

PURPOSE To show how people sometimes hide behind masks instead of revealing their true personalities or their true feelings.

PREPARATION *Materials*

- Variety of Halloween masks: funny, scary, sad, happy, real people, make-believe characters
- Plaster bandage or "Rigid Wrap"
- Containers of water
- Scissors
- Vaseline
- Soft soap
- Towels
- Lotion

PROCEDURE Webster's dictionary defines "mask" as a covering to conceal or protect the face, or anything that conceals or disguises. It's fun to wear a mask on a holiday like Halloween or as part of a costume for a masquerade party or dress-up event. Unfortunately, masks are often used to cover or conceal an unattractive appearance or an unexpressed feeling. Masks are associated with HIV/AIDS in several ways, too. AIDS does not just make a person's life different, it alters it permanently. HIV/AIDS not only strips people of their protective immunity to the ravages of diseases but also of their appearance, dignity, independence, appetite, friends, family, and even mind. Many people with AIDS, as well as persons associated with them, want to hide. They want to hide their looks and their feelings. They want to disguise the truth and the threat. Not only persons infected with HIV/AIDS but everyone affected by the virus and the resulting disease must "unmask the fear of AIDS." Use masks in an activity to help the participants explore ways to begin to do this.

As a way of illustrating this theme, invite one student at a time to select a Halloween mask from the assortment available and to put it on. With the mask in place, ask each individual to dramatize the character or expression represented by the mask. Invite the students to be creative in using the masks. Talk about how masks are worn at Halloween so that people aren't recognized.

Talk to the students about everyday ways in which people wear masks, not the commercially purchased or homemade variety. People wear a disguise so their true self is not revealed. For example, some people try to be funny or always in the limelight, to be popular with other young people, or to show fearlessness or an image that is tough. Explain that sometimes when people wear masks it means "don't get close." Ask for examples of ways in which people mask their personalities and their feelings. Discuss the responses. For instance, a man may wear the mask of being tough and macho in order to fit in. Someone may wear the mask of being cheery and happy all the time on the outside, even though the individual is really hurting on the inside. Allow students time to share and discuss the various masks people wear in everyday life.

Ask if masks are associated with the HIV/AIDS epidemic. Request examples to illustrate the point that masks are worn by persons infected and affected by HIV/AIDS. AIDS is not a pretty disease. As the virus destroys the immune system of the infected person, many physical changes take place. As parasites and fungi invade the body and cause complications, infected persons lose weight, hair, physical control, and mental ability. Diseases such as Kaposi's sarcoma (KS) and pneumocystic carinii pneumonia (PCP) become life threatening. KS is a cancer associated with HIV that creates dark swellings in the blood vessels and eventually in the major organs. It kills by interfering with the body's functions. PCP drowns its victims in lung fluid. It is caused by a protozoan that lives in most healthy human bodies and is normally kept under control by the immune system. Other diseases drain HIV-positive bodies with diarrhea or blister their brains with lesions. People with these disfiguring and debilitating conditions often want to hide, not only because of their fear, but also because of the fear of persons with whom they come into contact. Discuss ways in which these fears can be unmasked.

It is also important to unmask the reality and the seriousness of the situation as well as the personal responsibility associated with the HIV/AIDS epidemic. Each person is responsible for determining his or her fate because it is personal behavior, not the behavior of others, that ultimately puts a person at risk of contracting the virus. Stress that it is not easy to get AIDS. It involves contact with an infected person that is so intimate that either blood or sexual fluids must be exchanged. Emphasize that people must remove the masks of fear and ignorance and learn ways to protect themselves against AIDS, such as:

- Don't get involved with drugs or with the people who use drugs.
- If drugs are involved, get help in getting off of them.
- Never use or share needles or works in drug use.
- Avoid sexual intercourse, oral sex, and anal sex until ready to deal with the risks involved. If anyone says that there are no risks, they are masking the truth.
- Be selective in the choice of a partner.
- If sexually active, practice safer sex.
- Avoid situations that could be traps. Heavy drinking or drug use masks clear thinking and conscious choices.
- Learn the facts to unmask the fear.

If desired, conclude the activity by making self-masks as a way to remind the participants of their personal responsibility in "unmasking the fear of HIV/AIDS." Try a technique involving plaster bandage, the material from which casts are constructed. It is available as a commercial art material called "Rigid Wrap," which is specifically designed for mask making. Arrange the students in groups of two. Distribute the supplies for the project: rolls of plaster bandage, containers of water, vaseline, and scissors. Tell the partners that they will take turns making masks of one another. Instruct each person to liberally cover his or her face with a thick coat of vaseline. Begin by cutting the plaster bandage into 4" strips. One strip at a time is dipped into the water, wrung out, and laid on the face of the first person. Tell the mask makers to continue the process until a single layer of plaster bandage covers the face, allowing space for the eyes, nose, and mouth. Be sure that the person having the mask made can breath during the activity. When the first mask is completed, remove it and set it aside to dry. Repeat the procedure on the second person. Allow time for the participants to clean their faces and hands after each turn.

Invite the students to bring their masks and to gather in a circle. Ask everyone to place the mask up to their face. Remind them that hiding behind a mask or revealing self is a personal choice. Honesty is an important factor, especially in the AIDS crisis. People can no longer hide behind masks but need to be honest in what they say and do. Invite the students to remove their masks and to keep them in a place that will remind them to "unmask the fear of AIDS."

1. Diana L. Hynson, ed., *To the Point: Confronting Youth Issues AIDS* (Nashville, Tenn.: Abingdon Press, 1993).
2. Elisabeth Kubler-Ross, *On Death and Dying* (New York: Macmillan, 1969).
3. Jaime Rickert, "Beautiful," *New Wine* (Suffern, N.Y.: Parish Mission Team, 1989). Used by permission.

Glossary

Acquired Obtained by exposure, experience, or environment rather than heredity.

Acquired Immunodeficiency Syndrome Disease caused by the Human Immunodeficiency Virus (HIV) which reduces the body's ability to fight disease.

AIDS Acquired Immune (or Immuno) Deficiency Syndrome, a disease caused by HIV which damages the body's immune system, making the infected person susceptible to a wide range of serious diseases.

Antibody Protein produced by B-cells in the blood in response to contact of the body with an antigen. It has the capacity to neutralize toxins and to weaken or destroy disease-causing organisms.

Antigen Substance that is recognized as foreign by the immune system and stimulates the formation of antibodies to combat its presence.

Anus Opening at the lower end of the large intestine.

Asymptomatic carrier Person who has an infectious organism within the body but feels or shows no outward symptoms.

Azidothymidine (AZT) A drug used to treat AIDS which is effective in controlling symptoms and prolonging life.

B-cell White blood cell that makes antibodies to fight infection.

Bacteria One-celled microorganisms that can cause disease, for example, pneumonia, tuberculosis, and anthrax.

Bisexual A person who is sexually attracted to men and women.

Blood donors People who give blood to be used for a transfusion.

Bone marrow Soft, fatty tissue that fills the cavities of most bones.

Cancer Disease in which body cells multiply out of control and may produce growths called tumors.

Candida albicans Yeast-like infection that causes thrush in the throat and mouth.

Carcinoma A malignancy, or cancer, made up of a particular kind of cells and with a tendency to spread.

Carrier Someone with no symptoms of a disease who carries a bacteria or virus and can transmit it to other people.

CDC The Centers for Disease Control, a federal agency that studies and monitors the incidence and prevalence of disease in the United States and provides health and safety guidelines for the prevention of disease.

Cell-mediated immunity Immunity provided by the T-cells.

Cellular immunodeficiency The type of immune deficiency seen in HIV infection, generally characterized by poor functioning of the T-cells. Other immune deficiencies affect the B-cells, the phagocytes, or the lymphoid cells.

Cofactors Agents or other factors that are necessary or increase the probability for development of a disease when the basic causative agent of the disease is present.

Condom Latex covering placed over the penis before sexual activity to prevent the transfer of semen, pregnancy, and the spread of disease. Also called rubber or prophylactic.

Contagious Spread of an organism that causes the disease from person to person, directly or indirectly.

Contaminated Made dirty or impure by the introduction of a foreign or undesirable substance.

Contract To get or incur.

Cytomegalovirus Commonly known as CMV, a herpes virus often found in AIDS patients, capable of producing serious illness in infants, weakened persons, and individuals with suppressed immune systems.

Deficiency A shortage or lack.

Disease A destructive process in an organ or organism with a specific cause and characteristic symptoms.

Disinfectant Substance that destroys harmful bacteria and viruses and makes them inactive.

Drug abusers People who use drugs to change the way they feel, not to make themselves well.

ELISA Enzyme-linked immunosorbent assay, ELISA is the most inexpensive and widely used test to detect HIV in blood samples.

Epidemiology Study of relationships among various factors thought to determine the frequency and distribution of diseases in humans.

Factor Conditions that bring about a particular result.

Factor III One of the clotting factors in the blood, often used in the treatment of individuals with hemophilia A.

False negative A type of erroneous result in an AIDS antibody test that reads negative when there is actually antibody in the blood.

False positive A type of erroneous result in an AIDS antibody test that reads positive when there is actually no antibody in the blood.

Gamma globulin Serum proteins in the blood that contain the antibodies.

Gay Term used for men who are sexually attracted to other men.

Hemophilia A rare, hereditary disorder found mostly in males in which the blood does not clot normally and prolonged bleeding occurs, even from minor cuts and injuries. It can be treated with Factor VIII, a product made of human blood.

Herpes simplex Virus that causes cold sores around the mouth and genital area, often transmitted by sexual contact.

Heterosexual A person who shows sexual preference for another person of the opposite sex for romantic or sexual relations.

HIV antibody screening test Test performed on all donated blood that reveals the presence of antibodies to HIV.

Homosexual A person who shows sexual preference for another person of the same sex for romantic or sexual relations.

HTLV Human T-cell lympotropic virus, the first retrovirus shown to cause cancer in humans.

Human Immunodeficiency Virus (HIV) Virus that causes AIDS by attacking and altering T-4 lymphocytes, thereby neutralizing the body's immune system, greatly increasing susceptibility to infections.

Immune Protected from or not susceptible to a disease.

Immune deficiency A condition in which the body defenses do not function properly because some of the B- or T-cells are missing or damaged.

Immune system A system in the body consisting of specialized cells and proteins that defends against disease-causing organisms such as bacteria, viruses, or other infections.

Incubation Interval between infection and appearance of the first symptom.

Infect To become diseased with a bacteria or virus.

Intercourse A type of sexual contact involving one or more of the following: (1) insertion of a man's penis into a woman's vagina, called "vaginal intercourse"; (2) placement of the mouth on the genitals of another person, called "oral intercourse"; or (3) insertion of a man's penis into the anus of another person, called "anal intercourse."

Intravenous Entering the body through an injection by needles directly into the blood veins.

Kaposi's sarcoma A rare cancer or tumor of the blood and/or lymphatic vessel walls to which persons with AIDS are unusually susceptible. KS appears as pink or purple blotches on the skin.

Latency A period when a virus is in the body but is in an inactive, dormant state.

Lubricant Substance applied to condoms or sexual organs to make contact between condom and skin slippery. Only water-based lubricants should be used with condoms.

Lymph Watery fluid in the lymphatic vessels.

Lymph nodes Small collections of tissue that contain large numbers of lymphocytes and filter out foreign particles and cells carried in the lymph.

Lymphadenopathy Enlargement of the lymph nodes, often a sign of infection or illness.

Lymphocytes Specialized white blood cells, including B-cells and T-cells, that are involved in the body's immune response.

Macrophage White blood cell that destroys foreign substances and cells and cooperates with T- and B-cells in the immune response.

Malignant Cancer that becomes progressively worse and results in death.

Memory cells T-cells that have been exposed to specific antigens and are capable of multiplying and mounting a rapid immune response upon a repeat encounter with those antigens.

Neurologic Pertaining to the nervous system or brain.

Nonoxynol-9 Spermicide, available in some sexual lubricants for use with condoms, that has been shown to kill the AIDS virus.

Opportunistic infection An infection commonly found in the environment that causes disease in persons with weakened immune systems.

Pathogen Any disease-producing microorganism.

Penis Male organ used in sexual intercourse to transfer semen.

Perinatal Occurring in the period preceding, during, or after birth.

Phagocytes White blood cells that attack and eat invading organisms and chemicals.

Plasma cells Mature B-cells that reproduce antibodies.

Pneumocystis carinii pneumonia PCP, a rare type of pneumonia, caused by a protozoan parasite that occurs as an opportunistic lung infection in people with AIDS.

Precaution Care taken in advance to prevent disease or harm.

PWA Person with AIDS. This term is preferred over others like "AIDS victim" or "AIDS patient."

Quarantine To isolate in an effort to prevent the spread of disease.

Risk Chance of injury, damage, or loss.

Safer sex Sexual activity in which no body fluids are shared.

Secondary opportunistic infections A secondary infection that develops after the immune system has been weakened by an initial infection.

Secretion Substance generated from blood or cells that may have cleansing, lubricating, or other characteristics.

Semen Whitish fluid containing sperm, the male sex cells, released through the penis at the climax of sexual activity.

Seropositive Condition of having AIDS virus antibodies found in the blood.

Sexually transmitted diseases Abbreviated STD, diseases caused by organisms or parasites that are transferred from one person to another during sexual activity.

Side effect Secondary, unwanted, and usually unpleasant result or outcome.

Spermicide Substance used to help prevent pregnancy because of its ability to kill sperm.

Surveillance Monitoring and collecting data on incidence of disease.

Susceptible Easily affected.

Symptom Physical change or feeling in the body that indicates the presence of a disease.

Syndrome A number of signs and symptoms that occur together and indicate the presence of a particular disease or condition.

T-cells White blood cells that mature in the thymus gland and assist cellular immune reactions. T-cells are invaded and disabled by the HIV virus.

T helper cells Type of white blood cell that stimulates B-cells to make antibodies.

T suppressor cells Type of white blood cell that stops the activity of B-cells.

Therapy Treatment of disease or physical or mental disorder by medical or physical means.

Thrush Yeastlike infection of the mouth and throat, caused by a bacterium known as candida albicans.

Thymus gland Small gland in the upper chest that regulates the development of T-cells and makes hormones that are important in maintaining proper immunity.

Transfusion Process of putting fluid, usually blood, into a vein or artery.

Transmission To send, pass, or cause to go from one person to another.

Vaccine A preparation of killed or living but weakened microorganisms introduced into the body to produce immunity to a specific disease by causing the formation of antibodies and memory cells.

Vagina Opening in the female body through which semen is transferred during sexual activity and through which a baby is born.

Vein A part of the body through which blood flows.

Venereal disease Infection transmitted only or chiefly by sexual intercourse with an infected individual. Major venereal diseases include syphilis, gonorrhea, genital herpes, and AIDS.

Virus An organism consisting of genetic material, either RNA or DNA, enclosed in an outer protein coat. Viruses cannot reproduce on their own, multiply only within host cells, and cause diseases.

Western Blot Test used to detect HIV antibodies in blood samples.

Zoonosis Any disease that can be transmitted from an animal to a person, but not from person to person.

Resources

ABC Quilts. *Kids Making Quilts for Kids.* Gualala, Calif.: Quilt Digest Press, 1992.

Aiello, Barbara, and Jeffrey Schulman. *Friends for Life: The Kids on the Block Book Series.* Frederick, Md.: Twenty-First Century Books, 1988.

American Council of Life Insurance. "Teens and AIDS—Playing It Safe.." Washington, D.C.: American Council of Life Insurance, 1987.

American Red Cross. *Don't Forget Sherrie Workbook.* Washington, D.C.: American Red Cross, 1991.

————. "Teenagers and AIDS." Washington, D.C. American Red Cross, 1989.

Andrea and Lisa. Baltimore: Health Education Resource Organization, 1987.

Armstrong, Evan. *The Impact of AIDS.* New York: Gloucester Press, 1990.

Arrick, Fran. *What You Don't Know Can Kill You.* New York: Bantam Books, 1992.

Baker, Lynn S. *You and HIV: A Day at a Time.* Philadelphia: W. B. Saunders, 1991.

Bell, Ruth. *Changing Bodies, Changing Lives.* New York: Random House, 1987.

Beshara, Raymond, et al. *What You Should Know about AIDS.* Norwalk, Conn.: ERN, Inc., 1989.

Bete, Channing L. *Anyone Can Get AIDS.* South Deerfield, Mass.: Channing L. Bete, 1991.

————. *A Christian Response to AIDS.* South Deerfield, Mass.: Channing L. Bete, 1990.

————. *Dying to Get High—AIDS and Shooting Drugs.* South Deerfield, Mass.: Channing L. Bete, 1991.

————. *Let's Talk about AIDS: An Information and Activities Book.* South Deerfield, Mass.: Channing L. Bete, 1992.

————. *Making Responsible Choices about Sex.* South Deerfield, Mass.: Channing L. Bete, 1987.

————. *Sex and STDs—How to Stay Safe.* South Deerfield, Mass.: Channing L. Bete, 1992.

————. *Sex Is Safer with a Condom.* South Deerfield, Mass.: Channing L. Bete, 1991.

————. *What Everyone Should Know about AIDS.* South Deerfield, Mass.: Channing L. Bete, 1983.

————. *What Young People Should Know about AIDS.* South Deerfield, Mass.: Channing L. Bete, 1987.

————. *Worried about AIDS? Have an HIV Test.* South Deerfield, Mass.: Channing L. Bete, 1992.

————. *Young People Get AIDS.* South Deerfield, Mass.: Channing L. Bete, 1991.

Bevan, Nicholas. *AIDS and Drugs.* New York: Watts, 1988.

Blake, Jeanne. *Risky Times: How to Be AIDS Smart and Stay Healthy: A Guide for Teenagers.* New York: Workman, 1990.

Boulden, Jim and Brett. *Uncle Jerry Has AIDS.* Weaverville, Calif.: Boulden Publishing, 1992.

Check, William A. *AIDS: The Encyclopedia of Health.* New York: Chelsea House, 1988.

Colman, Warren. *Understanding and Preventing AIDS.* Chicago: Children's Press, 1988.

de Saint Phalle, Niki. *AIDS: You Can't Catch It Holding Hands.* San Francisco: Lapis Press, 1987.

Dodge, Joyce Northrup. *"Mommy, What's AIDS?"* Wheaton, Ill.: Tyndale House, 1989.

Eagles, Douglas A. *The Menace of AIDS: A Shadow on Our Land.* New York: Franklin Watts, 1988.

Fassler, David, M.D., and Kelly McQueen. *What's a Virus Anyway? The Kids' Book about AIDS.* Burlington, Vt.: Waterfront Books, 1990.

Flanders, Stephen. *Library in a Book: AIDS.* New York: Facts on File, 1990.

Fullwood, P. Catlin, ed. "AIDS News." Seattle: People of Color Against AIDS Network (POCAAN), 1988.

Girard, Linda Walvoord. *Alex, the Kid with AIDS.* Morton Grove, Ill.: Albert Whitman, 1991.

Glaser, Elizabeth, comp. *For Our Children: A Book to Benefit the Pediatric AIDS Foundation.* Burbank, Calif.: Disney Press, 1991.

Greenberg, Lorna. *AIDS: How It Works in the Body.* New York: Watts, 1992.

Hausherr, Rosmarie. *Children and the AIDS Virus.* New York: Clarion Books, 1989.

Hawkes, Nigel. *AIDS.* New York: Gloucester Press, 1987.

Hein, Karen, M.D., and Theresa Foy DiGeronimo. *AIDS: Trading Fears for Facts.* Yonkers, N.Y.: Consumer Reports, 1989.

Hermes, Patricia. *Be Still My Heart.* New York: Putnam, 1989.

Hoffman, Alice. *At Risk.* Berkeley, Calif.: Berkeley, 1988.

Humphreys, Martha. *Until Whatever.* New York: Clarion, 1991.

Hunt, Morton. *Gay: What You Should Know about Homosexuality.* New York: Farrar, Straus, and Giroux, 1987.

Hyde, Margaret O., and Elizabeth Forsyth, M.D. *AIDS: What Does It Mean to You?* New York: Walker, 1989.

———. *Know about AIDS.* New York: Walker, 1987.

Hynson, Diana L. *To the Point: Confronting Youth Issues AIDS.* Nashville, Tenn.: Abingdon, 1993.

Jackson, Tim. *AIDS: Just the Facts, Jack.* Chicago: Creative License Studio, 1988.

———. *What Are Friends For? HIV Safe Coloring Book.* Chicago: Creative License Studio, 1990.

Jordan, MaryKate. *Losing Uncle Tim.* Niles, Ill.: Albert Whitman, 1989.

Kerr, M. E. *Night Kites.* New York: Harper and Row, 1986.

Kerrins, Joseph, and George W. Jacobs. *The AIDS File.* Woods Hole, Mass.: Cromlech Books, 1989.

Koertge, Ron. *The Arizona Kid.* New York: Joy Street/Little, Brown, 1988.

Kuklin, Susan. *Fighting Back: What Some People Are Doing about AIDS.* New York: Putnam, 1989.

Kurland, Morton L. *Coping with AIDS: Facts and Fears.* New York: Rosen Group, 1990.

Landau, Elaine. *Sexually Transmitted Diseases.* Hillside, N.J.: Enslow, 1986.

———. *We Have AIDS.* New York: Franklin Watts, 1990.

Langone, John. *AIDS: The Facts.* Boston: Little, Brown, 1988.

Lerner, Ethan A. *Understanding AIDS.* Minneapolis: Lerner Publications, 1987.

Levert, Susan. *AIDS: In Search of a Killer.* New York: Julian Messner, 1987.

Levy, Marilyn. *Rumors and Whispers.* New York: Fawcett Juniper, 1990.

Lord, John. *Infection, the Immune System, and AIDS.* Santa Monica, Calif.: Enterprise Education, 1989.

Madaras, Linda. *Lynda Madaras Talks to Teens about AIDS.* New York: Newmarket Press, 1988.

Marsh, Carole S. *AIDS to Zits: A Sextionary for Kids.* Bath, N.C.: Gallopade, 1987.

———. *First AIDS: Frank Facts for Kids.* Bath, N.C.: Gallopade, 1987.

Merrifield, Margaret, M.D. *Come Sit by Me.* Toronto: Women's Press, 1990.

Miklowitz, Gloria D. *Good-Bye Tomorrow.* New York: Delacorte Press, 1987.

Minnesota AIDS Project. "Corey's Story." Minneapolis: Minnesota AIDS Project, 1987.

Morton, Carlos. *Risky Stuff.* Washington, D.C.: American Red Cross, 1990.

Mozeleski, Peter A., and Paul M. Mozeleski. *The Rubber Brothers Comics.* Wilbraham, Mass.: Rubber Brothers Comics, 1990.

National Hemophilia Foundation. *Let's Talk about Sex.* New York: National Hemophilia Foundation, 1988.

Norse, Alan E. *AIDS.* New York: Franklin Watts, 1989.

———. *Teen Guide to AIDS Prevention.* New York: Franklin Watts, 1990.

Opheim, Teresa. *AIDS: Distinguishing Between Fact and Opinion.* San Diego: Greenhaven, 1990.

People of Color Against AIDS Network. "AIDS News." Seattle: People of Color Against AIDS Network, 1988.

Randall-David, Betsy, and Amit Pieter. *Jeffrey Wants to Know.* Gainesville, Fla.: Florida Association of Pediatric Tumor Programs, n.d.

———. *Space Age Smarts.* Gainesville, Fla.: Florida Association of Pediatric Tumor Programs, 1987.

San Francisco AIDS Foundation. "Risky Business." San Francisco: San Francisco AIDS Foundation, 1988.

Sanford, Doris. *David Has AIDS.* Portland, Or.: Multnomah, 1989.

Schilling, Sharon, and Jonathan Swain. "*My Name Is Jonathan (and I Have AIDS).*" Denver: Prickly Pair Publishing, 1989.

Schwartz, Linda. *AIDS Answers for Teens.* Santa Barbara, Calif.: Learning Works, 1990.

———. *AIDS Questions and Answers for Kids: Grades 5–6.* Santa Barbara, Calif.: Learning Works, 1991.

Silverstein, Alvin, and Virginia B. Silverstein. *AIDS: Deadly Threat.* Hillside, N.J.: Enslow, 1991.

———. *Learning about AIDS.* Hillside, N.J.: Enslow, 1989.

State of Florida Department of Health. "Get the Facts." Fort Lauderdale, Fla.: State of Florida Department of Health and Rehabilitative Services—Broward County Public Health Unit, 1986..

Taylor, Barbara. *Everything You Need to Know about AIDS.* New York: Rosen, 1988.

Turck, Mary. *AIDS.* New York: Macmillan Child Group, 1988.

Udin, Sala, and Brian Clarke. "Rappin'—Teens, Sex, and AIDS." San Francisco: Multicultural Prevention Resource Center, 1987.

Wachter, Oralee. *Sex, Drugs, and AIDS.* Toronto: Bantam, 1987.

White, Ryan, and Ann Marie Cunningham. *Ryan White: My Own Story.* New York: Dial, 1991.

Wilson, Jonnie. *AIDS.* San Diego: Lucent Books, 1989.

Winterhalter, Sterling A. *Risky Business.* San Francisco, Calif.: San Francisco AIDS Foundation, 1988.

For Additional Resources

Locate: books, articles, pamphlets, adult curricula, journals/periodicals, audiotapes, videotapes

Contact: local, regional, national, and international organizations, denominations, data bases, hotlines, such as:

AIDS Office
Pan American Health
 Organization
World Health Organization
 Washington, D.C.
202-861-4346

Global Programme on AIDS
World Health Organization
Geneva, Switzerland
011-41-22-791-4673

National HIV/AIDS Hotline
Centers for Disease Control
800-342-2437

National AIDS Clearing House
Centers for Disease Control
800-458-5231